A JOURNEY FROM
PEW TO POWER

Pemba
Pennings

H A CHILVER

Ark House Press
PO Box 1722, Port Orchard, WA 98366 USA
PO Box 1321, Mona Vale NSW 1660 Australia
PO Box 318 334, West Harbour, Auckland 0661 New Zealand
arkhousepress.com

© H A CHILVER 2021
Unless otherwise stated, all Scriptures are taken from the New Living Translation (Holy Bible. New Living Translation copyright© 1996, 2004, 2007, 2013 by Tyndale House Foundation. Used by permission of Tyndale House Publishers Inc., Carol Stream, Illinois 60188. All rights reserved.)

Some names and identifying details have been changed to protect the privacy of individuals.

Cataloguing in Publication Data:
Title: Pemba Pennings
ISBN: 978-0-6453370-9-9 (pbk)
Subjects: Memoirs; Diary; Christian Living; Missions;
Other Authors/Contributors: Chilver, H.A.

Design by Matteo Bisato
www.matteobisato.design

Contents

Introduction 1
The Off 7
Airborne 21

Week One

Friday afternoon 32
Saturday 59
Sunday early morning 74
Monday 77
Tuesday 96
Wednesday 111
Thursday 120
Friday 152
Saturday 163

Week Two

Saturday evening 171
Sunday evening 174
Monday evening 186
Tuesday morning 206
Tuesday evening 211
Wednesday 213
Thursday 227
Late Friday night 237

Week Three

Saturday 241
Saturday afternoon 258
Monday morning 262
Monday evening 284
Tuesday afternoon 297
Tuesday bedtime 315
Wednesday early morning 316
Wednesday evening 318
Thursday 342
4pm 346
Author's Note 350

Introduction

Perhaps, like me, you have wondered what the key is, whether there is a heavenly formula that unlocks God moving in power in your life. A spiritual pathway that if walked could release the kingdom, which in the gospels Jesus consistently claims is 'here'. One might be forgiven for thinking that if it were possible, to be more like someone whose life already overflows with evidence of this kingdom, there could be hope ... Mmm. Since this story, this chapter of my journey was greatly accelerated when a kind friend called Kathy 'innocently' leant me a book about Heidi Baker, I'll take her as an example of the futility comparison breeds.

Heidi was born and grew up in a millionaire's paradise in America called Laguna Beach. I was raised with three siblings in a three-bedroom semi-detached red-brick home in suburban England. By the age of sixteen Heidi was preaching; I was fervently renewing my commitment to Jesus as Lord at regular intervals and optimistically going along to youth group anticipating romance. Heidi was exploring all things Pentecostal;

I was obliged to sit on a hard pew each Sunday declaring in doleful tones that he 'makes his chosen people joyful'. The complete absence of fun, laughter or anything remotely suggesting hilarity led me to the only possible conclusion: our church had not been 'chosen'. Heidi was learning to take risks and already adventuring in the power of the Holy Spirit; I was being warned. Warned that there were Christians who may 'need an extra baptism' but the general qualifications were deemed to be mental instability or possibly being an American TV evangelist, because any overt emotion was definitely not appropriate for a committed Bible-reading British Christian.

You can probably see where this is going but I will just finish. As a young woman Heidi experienced great passion and concern for other nations; I was busy avoiding any gathering where a missionary on furlough was showing their slides in case I got 'called'. Africa was a specific non-starter after a brief visit with grandparents living in Zimbabwe (then Rhodesia) introduced me to corruption, armed guards, poverty, intimidation and human need on a scale beyond my ability to process. Heidi studied, gained degrees (yes, plural!) and later a PhD. I didn't even go to university. Heidi was working on the streets in London seeing homeless people's lives radically turned around as she introduced them to Jesus and I was preparing to walk up the aisle and on into middle-class motherhood.

I don't want to be another Heidi, but any of us who feel ordinary or normal in comparison can be hungry to be in a relationship with our heavenly Dad that overflows with power and love to the world around us. Wanting to be just like another person, striving to emulate someone else God is using, will not fully release God moving in power and is likely

Introduction

to be a distraction or even a trap. 'Fix your eyes on Jesus' is in the Bible because nobody else will do.

The one thing we can share and do need to have in common has nothing to do with our upbringing or standing in life; it is a heart posture. A posture of hunger, desire, longing for God. It is the description of this hunger that so powerfully challenged me as I read the book.

By the time I visited Kathy I had been exploring living in the fullness of the Holy Spirit for twenty years. I was passionate about seeing Jesus loved and celebrated but miracles, signs and wonders were painfully conspicuous by their absence. I read Heidi's story because I had heard tales about God for which I had no personal point of reference and I was desperate for more of him in my own life. That day, when I got to the part where Heidi's hunger for more resulted in God coming so powerfully on her that she was, in effect, glued to the floor for a week, I spontaneously slipped out of my chair and found myself continuing to read on the carpet.

There was nothing at all 'British' about the experience she described. She was embarrassed, uncomfortable, and helpless to the point of absolutely no control over her situation. My reading ground to a halt as I tried to imagine. It didn't compute. What about the bathroom? What about eating and drinking? No. It was totally extreme, surely that couldn't be part of God's purpose in 'the normal Christian life'? Aagh … could that be the point?

I had had 'normal' for years. What if …? I sensed an invitation. It was unexpected and it came unannounced on an ordinary autumn afternoon in England as I waited for Kathy to return from work. The thing is, I didn't have to accept. I let choice hang in the atmosphere as I took a deep breath and decided to read on.

By the end of the book Heidi was seeing God do many miracles. After visiting Maputo Kathy told stories of the blind seeing and deaf hearing in Mozambique. I had also noticed in recent months that her prayers were different, more direct with a new authority. Kathy had prayed for me over the phone and my chest infection had cleared. So it was obvious to me that the encounter that Heidi wrote about was a catalyst in her life with God, as though the awfulness of feeling humiliated and embarrassed, and particularly being unable to control anything that happened, in some way catapulted her into a new release of God moving in power.

I pondered: what if in order to see signs and wonders in my own life, a similar experience is required? I don't know if the Holy Spirit holds his breath but in that moment I stepped back from the detail. Basically I was looking at a person moving from being glued to the floor in public to seeing God bring dead babies back to life with countless other miracles in between. How could I hold back when those were the possibilities? As I lay on the carpet and said yes to whatever it was Love was drawing me into, I felt heaven sigh with pleasure.

A few years later: piercing electric-blue eyes combed the upturned faces as she pondered response. Most glistened with humid sweat, many streaked with red dust; all were focused on hearing the answer to the question. The air was pregnant with expectation as hungry hearts from many nations ached for resolution. It was hot, flies were busy and everyone was sitting on the cement floor in the meeting hut in Pemba, Mozambique.

Harvest School 21 would soon be over and we had a final question-and-answer session with Heidi. Janice had voiced the heart cry of

Introduction

249 other students: 'Heidi, we have been here for nine weeks. Many of us have connected with children; we have been involved in all the activities and loved serving where we can. But we are all going home tomorrow. Just … leaving. Some of us sponsor children but what more can we do? We will all be back in our own nations but is there anything we can do? Is there any way we can continue to make a meaningful difference here?'

Smiling, Heidi spoke; slowly turning her head as she did to ensure every student was included. 'Some people give up a month each year and come to help us. That's fantastic and we really appreciate it. How can you help? The thing each of you can do, the thing that really is the most help, is to tell people, leave here and tell your story.'

I heard Heidi's voice but it was God who spoke to me. Excited hope stirred. Just over a year before I had begun writing about Pemba but had got distracted, and then convinced myself that it was unlikely anybody would ever want to read my ramblings anyway. The project lay incomplete in the labyrinth of documents and folders on my laptop. Now, many months and even more writing hours later, this is my story.

The Off

Dearest Ma,

Here I am on the 12:26 from Exeter St David's to Waterloo. It was good to chat briefly on the phone. Sorry the Auckland summer is less than you hoped but at least if the roof is fixed you can relax. With little phone or internet contact where I'm going, I thought I'd just get you up to speed with a couple of letters as I set off, and then I could be out of contact for a while whilst I venture into the unknown. I suspect I will be able to email you in just over three weeks from the airport in South Africa, once out of Mozambique and on my way down to Australia.

Rather a lot to catch up on as things have gained momentum so I'll try and start at the very beginning. To be honest chatting to you about the adventure as it begins makes it feel less lonely. I really appreciate your support, even though I know a part of you probably wanted to dissuade me. I do admit to feeling completely blown away that God would orchestrate such an unexpected turn of events. But in my spirit I hear him clearly. He's saying, 'Come on, Haze, further up and further in,' and I am magnetically drawn by love to respond.

The weird thing is the train looks just the same as it does every day, exactly as all the other times I have caught it. My suitcase, with fluro-pink strap clicked firmly around its bulging midriff, waits patiently in the corner rack. I like to wedge it outside the other bags, poised for a smooth pick-up as I exit en route for the Tube. I'm sitting in my preferred spot: an aisle seat at a table facing the way the train is travelling to defy nausea. (Even going the wrong way on the train makes me feel queasy since I had that paroxysmal vertigo thing in my ear last year.) My preference is the first table that offers a view right down the length of the carriage. I like light and space even when I'm travelling. I can't bear the bulkhead seat in a plane, like being tied up and dumped in a dead end.

So, on the surface this journey looks for all the world like just another routine trip home to Australia. Only there is actually nothing routine about this journey. From the foreign objects of mosquito net and water filter through empty jewellery pouch in my case, to borrowed 'Fitness First' rucksack replacing stylish leather handbag, to crisp new visa on page 11 of my passport. Golly Ma, nothing is 'normal'.

Sometimes when I travel friends give me a card to wish me well. This morning (remember I have been renting space in the large shared home in Exeter) it was 'house prayer'. At 7am I was striding the canal bank and deep breathing, gulping in the last Devon air for a few weeks. Others gathered in the lounge to pray and later I received an envelope bulging with encouraging notes, pictures and Bible verses God had prompted them to share with me.

True to the creative nature of the household, as I opened the envelope just now a golden shower of glitter erupted. Bursting with relief at

The Off

being released, it enthusiastically coated as much as possible within its reach. The unsuspecting gentleman opposite tried not to respond (how very British!) as his *Daily Mail* took on a lustrous shimmer. I thought of Joanna chuckling as she stuffed the envelope. Hopefully it will prove to be a prophetic sign of God's presence visiting me in power. I do know of meetings where 'gold dust' appears on worshippers but I only experienced it that one time when the Toronto blessing was influencing things in our church in Petersfield. I'll keep you posted.

I didn't have time to go into the detail on the phone Ma, but honestly, this journey only really began in earnest four weeks ago which is why I am feeling pretty breathless about it all. You remember I went to that conference in Cardiff? It was actually a training school intended to equip and teach us to pray for people to receive healing from God.

At lunch break on day two I met a young couple called Fred and Chloe. As we chatted I shared my frustration and longing for God to break out and transform the lives of the desperate homeless people I have been getting to know in Exeter. As she breastfed her tiny daughter, this young mum calmly levelled her gaze on me and said, 'Hazel, I think you should go to Mozambique.'

In the next session I went forward for prayer and received a prophetic word: 'A new chapter is beginning. It will be bold. It is a long chapter.'

The following day I connected with Fred and Chloe again. They prayed for me and Fred said, 'I see you on a stage with a spotlight on you. It's God shining the light. His attention is specifically on you. This is a time of preparation. It will be short so savour the process. I feel God also reminding you that he saves the choicest wine till last.' With mellow thoughts around Pop and his passion for Châteauneuf with beef, I went happily into the next session.

Randy Clark shared that he had been in a meeting where Mrs Mahesh Chavda, Bonnie, described seeing a number of angels, all about six-foot tall, moving among the people and strengthening the saints. She then saw three huge angels, all over nine feet tall who went to just a few and handed them commissioning scrolls before stamping a number on them. Randy said God had told him there were a number of people who were at the conference to be commissioned and that there would be opportunity, specifically for those who knew it was for them, to respond later in the week.

Something leapt to attention inside me. I resolved I would be among those responding. At the time it didn't feel like an issue that I had no clue what a 'commissioning' may look like. I just knew God drawing an unconditional response from my heart and felt a deep excitement about being in the right place at the appropriate moment.

When it was time for those of us who identified with this sense of being drawn into a specific new chapter to respond and to receive a commissioning, I went forward with a huge 'Yes' in my spirit. When Randy spoke about the likely cost and gave people the opportunity to return to their seats many did but in my heart I had already stepped off the cliff.

As Randy prayed for me God's presence was like a soft, heavy cloak covering my whole body. It was heavy and I fell to the floor. As I lay on the ground I had thoughts about Heidi Baker and heard the words, 'Spend time in Heidi's shadow and write about it.' Much later, as I came to as if from a deep, peaceful sleep, that phrase was going round and round in my head but I had no idea what it could mean.

How could I begin to support or connect with an international miracle worker? Was God planning for me to work for Heidi or 'carry her bags' for a season? That would obviously be a season when she was going to be in Europe then.

You know, from time to time in life somebody will say something and it has a 'ring' to it, a sense of purpose all its own, a prophetic edge? Chloe's comment was one of those and her dart landed a bullseye. However much I wriggled I couldn't dislodge it.

I had been back in Exeter for a week and the thought of emailing Heidi Baker surfaced every time I began to pray. Googling her I found a contact address. It was in Mozambique. I had no intention of actually going there but God's spotlight was on the next stepping stone and I knew from experience only obedience would move the light to the next step. Surely he would show me the turn that would enable me to fulfil what he was asking but just in that moment the process required me to email Africa.

Finally, I sent a tentative email of inquiry to Pemba (where, it turned out, this young couple had done a training course when Chloe was still pregnant). Obviously God was just testing me; had to be. He knows my heart, I want to follow him 100 per cent but he also knows I don't really do Developing World.

With missionaries in the family I have strong feelings; you remember me returning from visits to Nigeria and Zimbabwe as a teenager and announcing I need never return to Africa and I was definitely never going to be 'called'? And to make jolly sure, I have successfully boycotted any gathering or feedback evening that could possibly have even the vaguest risk of said 'call'. The word 'furlough' has sent shivers up my back since I was 17.

Pemba Pennings

My initial tentative inquiry about offering 'support' was greeted with a reply email that positively gushed joy and led to a request for 'basic information'. Reasoning no harm could come from my sharing simple details I quietly responded, all the while thinking how well God must think I was doing. Communicating with Africa of all places! Each time I pressed 'send' I smugly thought I'd hear nothing for a couple of weeks at least. God had other ideas.

Friends began spontaneously sharing dreams and words that could indicate a particular step of faith was imminent for me. Meantime the community in Africa (who surely would have all vacancies for short-term volunteers booked up well in advance), gleefully emailed saying, 'Welcome to Pemba. Please send your arrival details as soon as possible and we would love to meet you at the airport.'

In obedience to a prompting I had made a polite inquiry about the volunteer programme at Pemba. Convinced it was simply the next 'stepping stone' (in my mind there was no risk of my actually going there), I had placed my confidence in a friend's comment that only one in three applications to visit the base were accepted, therefore I was quite safe.

I know you will be thinking about the boys, Ma, and possibly feeling that responsible parenting rarely looks like placing sons under the strain of needing to ponder Mum's mental stability. I have been astounded ... in a wholly good way!

Firstly, when I got back from the conference and sat with Sam (who is now 30 remember), explaining all I sensed God might be saying, he was not in any way disparaging. He listened, asked a few thought-out questions and then endorsed my sense that this seems to be a God idea. Although admitting it was unexpected, to the level of 'flying pigs delivering milk' (we were actually able to laugh together about that), Sam agreed that I needed to pursue the idea and trust that the door would close if I were on the wrong track.

And Nathan? Having a son in an active war zone has been one of the hardest things I have had to walk through as a mum. I explained to God that the timing was all wrong because Nathan was due home from Afghanistan. I desperately wanted time with him. And then ... God brought him back two weeks earlier than anticipated. I wanted to discuss the detail of a possible trip and give him the opportunity to say he would prefer Mum not to be dashing off to 'the jungle'; probably he would gently say he would really like me to be around for his birthday. But God.

To say Nathan was excited is an understatement. He leapt up and immediately ordered me a top-notch mozzie net and a water filter flask such as the army issue, then whisked me off to purchase antimalarials. I could not have felt more supported. I was stunned and blessed but I couldn't afford to just buy a plane ticket and my air miles are all with Qantas, who surely don't fly into Africa?

Next, the travel agent found a Qantas ticket was available and, unbelievably, as I sat at her desk (registering exactly where Mozambique was on the house-sized map on the wall), an instrumental version of that worship song 'As the deer pants for the water so my soul longs after you' began playing. I presume everyone in the office could hear it? I managed to wade through all the forms and successfully submitted my visa application but with *no* payment; the visa was granted anyway and I paid later online. I began to feel 'snookered'.

Ma, I hope you are sitting down ... I am on my way to Mozambique.

Pemba Pennings

Pens and notebooks are packed and I'm lining up to produce a great piece of writing. Not quite sure yet what it will look like but I am only in this position because of obedience so I'm asking the Holy Spirit to unfold it.

My friend Joanna and I felt sure some 'normal Christian' young woman must have made this journey from traditional church to seeing God move supernaturally, and written about it. But no ... we could not find a book. Maybe I am to write something that will inspire others who are longing to see God move in power in their everyday lives. Got to dream big Ma!

You may not have noticed but conferences and Bible weeks were part of life for some years. Then I found I was having a painful, ongoing conversation with God and it became depleting so I stopped going. I was flummoxed.

What I churned over was that Jesus took twelve ordinary men and totally transformed life, the whole course of history. I would be standing with 10,000 others. We all loved God and most of us were filled with the Holy Spirit but I knew we would all be back again the following year and what would have changed in the nation? My heart would be crying 'What are we missing?' It just got too hard so I stopped going.

Years later I was challenged by the BBC series about the value of silence in our lives and then learned about the power of resting and simply soaking in God's presence. Life gradually became more about making space and time for God's presence to remain and then overflow from my life. After reading about Ffald-y-brenin and visiting Wales, God's presence seemed to linger longer and deep hunger was aroused.

After receiving prayer at a gathering in Birmingham I was able to pray with more authority and the training days in Cardiff seemed a natural progression which have resulted in others receiving God's love through me in a more meaningful way.

One of the most unusual examples is a ticket collector on the train who stopped to chat. He was telling me how he had helped a passenger recover some lost property that day. As he made to continue down the train I just put my hand on his arm and said, 'God bless you; you do a great job.' Nobody was more surprised than me Ma, when half an hour later he returned and, reaching over to check the ticket of a lady who was now in the seat beside me, he said, pointing at *moi*, 'This lady here is welcome on my train any time but look out, she made me cry.' Turning to me he said, 'My arm is still tingling where you touched me, you know.'

I began to hear God telling me to reach out in particular ways to identify more with the homeless. I was working on that project to raise awareness for The Big Issue Organisation. Volunteering in the local depot and visiting the street pitches where they sold the magazines, I got to know vendors by name and several shared their stories. I had prayed with a number of those living on the streets and in hostels and they would often appreciate a hug BUT their lives were not transformed. At the end of the day I was going home to a meal and a warm bed and they ... were not.

On one unforgettable occasion the Holy Spirit told me to buy lunch for a particular magazine vendor. This wasn't unusual but the instruction to then sit on the pavement in the main street and eat my own sandwich beside him was. Obedience is crucial I know but I have to tell you that self-conscious nowhere near describes how I felt, especially when ladies I recognised from church scurried by without even greeting us. I became convinced that if Jesus (or even Heidi) were on the pavement, those my heart was aching for would encounter loving power that could influence their circumstances. I lay in bed at night reliving conversations and events, trying to discern what I was missing and crying out to God for whatever I needed or he wanted to do in my life to take place.

So for some years now I have been praying specifically, asking God to make my life a clear pipe through which he can pour himself in power, into the lives of anyone he wants to love through me.

Recently I have been tearful for no reason and want to lie on the floor for hours with worship playing. I have been feeding on teaching by Bill Johnson who is a leader at Bethel Church in Redding, California, and also Heidi Baker. I feel like a sponge that just can't hold water; it needs to be held under to stay wet. I want to hug the lonely and infuse the hopeless with hope. God isn't just teaching me about compassion but is somehow changing me inside so that mysteriously, others experience his love and compassion when I am with them.

Today I set off but I am nervous that being in a situation where need on a huge scale is a way of life, I might be totally overwhelmed. I wonder what Jesus felt like when he was here on earth … really? What will I feel in the presence of hundreds of children who have no mums or dads? How will I cope if I am asked to cuddle a baby recovered from the rubbish tip, whilst it dies? Am I going to be among weary, overstretched missionaries or will joy truly abound in the everyday? It is widely known that, through Heidi, God has opened blind eyes, given deaf people hearing, cripples run and dead people climb out of their coffins but I have never witnessed this power.

Those in the office of 'Pemba Hospitality' who vetted my application and read of my journey with God so far seemed genuinely excited as they extended the invitation for me to visit for a few weeks. I had a sense they knew something I didn't.

They wrote that they would pray and ask God about my visit. They wanted to know what I felt I could offer. The million-dollar question! I can't imagine what I could possibly offer to a community who ostensibly experience as normal life, activity of God I have only dreamed about since Sunday school.

Anyway, as I've prepared I'm as willing and clean as I know how. People keep telling me how unlikely it is that I will see Heidi, implying it would be more sensible to visit another conference where she may be speaking than strike out on a whim for 'darkest Africa'. But God told me to 'put myself in her shadow' and I know for certain that this is not my own idea so I will trust him.

I have settled in myself that it is unlikely I will catch even a whiff of Heidi's perfume (she and her husband Rolland travel for a large part of each year) and I may not witness a supernatural act. I kept in contact with Fred and Chloe and they were excited on my behalf though explained that in three months in Pemba they had not seen a miracle.

But God wants me to make this journey and my heart is changing every day. Being obedient and going just because I want to please him, not demanding certain experiences, feels important. Ma, I want to have a life that he inhabits so completely that he bursts out all over, meeting need. It's weird but I think he is saying that the poor hold a key.

Last week I was reading Heidi's book *Compelled by Love* again, thinking it might help me get 'into the zone'. I was mulling over whether God is showing me something about keys. She writes, 'Children have keys to the kingdom'.

I know there are more children than adults in Pemba and the whole work has grown from Heidi and Rolland's initial contact with street kids.

Then, the day before I left, I had this strange experience when I was walking past a street-side booth selling clothes in Exeter town centre. The sleeve of a blouse caught my eye because it was that lovely romantic lacey look with a frill at the cuff. It was cream, though, which I never wear. Wearing cream makes me feel slightly 'off colour' since learning that I am 'Winter' and therefore look really well in crisp white. It's not just that I am easily influenced; I genuinely feel more alive in white. Anyway, the girl told me the blouse does come in black but she didn't have any.

I continued with shopping and was making for home in a steady, grey drizzle when God said, 'Go back and buy that blouse.'

'Er, Lord, I think you may be forgetting ... I don't do cream.'

'Go back and buy the blouse.'

'Lord, it's starting to really rain and it's probably expensive.'

'Buy the blouse.'

I reluctantly retraced my steps pondering the clarity of 'the voice'.

'Hi, I know I said I don't really wear cream but I wonder if I could just try the blouse on?'

Averting my gaze from the disquieting gothic mannequin in the corner (sporting a bondage-style Victorian corset over a garment held together with chains), I fervently hoped nobody I knew was passing by. I stepped behind the makeshift screen. I was stunned as the blouse was handed over to see that the top button had a bronze loop beneath it and a small bronze key hung down.

The Off

I bought the blouse and wore it to church as a private, prophetic statement of my accepting that I sense God speaking that something in me needs permanently unlocking so that he can be fully released in my world. From what I have read and heard and sense God unfolding to me, there is a risk I may find that key in Pemba. So for me, today, this is what faith looks like. God has indicated he has a specific purpose in my going. I am trusting him.

It is a risk and so much is unknown. But I cannot afford the greater risk of missing what he wants to teach and show me. Just living one day after comfortable day with the odd answer to prayer is no longer an option. I want as much of God as he can possibly pour through me. I think … at any cost.

There was one other part in *Compelled by Love* that just briefly touched a spot as I read last week. Heidi writes,

> *The Lord is calling for servant lovers who will call in the outcasts, who will go into the dark corners of the world and compel them to come home … Who will go and leave their life of comfort and call in the broken? Who will go and be a learner? Who will go among those who are mourning and lay their life down for Jesus? … It is time for us to go to the poor, to the broken, to the homeless, to the dying and to the lonely … Thousands and thousands of 'sent-out ones' need to go out to the darkest places, to the poorest places, … forgotten places, because the wedding feast is about to begin. So many still must be called.*

I don't know exactly; it's all outside my life experience but something about the depths of wretchedness she describes touched a chord and I had a fleeting impression that reminded me of a news report about

Aboriginal people at home in Australia.

Golly Ma ... surely after all these years I won't get called to Africa? No, couldn't be. But then I really have to go on a 'no holds barred' basis, don't I? Otherwise it makes a mockery.

Oh ... please just be praying for me.

Amazingly, I normally fill a journal a year on my spiritual journey but here we are in April and my current one finished this morning. I brought a packet of my favourite tea back to the UK with me in February and with my morning pot today, I finished the packet. As you know, I've been writing about God's faithfulness through the dark days of divorce. The book has been a huge journey and yesterday I wrote the final chapter of *embers*. These endings seem strangely significant. I have an unsettling impression that my life is never going to be quite the same.

It's a long journey so I will aim to write a bit more before arrival but will sign off now. I've arranged to spend the night with wonderful friends in Park Drive so I am near the airport for tomorrow.

Don't worry about me Ma, I feel quite intrepid. I wonder if Pop has a window in heaven? Perhaps all along he was adventuring with God when he visited missionaries working under the banner of Tear Fund, when it just looked like 'business as usual' to me?

Yes, I've had all necessary jabs and am being sensible about my antimalarial medication though a possible side effect of photosensitivity could be a hindrance.

ALL prayers gratefully received.

Big hug for now x x

Airborne

Dear Ma,

I had a great night's sleep and it was a good plan to be in London. I decided not to risk any delay with such a big journey ahead. Nathan called me at the airport and Sam emailed so I felt very loved. They have both been supportive and I hope Mum going off on an adventure will be inspiring rather than cause for concern.

The atmosphere around my checking in at Heathrow seemed unusual from the start. Kate was on the desk and as she weighed my first bag she said, 'Right, it says here only one bag.' (Strange because I always have an allowance of two bags and I am on a Qantas ticket so I felt perplexed.)

I thought it best just to explain and I launched into telling her I was going to a project working with children, many of whom have lost their parents to Aids, so was carrying bedding and various things to leave with them. She asked me why I was going and I told her, realising as I did that for me things are polarising into the suspicion that I am actually going in order to learn how to love the poor, really love them in a way that is meaningful for them.

We had a great chat about the face of Christianity today in England and then she pressed a few buttons, blithely announced, 'OK I think we'll just lose that bag in the system; no problem.' That was that. She seemed excited and wished me a great trip as if she were an old friend.

My overnight host generously gave me some leftover money from a recent business trip to India. I felt defensive when he offered it and had an overwhelming urge to clarify that I am not in any sense a *missionary* (how can a word feel like a chicken bone stuck in the throat?) so he didn't need to feel he *had* to. Sensitive? *Moi?* Well ... in my defence a flight booked on Apollo 13 would feel less challenging than this particular journey.

When I went to exchange the rupees the cashier asked where I was going. So I told her. She wished me a good trip and said she would be praying for me! A stranger praying for me? I was so caught up with wondering if she knew something I didn't about Mozambique, I managed to leave my passport and ticket on the counter. I had been walking for about ten minutes before I realised and I confess to a moment of, 'Wow, if they are stolen I can't go; maybe it has all been a test after all?!' but I couldn't help being heartily relieved to find them still there when I rushed back.

I sank gratefully into the familiar surroundings of the Qantas lounge and tried to collect the thoughts that spilled all around me like a picnic hamper tumbling from the back of a moving vehicle; contents strewn all over the road. In light of the fact that the menu in Pemba is likely to be somewhat spartan, I decided a small personal ritual was called for.

Airborne

My sensitive personal radar had picked up in recent weeks that Mozambique is rarely mentioned in a sentence that doesn't also include 'rice and beans'. I relished a wholegrain egg sandwich and a small piece of carrot cake before boarding.

I couldn't help wondering what a lifetime without carrot cake would be like. I felt so blessed when the plane was only half full which meant I had a bit of space to spread myself and I got some shut-eye.

Johannesburg airport felt like a vast marble maze; I don't think I have ever walked so far to show my passport. I was completely unprepared for how un-British the customs hall was. I suppose most South Africans I know — well, all actually — are white and speak English. All the employees here were black Africans (is it appropriate to call them indigenous? Is a white person born here called indigenous? So many questions …)

I was perplexed by the guessing game as queues of us tried to gauge which particular booth was open for business. There appeared to be a person at most desks but body language did not communicate 'next please'. With some staff in uniform and some in casual shirts, all avoiding eye contact, it was impossible to tell who was working and who was on a break.

A small group of Asians were being herded along the line of desks by a rotund African in khaki trousers and short-sleeved shirt. His snug shirt buttons oozed job satisfaction. Ushered past the first desk the bemused group hesitated in front of the second, the occupant of which glanced up and flicked his hand to indicate they should keep moving.

So it went on down the nine desks until finally they were ushered back to desk four, where the occupant who had indicated he was not actually working, seemed to take a sudden interest and processed their papers. An exchange where nobody understood what was being asked culminated in the African official waving a languid arm to indicate they were free to continue into the luggage hall.

I kept thinking about visiting Dave in Hong Kong last year and the military precision with which we were processed on arrival. I couldn't help thinking that any official from Hong Kong airport would be apoplectic if dropped into this work environment. We were sort of guided, over time, to various desks in the line and eventually I collected my suitcases and made my way to a South African Airways check-in because I had to have a separate ticket for the Johannesburg to Pemba leg.

As I approached the row of desks I entered a wide rope cordon with the usual sharp turns designed to slow progress and challenge luggage-trolley driving skills. At the first bend stood two burly Africans in casual clothes with a pair of scales ominously erect between them. They didn't appear in any way official and I felt clammy. I didn't want to let go of my cases for fear of being expected to hand over money. I didn't have any local currency.

I indicated I was happy to keep my luggage with me and one of them asked where I was going. I said Pemba and they moved one either side of my trolley indicating I should go with them. My pulse quickened. They escorted me around the corner to a fresh row of desks and I was called to approach one.

My new companions made as if to accompany me but I made it clear I could lift my own bags onto the scales so they stepped back and hovered. I was very conscious of them but the girl on the desk in front of me had my attention. She seemed to be indicating that one bag was too

Airborne

heavy. I thought I was asking clearly if I could take two bags if one was lighter and she seemed to affirm that.

I made some excuse and headed for the nearest stair well. By manoeuvring the trolley and assuming a little-known version of the squat position I began the process of weight redistribution. I decided if I put some of the heavier things in my rucksack I could just carry them myself for this last leg, then other bulky items could go in the second case, which was small enough to be cabin baggage (hopefully nobody would ask to weigh it). Then by stuffing my handbag into the rucksack I should pass muster.

Something had to be compromised but it was hot and I was keen to wear sandals. I pushed my shoes into my bulging rucksack reluctantly draping the jumper whose space they took over my shoulders. The heavy, black, wool overcoat that would be essential for my return to a Perth winter wasn't the ideal garment but maybe it would be cool in the plane. Desperately hoping the rivulets of nervous perspiration streaming down my face would not attract attention I made my way back.

I queued, causing some confusion. Anxious to return to the same check-in desk I held back, encouraging others to overtake me. But when I finally got my bag onto the scale I realised at close quarters it wasn't the same girl at all. I launched into an explanation that I had been told by her colleague it would be alright if I moved some heavy objects but with a happy smile she just checked both bags through, issued a boarding pass and waved me on. My legs felt dangerously close to not being able to support my body weight as I searched the sky for signs to the lounge. Then I remembered this was a separate flight with no lounge access.

I thought to myself, 'Let the Africa experience begin.' I had about four hours to wait and I found my way to a hall with a number of departure gates. They all had exits directly onto the tarmac. It quickly became apparent that 'last call', 'emergency', and 'flight closing' all have slightly different implications in this African context. The most 'final calls' I heard for any particular flight was seven. It was becoming apparent that 'hurry' is not a cultural precedent. Meanwhile I had no access to refreshment so I decided it was time to bring out my filter flask and then I could have water.

Modern rest rooms were designed with slim hands rather than chunky flasks in mind so I spent a happy half hour seeking out a tap with enough space below for me to access water. Feeling thoroughly plucky and resourceful I shuffled thankfully back to my seat delighted to feel fresh air around my flip-flop-clad feet and glad to remove the wool coat. I remembered a snack pot of fresh almonds Joanna had handed me as I left Exeter and sat happily munching and slurping as a cloud of well-being, such as would be worthy of a Famous Five picnic (à la Enid Blyton) descended.

There was plenty to look at as you can imagine with various forms of national dress, businessmen, older ladies travelling with much loved pooches and countless children scuttling about. The time didn't really seem to drag but that could have been to do with the fact that I suspected this plane could be rather smaller than I am used to and I was in no hurry to have my suspicions confirmed.

Eventually it was time and we moved through the gate onto the waiting bus. An unusual shaped bus, it had a wide cab at the front with two driving positions, which I found strangely disconcerting. We pulled out onto the tarmac joining various cranes and planes, some stationary, some moving slowly. Huge trucks bearing luggage careened past and a lorry loaded with steps and ladders veered across our path. The driver was on his phone, oblivious.

The reason for two 'drivers' soon became clear. The second 'driver' was clearly the eyes of the first. The first man now sat frozen over the wheel, face set, eyes straight ahead whilst the second searched frantically for a glimpse of a clear path shouting staccato instructions which produced robotic response from the man at the wheel. There were fifteen of us on board including the drivers and ground staff. Following the line of the driver's gaze I could just pick out, on the far side of the airfield, a model plane; it looked like one of those remote-controlled things that buzz around the park. You can imagine how I felt when we finally pulled up alongside it!

As I write I am airborne Ma, and gazing down on a vast expanse of scrubby bush. The plane is tiny with only single seats down one side of the narrow aisle but I'm OK as I'm imagining this little bird to be strapped on the back of a gigantic angel and I am focusing on the beauty below. There is a streamer of gold ribbon unfurling between ocean and bush, an opulent banner rippling into infinity. This is the coastline of Mozambique.

I'm remembering that South African farmer I met in Canberra some years ago, who had a farm out here and offered to show me a good time driving up this stunning coastline if I flew to South Africa to meet him. I hesitated because I suspected he was a widower on the look-out. When I met him in Australia he was comfortably off and had a weak heart so there was some appeal.

Poised aloft today I wonder if I was rather hasty. But then this incredible adventure deeper into God's heart wouldn't have been on the cards. Chivalrous to the point of Bourgeoisie, freelance exploration for any wife of his would have been well and truly off the cards.

One of his sons still works a farm in Maputo but I doubt there will be a chance to make contact. Maputo was mentioned in the information I received about travelling here. It stated that it is three days 'risky driving' from the capital up to Pemba in the northern region of Cabo Delgado. I haven't pressed anyone for a definition of 'risky' in this part of the world but I'm guessing that both pot holes and bandits feature. Iris Ministries do have another base outside Maputo, which is said to be, 'more geared for visitors and much less rustic' but God clearly highlighted Pemba to me.

I'm quite apprehensive about landing and going through customs in Pemba; cloak of invisibility Lord? Guardian angel? I have been careful not to bring lots of packets of things that I may be accused of intending to trade as it was explained that if I did, import tax could be demanded. But I would still prefer not to have my bag rifled through at gunpoint.

Once 'out' how will 'they/Iris' find me? Who are 'they'? They emailed me saying they are 'easy to find' but they probably operate on African time. I was chatting to a friend the other day, concerned about how I would be 'found'. She soberly pointed out that I am white.

It's a small plane and not full so I have moved to a double seat. They offer a snack with beef but I'm still rather conscious of the horsemeat scandal, in fact haven't eaten any processed meat since it was exposed, as I just can't bear the thought. A vegetarian pasta option tasted really good and I had two delicious chocolates, an unexpected blessing, which I deliberately savoured with a relish that means if I never see chocolate again, our final parting was worthy.

Five of the other passengers are Filipino men who are together and have the word *Salutug* on their travel documents. Pemba is a large, deep, natural port so I imagine they are coming to work on a vessel. (I can't help thinking about all those who died recently in the lifeboat drill of that cruise ship.) I wonder if these men are being 'shipped in' as cheap labour and whether any of them can swim. There is just an air of vulnerability about them and they don't understand the English on board or have local language.

We've got half an hour to go. 'They' didn't mention what kind of vehicle they would collect me in, if we would have to get a local bus or how long the journey might be, but I'm meditating on Psalm 37: 'If the Lord delights in a girl's way, he makes her steps firm.'

Before I left Morna texted. She is so familiar with exploring and experiencing the cultures of different nations, especially low income Africa. She wrote, 'my tip is, if you struggle with anything uncomfortable, don't verbalise it. It gives it a reality.' AJ commented (I tell myself to value his brotherly love!) that not being judgmental could be my greatest challenge (ouch). I have taken both on board. I'm just wondering if Mr Brown-Eyes across the aisle could be a dynamic (single?) South American pastor coming to Pemba? Well, I'm always being told I need to be open ...

Coming in to land now. More soon Ma. Oh my word, I am really here! I can just see a bright blue and yellow plane on the ground with 'Iris' on the side; it must be Rolland's. Hope you are praying for me. I feel so out of my depth but am trusting for safe passage through the airport for starters! I'll let you know. I love you x x

week one

'We don't use the word prostitute.'

Friday afternoon

Whoa Ma.

Been here almost 24 hours. Golly, so much to tell.

Right: so the first thing.

I have to tell you 'work', as in writing, is just not an option. My breathing is almost back to normal but I don't know if I can properly describe what I am experiencing. I'm really not sure I can put into comprehensible language the enormity of it all.

Oh Ma. I'm reeling.

I am hiding behind the elongated hut-style building my room is in. This barn-like construction is split down the middle inside by a partition wall, which ends several feet before it meets the roofline, leaving several feet of airspace (privacy nil!). This 'almost wall' splits the building into two rows of dormitory-style accommodation so the lines of rooms are back-to-back, sharing the high roof.

All rooms have a door directly to the outside. One side opens onto the main central area in the visitors' centre and then the area where

Friday afternoon

I am crouching is a line of currently unoccupied rooms. Doors open onto a walkway with small areas of scrub butted up to the rear of other outbuildings. I felt desperate to find a spot where there is enough light to write but without people. Every limb is sticky with perspiration just sitting here.

It's overwhelming.

As a nurse, I am at a loss. I have already seen several indications of people suffering infections: angry red and yellow cuts; swollen, weepy eyes; green noses; wet coughs. Keeping any wound clean must be a huge challenge in this environment with dirt and dust everywhere. Antibiotics are thrown out by the bucket load at home as patients don't complete courses, dates expire or new drugs come in. It's clear that for local people 'hygiene', 'sterile' and 'antiseptic' (all so normal at home) are about as obtainable as the crown jewels.

And then there are those who are disabled. I literally saw one man with stumps for legs shuffling along in the filth, pulling himself on his forearms. Shock kicks me in the stomach and I'm gasping for air. I can't help wondering if western preventatives could have saved them from a life of daily challenge: challenge beyond anything the average westerner living on disability benefit with an adapted home and probably a vehicle as well, could begin to imagine.

As a mum ... I see hundreds and hundreds of beautiful children who feel somehow totally 'unparented'. Not the children who live here, being loved by Iris. They have a warmth about them, a confidence that marks them; but literally hundreds of others from the surrounding area come for a simple meal each day.

I know life looks totally different here. I'm just trying to ... process?

Pemba Pennings

Absorb reality? It's all swirling, gnawing my emotions. A physical pain: it hurts inside to feel the pull from so many gorgeous little people just starving for love and affection. The atmosphere is loaded with longing and no amount of brief hugs is going to substitute. I feel my heart is cracked.

Then there are the women. Dozens of young mums and girls wandering around with empty eyes. Older ladies shrivelled and bent. I don't think women are valued or cherished. I feel traumatised by the raw absence of care that at home we take for granted. I am teetering on the lip of a vast chasm of need with no hope of safe crossing. From where I stand, this looks like a three-week experience that threatens to squeeze life out of me.

All this Ma, and then … as a Christian how do I process this level of human suffering? Lack and poverty such as I have never encountered. All senses reeling. Who was that woman who blithely thought she would visit the orbit of Heidi Baker in Mozambique and 'write about it'? I have spent 24 hours thrashing around internally. It seemed so clear that God was asking me to write here but working in this state where every sense is overwhelmed or screaming in pain? Impossible. You're probably very surprised to get a letter so soon so I'll explain.

I retreated, alone, a maelstrom of emotion, about an hour ago now. Need to sort myself out. No way I can write or even think coherently in this state. Never imagined this level of impact. As I sat here trying to pull thoughts and feelings into some kind of order, I heard a Holy Spirit whisper,

'You could write letters to your mum. Pour your heart out to her. You usually write home when travelling.'

Relief came in that moment! Could you believe it? I think that is my

Friday afternoon

'assignment'. How sweet is the familiar? To simply write to you as I make the journey here. That I think I can manage ... with divine help.

So brace yourself, Ma. This is the first of a few missives and thank you for sharing the adventure in this way. Even writing now I feel a measure of comfort.

At one level it could feel too enormous to write but I sense that if I don't set myself to record and share as I go along it will be a mountain of experience I am never able to recall or recount accurately.

I sense also that if God says or does significant things in me it could be very valuable to have recorded those as 'in the moment' as possible; we all know how committed the enemy is to robbing, blurring and generally undermining whatever he can.

So, letters to you feels manageable.

Keeping a record as a piece of work? Beyond attaining! I think he has a purpose. It will be challenging to process 'aloud' plus you know how brilliant I am about sharing emotions (not!) so I will picture us on the white chairs in your garden just chatting over coffee and set myself to find courage.

I admit I am apprehensive. Sensing that God's heart of compassion needs to be somehow deeply impressed into mine and conscious that if it involves some kind of humungous 'letting go' or visible emotional response ... well, my roots are British and I am my father's daughter! It isn't totally reassuring that Heidi and Rolland's stories appear to be peppered with the uncomfortable and more than slightly daunting word 'wrecked'.

One is daring to hope that this is just a rather American euphemism (for some part of experiencing the love of God that is 'normal Christian living') but one has to confess to a disconcerting tremor of doubt. Right. Enough introspection. Knowing you love me unconditionally is so fantastic and I just won't let myself think about the possibility of any other readers. How incredible would it be though, if God could use my experience here to lure others deeper into the wild romance that I relish?

As we approached Pemba in the plane, the water was every shade of green, blue and turquoise I've ever seen and the white brilliance of the sand was incredible even coming up through fathoms of ocean! I almost forgot the size of the plane. The inhabited area was vast from the air, huts and bits of roofing stretching for acres and acres. We are on a peninsula and I am told Pemba is one of the deepest natural harbours in Africa. I didn't really know what to think as I walked down the steps of the plane.

Of course the sticky heat (particularly if one happens to be coming from winter and wearing a black wool overcoat) is the first thing to impress. But then nothing at all is familiar, be it sight, smell or sound. I quietly pictured myself slipping my clammy mitt into a large, cool, divine palm, took a deep breath and found my flip-flops taking me gently across the steaming tarmac towards …

I was about to write 'the terminal building' but the reality is a small man, his face glinting like burnished ebony, was brandishing large plastic lollipops on the tarmac. Once we exited the plane he used them to indicate we should head for what appeared to be a white tent. I noticed this tent had windows, just like a wedding marquee. Then I realised that was because the arrivals terminal was indeed a marquee.

This was a bit disorientating as we approached because the messages to my brain hinted at trays of pink champagne cocktails offered by a

Friday afternoon

penguin person prior to the reception line. These wispy thoughts were not half as disorientating as actual entry to the 'arrivals hall'.

The side of the tent appeared to be hooked onto one end of a wall that was almost holding up a low building, but the building was only half built (or half demolished, I couldn't tell). The overall effect was akin to that of a big night out, as depicted by Hollywood, rendering wall and tent in a state of inebriation and thus only able to remain upright by leaning into each other.

This was the part of the journey I had awarded generous prayer time. It stood me in good stead. The handful of us who had disembarked hovered. Gazing around there was a confusing cluster of what appeared to be large, upturned cardboard boxes. I mean of the genre we have washing machines or refrigerators delivered in and children then adopt as 'home'.

Behind each box stood or sat an African male. One was huge with a broad shiny face above full military uniform. A couple of guards lolled beside what looked like a freestanding old-fashioned x-ray machine. (I had the impression they were armed but that may have been me anticipating 'menace'. I deliberately focused on keeping my line of vision above the belts where weapons would be carried.)

The notes from Pemba Hospitality had stated that this machine was new to Pemba and only used intermittently. I had memorised the phrase, 'If the machine is not in use collect your bags and walk straight out.' My jittery gaze briefly took in a few random notices. They looked to be written on more bits of cardboard box with a fat marker pen. The words 'Passport', 'Visa' and 'Baggage' hung in the air on lopsided lengths of string. Conspicuous by absence was the word 'Exit'. Nobody moved.

The heat was stifling. I studiously avoided eye contact wondering if 'Iris' were within earshot.

A trolley was pushed from the plane and the suitcases shuffled into a sticky pile on the dusty ground. With a huge surge of relief, clearly out of all proportion but sufficient to propel me the six feet needed, I spied my bag on the outer edge of the jumbled heap. I lunged for my case thinking I would head straight for the only opening in the tent other than the one through which we had entered. Wishful thinking!

My movement galvanised one of the guards who grunted something. Gesticulating with both arms he indicated I should retreat and show my passport at the first box counter before just blithely sailing out with my luggage.

The official at the 'desk' studied his fingernails while I stood, now weirdly grateful for the familiar comfort of my coat in spite of grimy rivulets trickling down my legs. I breathed in and out and held my nerve. Suddenly he thrust one hand out at me and I placed my passport into it.

Would a smile appear flippant or disrespectful? Would a serious face be perceived as haughty? My passport was handed to the adjacent desk and I meekly followed, probably looking slightly delinquent since I had yet to settle on an appropriate expression.

'Here,' a gruff voice and an arm waving my bag towards his machine. OK, this was it then. What would look suspicious enough on the screen for me to have to be 'searched'? (That scary time in Harare, when the man wearing a huge machine gun wanted some of my things and I didn't understand about bribing, scarred me for life, Ma! As you know, I was never ever going to Africa again … But God!!) If I stepped up to the

Friday afternoon

machine I would cross the invisible line in the sand that had provoked the earlier reprimand. If I stepped away I might look guilty. I froze.

Then suddenly the traveller behind nudged me. Everyone was waiting for me to pick up my case. I was free to go. I was aware of a cluster of men gathered outside the tent. Just visible through the open flap, a few bodies languishing in the shade of the half wall. Iris were probably in the real arrivals hall with a banner or a badge or something. If I stepped outside how would they find me?

Too late. It was only a step from the machine to the outside and there was nowhere else to go. I found myself in the glare of a cloudy alley with assorted chunks of rubble visible in the swirl of brick dust from the building works. But nobody yelled or grabbed me so yanking my unwilling case after me I moved slowly on the uneven surface, attempting to emanate an air of nonchalance that would suggest, to anybody waiting to pounce, that I knew exactly where I was going. If I could pull it off maybe no one would try to sell me anything or usher me into their waiting vehicle.

On a corner that looked as if a road ran past the end, there was a short flight of steps up the outside of the building. Moving slowly and longing for 'Iris' to spot me, I came to rest in the shade of the rough wall and leaned gratefully against it. One or two white faces hovered at the top of the steps. I was reassured.

Would 'Iris' be black or white? Male or female? A number of 'possibles' broke away from the cluster at the other end of the alley but one by one ambled past my spot without speaking. I felt slightly wistful as an efficient-looking man with a clipboard ushered the Filipino men from the flight out of the alley and into a waiting jeep.

Pemba Pennings

Never mind, it was daylight and I had a spot of shade. 'Iris' would come soon. All other passengers had gone and I gazed down the alleyway hoping I was in the right place. Suddenly a lanky silhouette came loping into view. With afternoon sun behind him I couldn't discern detail but flip-flops and baggy shorts were suggestive of youth. (I made this assumption before arriving on the base and discovering this outfit is uniform for males of all ages.)

'Are you Hazel?'

'Are you Iris?' (Knees weak with relief.)

'I was expecting you to be a group. I'm Ben.'

'Er no, I've come alone, just me.' Was I a disappointment already?

'No worries then; welcome to Pemba.'

Then taking my case, 'Shall we?'

I threw my coat onto the back seat of the dual-cab chunky truck/Land Rover-type vehicle and climbed up into the front passenger seat. (You can imagine the apprehension churning my stomach.) The short drive to the base is something of a blur. Travelling through an assortment of crude buildings and a number of junctions, the impact of turning a corner and finding the sparkling Indian Ocean lapping sand beside our route was very disorientating. I think because of that 'holiday feeling' normally attached to the beach.

With the ocean still on our right we turned left and Ben acknowledged a guard in uniform in the wide gateway. A large sign announced we'd arrived at Arcos Iris which I'm told means Village of Joy. The track ahead was thick, sandy dirt and rose up a slight incline for some distance in front of us. A large sports field spread out to the right and the left looked like a building site, with one completed structure beside the

Friday afternoon

track. Ben explained that this is the new clinic. They are hoping to build a hospital and provide maternity services on the same site, which will be fantastic for local people.

There were clusters of children and young people everywhere. Most were barefoot with raggedy clothes. Many of the slightly bigger children had bundles of faded fabric on their backs. As we drew closer each bundle had brown limbs dangling but the air of solemnity defied all initial thoughts about games or piggy-back.

It was bemusing for me to see so many children obviously in sole charge of another; many of the small bundles looked little more than a baby. A large cement-floored shed rose up on the right. It looked like a cross between a large farm building and an aircraft hangar and was spewing children from its small doorway.

'That's our church building and we feed a crowd of village children every day between one and three. You'll see,' Ben explained.

A set of smaller rustic-looking gates lay ahead, creating an 'inner' and 'outer' feeling as the guard here indicated we should slow. He appeared to recognise Ben and waved us on through.

A noisy motorbike overtook us and disappeared up the hill leaving a sheen of rusty dust on the windscreen. A chunky lorry with light-green canvas stretched over a frame lurched towards us. The Mozambican driver acknowledged Ben with a slight movement of his right hand. He appeared rather low behind the wheel, just visible beneath a cap. Dark-rimmed glasses were escaping down his glistening nose, coming to perch just above wide nostrils.

Some interesting stonework formed walls and paths that wound away to the right and Ben indicated that a large umbrella-shaped roof was the prayer hut. 'Sunrise here is stunning if you are up in time.' He swung the vehicle into a short laneway with buildings on each side. It was a dead end and we drew to a halt in front of a small fenced-in area that had a construction like a pump or water tower of some kind in it.

Ben opened his door and pointed to an opening with solid wood gates swinging from chunky posts. I had to push down that uncomfortable feeling, from years ago visiting Grandma and Grandpa, when I saw the lock and high gates like they used to have in Zimbabwe; it feels so intimidating, especially in a culture where I don't have the language. We entered up two rough concrete steps. To my right it looked as if someone had tripped carrying a bucket of cement that had dried before anyone managed to clear it up but closer inspection indicated a 'disability ramp' (with only a three-inch lip at the top!).

Ben spoke, 'Here we are. This is the visitors' centre; it's fully enclosed to offer some privacy and the chance to rest. I think you are in "Kindness". Now, we are currently undergoing renovations so things are a bit messy.'

He pushed open the heavy gate with his shoulder, hitching my case over the final step and almost knocking over a man in guard's uniform in the process. He was unsuspectingly hovering on the inside. They exchanged greetings, Ben introduced me and we shook hands. I was thinking, 'Golly, what do we need guarding from?' I felt the guard's eyes on my back as I picked my way slowly along the crazy-paving path.

Immediately inside the gates was a roofless circular hut with workmen poised aloft redoing the struts and raffia, which looked like the Mozambican version of thatch. The bamboo scaffolding looked rather flimsy; I didn't want to stare but I noticed the exposed green wall had

Friday afternoon

a scripture emblazoned on it. There was lush foliage and evidence that somebody was keen to establish something of a garden with climbing shrubs and a few pots.

The centre is basically a rectangular-shaped compound with accommodation on the two long sides. It's on a slope so the upper side is raised with several flights of steps leading from the middle where a number of trees and plants are in varying stages of health and growth. At the end nearest to the gate there is a small office and the opposite end has a row of latrine cubicles (holes in the ground) with doors and a laundry area. All rooms open on to a covered walkway that provides crucial shade.

Dormitories are named after fruit of the Spirit, serving as a helpful reminder about attitude. 'Kindness' is a room with three sets of bunks and one single bed. It took my eyes a while to get used to the dusky light in the room. The ceiling is high; it's a pitched tin roof with a few holes. I wondered at first why the wall didn't join the roof but I realise now, as I mentioned earlier, that the wall is in effect down the centre of the long construction as a partition and the large ceiling fans suspended periodically (ditto for their functionality!) cater to the needs of bedrooms on either side of the wall

There are no occupants in the other side of the building at this moment. The two window-shaped holes are glassless. They have metal grid-style bars across them and look out onto the covered walkway, so light cannot really penetrate the depth of the room but I think the airflow will be lifesaving.

The only thing in the room apart from bunks is a freestanding fan but when I tried to plug it in, the socket just plopped out of the wall so I'm not sure how much actual fanning will be accomplished. A box of bottled water and a toilet roll were thoughtfully left ready for me.

Ben told me that my roommate is on a bush outreach for two nights with all the other current visitors (except two who are unwell) so things are pretty quiet. He gave me a brief orientation. The main points that have stuck with me are that we are asked not to give anything to anyone without conferring with a permanent Iris staff member. Then there is the question of amenities.

There was some mention of 'village boys', which was a bit confusing since I thought we were living in the village. He explained the base is called 'Village of Joy' but 'village' generally relates to those not currently living as part of the Iris community. The base here is positioned as if it were in the hollow part of a horseshoe shape. Opening onto the road by the beach with 'village' living all around in a giant U and stretching a long way back inland. We're talking real mud hut, no mod cons, genuine African village.

My initial impression is that there are many more women and children than men. Haven't seen an elderly man yet. Ben confirmed that the centre is not busy, as in not fully occupied at the moment. With only two showers and two toilets I am quite relieved as I think they can have nearly seventy visitors in the centre in a busy time. Ablution facilities then are pretty basic but I don't think I will be hankering for hot water anyway.

They have just had three weeks without any running water or power in the wake of a huge storm. The toilet priority is that nothing at all that has not been through the body can go into the toilet. (Holiday musings and thoughts of Gerald Durrell and his unfortunate sister in Greece wafted in.)

Ben brought me back to the present: 'This is very important and we

Friday afternoon

ask you to get a stick and fish out anything you drop in the toilet in error.' Right, message received. The padlocks on the outside of the toilet cubicles are because if the water is off for any length of time toilets are locked and latrines must be used. (Padlocks? Presumably previous guests have a track record of non-compliance, thus totally blocking the system rather than using a hole in the ground.) Flushing when they are in action is initiated by pouring water into the toilet with a jug or beaker filled up from the big bin provided. Guests are responsible for keeping shower area and kitchen clean … all joy!

In a second hut, identical to the one that is being worked on, Ben pointed out a tiny kitchen area for communal use. The encouraging notice over the sink reads:

To prevent sickness wash dishes with either …
1. Hot water and detergent (heat water on stove)
2. Cold water and detergent + half a cupful of bleach

What it doesn't explain is that using the stove entails taking your life in your hands as it is like something from an old movie, with a rusty pipe feeding into a gas cylinder, which is to be switched off manually after each use. The noisy gutterings and poppings, which threaten imminent explosion on each use, mean I have no intention of risking it.

There is a kettle so whenever there is power I am boiling it twice before using the water. I'm not at all sure that the cooker is safe but people here must be aware so I am just praying whenever it's in use and keeping my distance. I'm not judging. It's great there is a cooker … I'm not verbalising because everyone can hear and see it. Maybe it is an intended part of the Pemba experience to promote longsuffering? Come to think of it, I haven't seen a room called that: probably too many letters to fit on the door sign!

Pemba Pennings

That was about it really and then Ben went off, leaving me to settle in. I found a pile of dusty net curtains on the bunk above me that turned out to be mosquito nets. A hook suspended from the underneath of the top bunk offered a centre point but I think it could be pretty claustrophobic if I had to attach the net within the confines of the lower bunk and I would be bound to keep catching it. I am not thinking about what can crawl in the dark and I am really pleased I worked out a way to be able to place the net under the top mattress so it drapes right down and there is enough to tuck in.

A piece of string that was left tied washing line style between bunks, gave me a focal point and I got out the clothes pegs I brought with me and pegged up one or two items to make it feel a bit more homely. A flannel, a pretty pink bag and then I sorted into another bag, which I hooked over the end of the top bunk, things I will need every day such as malaria tablets, sunscreen, insect repellent.

I opened my box of water and began the first bottle. Ben did mention hydration being a key issue but I love water and in this heat it won't be hard to drink plenty. $15US for twelve bottles holding 1.5 litres each seems a good start but anyhow, I've got my flask with the filter from Nathan and then also some steri-tabs so I should be fine.

When I arrived the power was on but the water off so I sorted myself with an old plastic tub (I think ice cream?) I saw lurking under a bench outside and put it ready with a flannel under my bed. Once I have empty plastic water bottles the routine here is to fill them with tap water (when it is running obviously) and then keep them under your bed ready for washing when the water goes off again. I love a good system but last night I had no option but to wash with bought water. I stayed calm and

Friday afternoon

am determined to see any new experience as part of the adventure.

Speaking of adventure, I had been here about two hours when a loud gong reverberated over the centre and I knew it was time for the evening meal. In the communal hut area by the kitchen here in the visitors' centre there is a large wooden table with benches and a smaller table to one side. A low daybed with wooden frame offers hammock-style relaxation.

Molly was reclining on the daybed when I got there, apparently sleeping off whichever ailment had prevented her from going on outreach. Two scrawny cats were snuggled into various parts of her anatomy and I couldn't help wondering how big a part they play in the life of the centre. The words 'flea' and 'worm' hovered.

Clara was awake and watching over her friend. Introducing them as part of a missions team from the US she explained in a stage whisper that didn't disguise her broad (I think Texan) accent, that she had most likely had malaria herself but the blood tests would soon show. She rolled her eyes dramatically as she commenced a detailed catalogue of symptoms, including exhausting sounding visits to the 'rest room'. She broke off mid-sentence to ask me if I wanted to eat. Explaining she and Molly were forgoing the pleasure out of respect for their own digestive systems she encouraged me to go forthwith, so as not to risk there being nothing left.

I confess that I felt daunted about stepping out of the visitors' centre. In the space of a few hours the centre had become familiar. I knew the layout. I had my spot. However, food was not going to find its way to me. The information I'd read stated that all visitors were encouraged to eat with the children and those Iris staff living on the base.

I collected my plate and the plastic fork I brought with me and tucked my antibacterial hand gel into the lightweight shoulder bag a friend leant me. (She said I could leave it behind when I leave.) It is not pink and it's not exactly beige and the front flap is sort of petal shaped. It's not at all 'me' but then I don't think it was my friend either. It has the distinct feel of an unwanted Christmas gift from a spinster aunt; this is enhanced by the fact I want my hands free so am wearing it across my chest (you get the picture ... basically, any notion of feeling anything akin to 'myself' is long gone!). But this isn't a fashion parade and I'm grateful to her, because I sense carrying a handbag could only be a hindrance.

I have the feeling that keeping things 'safe' will be a challenge. Ben mentioned keeping everything shut in bags or cases and not leaving things 'open to temptation'. He also made it clear that wandering out of the base or down the road is not safe with less than three. An even larger group and a male presence are required after dark.

I felt self-conscious just walking past the guard who was resting on a white plastic chair (only one leg cracked!) by the gate, never mind walking out onto the main track and turning into the shadowy human coils snaking their way, in what I assumed to be, the direction of food.

What would I do if someone spoke to me? It probably sounds mad but I was so apprehensive about coming here that I didn't even go on the website. I just felt the less I knew the better able I would be to embrace the adventure as it unfolds. The stories I had heard all implied children wanted to just cuddle visitors.

I didn't have to wait long, although the young man who approached me was definitely too big to be cuddled; he spoke polished English. As you know, I've always loved young people and enjoyed their company but honestly Ma, I struggled as intimidation got me in a headlock and

Friday afternoon

my throat constricted. I've never thought about skin colour influencing my ability to read facial expressions, eyes so dark.

I am an alien here; thoughts were straining but I failed to come up with a single thing I might have in common with this young man: my well-covered frame to his bony lean; his black, my white; his worn threads, my well-made garments (even though second-hand bargains).

'Hello Mama' (they all greet me as Mama but I think it may just be the normal greeting for a woman ... I'm not sure yet exactly why).

'Where are you from?' He thrust his hand out for me to shake. As the spectre of sickness hovered I fervently hoped I would have the chance to reapply my antibacterial gel before coming into contact with my food.

'Are you going to eat?'

We had a brief chat and I explained I had just arrived and it's my first visit to Pemba. We reached the food hall and he held back.

'I won't come,' he said, 'I live in the village.'

With a jaunty, 'I see you later Mama', he melted into the shadow of the building and I knew a fleeting frisson of pleasure. I had made my first connection with a Mozambican. I felt it went well. Perhaps I had a new friend? I was bemused by the whole 'not coming to eat' thing but couldn't dwell on it as the current of bodies carried me towards the eating hall.

The moving throng slowed and as I got nearer the front of the line I saw everyone stopping by a big plastic bin (we're talking large dustbin size just like in the showers back at the centre). My hands were pulled over the bin and water that had the faint aroma of bleach was sloshed over them before the tide carried me up some concrete steps and into a cacophony of noise and food.

Pemba Pennings

A cement floor and the glare of fluorescent strip lights reveal the food hall as another big rectangular shape. Walls with various gaps for doorways and some large grilled openings looking out onto what appeared to be huge play pens. (I now know this to be the accommodation for the smallest children; pre-schoolers who live and eat in their own area.)

The noise was overpowering, the smell unfamiliar and the heat heavy as the light outside faded fast. Down the middle of the open-sided hall stretched a long line of tables end to end with benches on either side. A few tables and benches were against one of the sidewalls and people were just wandering in to sit wherever they liked.

I turned back towards the serving hatch on the short end wall that was the focus of attention. The queue was long and I could see no other European or anyone who looked even vaguely like a missionary. I stood patiently as boys filed past me with plates laden with rice and some kind of sauce. OK this was it ... first meal in Pemba.

Two other young men came to greet me, shaking me politely by the hand. Clutching my plastic plate to me I surreptitiously managed to flip the lid and re-gel the shaken hand all within the confines of the little beige bag. I felt desperate not to offend anyone but maybe more desperate not to be ill. As I came to the front of the queue I tried not to stare ... and failed as my lower jaw sagged.

Two male youths were on stools each with a pot resembling a vat in front of them. The first pot (they each looked suspiciously like the bottom half of a large petrol drum) contained white rice and the young man serving was armed with two plastic plates. With a kind of scooping motion he was working hard to keep up with demand as a stack of empty plates on a large board balanced between the pots was constantly

Friday afternoon

replenished. The portions were generous.

The contents of the second pot were greenish and liquid. It was being stirred by a piece of wood that had all the appearance of having been recently pulled from a tree. His face streaming with perspiration the second young man wielded a large ladle. I could see no other appliance or utensil that would indicate the area as a kitchen.

Through an opening at the back of this serving area I could see a huddle of people squatting in the shadows. They seemed to be leaning in to a central point on the ground. When a woman emerged with a stack of fresh plates it dawned on me that this was the washing-up area. I handed my plate over and tried to slow my heart rate.

I felt totally self-conscious, conspicuously well fed and obliged to sit on the spilt rice that was all over the bench seat rather than appear to be fussily flicking it onto the floor. The green sauce was quite tasty and reminded me of well-cooked spinach; too runny to be labelled 'purée' it gave the plain rice a tasty moistness.

I was by this time hungry and had agreed with the Lord I would be properly 'in the zone'. It was not as if I had tasty snacks or muesli bars tucked away as an option. This was it until the promised bread roll that constituted breakfast, which is available each morning from 6am except for Saturdays when it will be an hour later.

I tucked in and rather enjoyed what I now know to be a traditional meal of *matapa*, which is made from cassava leaves and is part of the staple diet. It looked similar to a rather watery spinach. Several other young men spoke to me and I noticed a group of teenage girls sitting apart on a smaller table.

As I emerged from the meal it had become dark. It's very similar to visiting the relatives in Queensland in that way, Ma: the sun goes down and 'lights out'. I had no idea that it would only be one hour's time difference when arriving from England but I am so thankful I won't have to contend with jet lag on top of this humidity.

As I turned the corner to return up the main drag to the visitors' centre my new 'friend' emerged waving a flip-flop. He began to spin me a tale of woe involving him breaking one of his sandals and having no other shoes. He lamented that he now had nothing to wear on his feet.

My stomach contracted and I could feel pinpricks of damp on my upper lip as he asked me what I could do for him. He must, after all, be one of the 'village boys' who sadly know how to 'work' visitors. I could only feel acutely aware of how much I have but I truthfully said to him that I only have the flip-flops I was standing in.

'Do you have money?' he wondered

Thankfully I had not changed any of my dollars to local currency so could say 'no' truthfully. I felt so awkward and completely foolish as he shrugged and walked off unimpressed. How will I know if people are only talking to me in hopes of getting something from me? Was it some old broken flip-flop he had picked up or was his really broken? Do other westerners feel guilty all the time because they also have so much when those around clearly have so little? I have questions.

Molly had surfaced from her healing slumber when I returned to the visitors' centre and introduced herself, adding a few details of her bodily functions that I could have managed without. In a broad American drawl she inquired as to my supper plans and was aghast when I explained I'd eaten in the dining area.

I proceeded to the kettle to boil water in which to wash my plate

Friday afternoon

and fork. Following me into the tiny space Molly explained that she had previously offered to help in the 'kitchen' ... and not eaten there since. I tried to appear attentive whilst consciously letting words like 'grease', 'slime' and 'germ' slither past. I knew I couldn't afford to let them 'lodge' because I am looking at another 20 days of communal eating.

Molly has rounded features and shoulder-length brunette (with colour in) hair. I suspect she has a healthy sense of humour but she is obviously feeling unwell; I think getting to know her will be fun. She explained that she and Clara are part of a bigger group of students who have just graduated from the first Harvest School in America.

This was a pilot course of the training programme I mentioned that they run here in Pemba twice a year. They are now on their compulsory end of training 'mission' experience and chose to do this in Pemba. The students have a full schedule of activities, prayer times and sessions together for the two weeks they are here. The others are due back from outreach tomorrow afternoon so I will meet them all then.

The water was still off so I did my thing with my little pot of water in my room. I couldn't work out how to clean my teeth without spitting (I didn't want to swallow the toothpaste) and couldn't face going out into the dark or padding along to the tiled gathering place for bugs where there was no running water to carry my spit down the plug. Anyway, I imagine the mozzies are attracted to the lights in the shower area so a sensible risk assessment concluded teeth could wait till the morning.

All these decisions wore me out and I was thankful to slip onto the clean sheet. Actually I put my own over the top of the Pemba one just for the luxury of having one more layer between my body and the mattress, which was presumably as well used as the less than pristine ones that lay on the vacant bunks around me.

I managed to wedge the socket so the plug of the fan stayed in the wall with only one initial blue flash. Luxury to feel cool air on my skin. I drifted off to sleep pondering the amazing way in which events have unfolded to bring me here at all and hoping the mosquito net was properly spread out so that no bugs would get in. I tucked my watch and my head torch into the top of my pillowcase so that I wouldn't have to reach outside the net in the night.

I slept soundly till 4.30 when a distant wailing (which I now know to be the Muslim call to prayer) dragged me to the surface. I fleetingly thought of Ben's 'sunrise' comment and promptly went back to sleep. The next time I woke light was trickling over the bunks and my watch said 7am. Fear of missing my bread roll propelled me from my bunk.

We are each given a key to our room and have to pay a deposit because so many are lost; Ben said keys are expensive here. Locking myself out after dark (and office hours) is a daunting prospect so I wear it round my neck and am hanging it by the door on the light switch overnight so I really can't miss it.

As I made my way along the walkway a cheery, 'Good morning' emanated from the kitchen hut. I came down the steps onto the same level and was greeted by Al. Molly was there and introduced him. Al is a friendly, cheerful Singaporean. He hugged me (a proper warm godly embrace, none of that Christian, play safe, twiglet business ... you know where the men contort to ensure any bumps meet a space and affection cringes) in a warm inclusive way.

It was like Jesus saying, 'Welcome to breakfast Haze,' as Al expansively welcomed me to the table. He had collected enough bread rolls for

Friday afternoon

those of us in the centre and had also boiled a number of eggs which he explained he had been out and bought from a *barraca* (this is the equivalent to a roadside stall or basic shop). Obviously a male can wander about at will then.

It was a gourmet breakfast and such a scrumptious surprise. Heidi writes about 'our delicious Mozambican bread' in her books and I confess to presuming she was exercising the power of positive speech but truly the fresh, white, fluffy roll was delicious and sliced hard-boiled egg was a complete bonus. I drank hot water that I was careful to boil twice and had in the thermos mug I brought with me. It felt like a banquet.

So it was Day 1, Friday morning and I wondered how to spend the day as I prayed God would let me feel his presence. A young woman appeared at the table and I introduced myself. Gina explained she is here for three months so officially a 'short-term' staff member. A family from her church in Cambridge, England, is living here because the husband is helping roll out a project called 'Stop for the One'. Anyway, Gina came to help with childcare so the parents can be free to work and she also has a role in the pre-school here.

I had just been mulling over how to get started in terms of being engaged with activity on the base when Gina brightly said, 'What are your plans for the day? You can always come and help in the pre-school.' I made a swift decision to accept her invite. It seemed a double blessing when she added, 'It's Friday so we take the children to play on the beach this morning. Why don't you come down and join us there about 9.30?'

As she wandered off I remembered reading 'children have keys to the kingdom' in Heidi's writing and felt a surge of anticipation. Also relief if I'm honest; I was thinking, 'OK, children I can do.' Plus, even in the few

Pemba Pennings

hours I had been here, I was struggling with the sea shimmering literally at the end of the driveway.

I can't leave the centre to go anywhere on the base without the tantalising view of crystal water. I am so hot most of the time it's a challenge to manage not being able to plunge into the waves. It is a Muslim region so I would have to be more or less fully clothed, but still. I'm going to find it hard I think. At least it sounded as though I could paddle with the children ... joy!

It must have been around 9.25 as I approached the end of the main drag. The sea sparkled on the other side of the road and the dirt scorched my feet where it flicked into the space between the soles of my feet and my flip-flops. I covered up with long sleeves and my cap because of the antimalarial tablet issues. Apparently one of the side effects of doxycycline is you can burn really badly with it. I remember Nathan saying one of his men was badly affected in Afghanistan so I have let go any dream of returning sun-kissed.

I was excited to think I would be 'hands on' with the children and was looking forward to it but I felt quite anxious about crossing the road and then walking along the beach alone. As I walked God reminded me of something.

I had emailed my friend Catherine to say I was coming out here and she'd replied in a state of wonder. 'Hazel, that's amazing! I had a dream about you a couple of weeks ago and that makes sense now. I dreamed you were kneeling in the sea and waves were washing over you ... I didn't know what it meant but now I think it means that in your humility and willingness to kneel before him, waves of power and refreshing will wash over you and you will not be overwhelmed, it will just keep coming

Friday afternoon

as long as you kneel in those waters.'

Golly Ma, just realised this is a marathon of a letter; sorry, there is just so much to tell. I hope there is a night with nothing much on the TV so you can read this! I'd better stop soon or you'll give up; I'll just finish this bit because it was special.

As I approached the gate wondering if it would be safe to continue, who should appear from under a big tree but Al! Cheerful as ever he inquired as to where I was going and immediately offered to walk me over the road and along the beach to join the others. What blessed timing.

I felt a huge sense of well-being on the beach. I just felt I was in the right place at the right time and a surge of love came over me when a small boy called Roland cut his toe then climbed onto my lap and snuggled in for comfort. One white feather was suddenly dancing in the wind coming in off the ocean right in front of me. Feeling a sudden whoosh inside I wanted to catch it, capture the moment. I leaned over Roland to grasp it and it swirled just out of reach and then was gone so quickly I was left with a quiet sense of awe.

Then I felt a God whisper about kneeling in the water's edge. I felt a bit self-conscious but I did it as a symbolic act, receiving the promise of Catherine's dream as children scampered and splashed around me. It was so hot I don't even remember when my skirt dried.

Christy is the amazing young woman who runs the pre-school and has been here nine months with every intention of continuing. She clearly loves the children and understands how to help them as they arrive in the group often traumatised and starved of affection. She has a presence about her that makes the children feel safe. I had a quiet afternoon and then an amazing evening but I'd better save that till my next letter.

Pemba Pennings

Thanks for sharing this journey Ma. It feels incredible to think I have three whole weeks to experience all God intends for me here. Still can't really believe I am actually in Pemba. Oh my word ...

All my love for now, more soon, hoping all well your end,

Big hug, Hazel x x

Saturday

Dearest Ma,

Well, Saturdays are a bit of a rest day here so I can catch you up on what I didn't write yesterday. I feel as if I must have been here longer than 2 sleeps.

'Rest day?' Mmm ... well my room-mate Aya is back from outreach and another girl Katie (who works in another part of the country as a missionary with a different organisation) is here on a kind of retreat/refresher break. So now there are three of us in the room.

Katie has been here several times and is enjoying renewing links with a group of girls who are growing up here. Aya is from Tai Wan but lives in Brisbane and is probably in her late 50s. She is tiny and can sleep on her bed, the only single one, by the door, with all her possessions lined up against the wall on the bed beside her. She doesn't use a net.

I'll pick up where I left off so you don't miss anything. Returning from the beach yesterday morning with the children I joined them for a Play-doh session (no language needed!) in the cool shed that is their learning area. I felt strangely awed when Gina suddenly announced the little boy I was playing with was Heidi's grandson. Then puzzled because I know Heidi and Rolland have two fair skinned children living in America and have adopted a number of others. Joel is a yummy caramel colour and Gina explained that his mum is white American and his dad was born and grew up here (I think he must be one of Heidi's adopted sons).

I was completely stunned Ma, to hear Gina saying to this little chap, 'Yes Joel, and Grandma Heidi will be here next week won't she? How cool will that be?' I didn't trust myself to speak but had a pins and needles sensation all up my back. Imagine if God actually brings Heidi here whilst I am around? I really had let go of that dream; especially since realising I could book for the Shine Conference in Perth after leaving here and hear Heidi speak when I visit the cousins. But how incredible could it be to *actually* be here in Pemba whilst she is home and working? Maybe she will preach in church?

It's not hero worship or anything Ma, truly; the presence of Jesus in Heidi is totally magnetic. His presence was tangible that one time I heard her speak; in a way that I feel something of heaven really could invade my own life. I know I may not even see her but deep down I continue to have a strong sense of God having an intention for me being in 'her shadow'.

Let's face it; we both know none of this was my idea! Even listening to her on YouTube a couple of weeks ago God spoke to me clearly. I just can't get my head around how much God loves me and is in every detail of this trip!

Christy has a beautifully organised cupboard stocked with activities for the children that look well cared for. Many are donated and she col-

Saturday

lects others when on leave. There is something very honourable about the way she is faithfully serving here and I felt graciously included.

Before lunch I was delighted to find the water was running. I had a wash, got my plate and went for my introduction to rice and beans. (Felt totally conspicuous again with no chance of blending in.) Truthfully? I found it tasty. The portions are ample and I really haven't been hungry between meals. I am persisting with my anti-bac gel routine and using my own plate and fork and praying over my food. God is certainly able to keep bugs at bay so I'll trust and be sensible.

Al offered me a coffee bag (gold!) when I came back to the centre. I poured water from the kettle onto it and was *mortified* when I realised that in my haste the water had not boiled. Then I had to thoroughly bleach and wash my thermos! What a missed opportunity, can't believe myself sometimes!

At the evening meal I got chatting to a lovely missionary called Hans who lives and works here, married to Annette who is Heidi's assistant when she is here. (There are other girls who travel with her.) I really appreciated sitting with him and chatting. It was good just to be with someone who could communicate and knew the children around him and I was able to relax for the first time at the table.

I spent time after that just trying to absorb everything and looking around a bit more. One of the missionaries who lives here came into the centre mid-afternoon to invite any of us who were free to join her for what she calls 'Rahab ministry'. The others were still on their way back from the bush so she said she'd return later to give us some orientation about the evening. Golly, what she is doing sounds amazing Ma.

Sara is British and is probably in her late thirties. By 6pm the others had returned and we gathered round. Rahab is the name Sara has given to the work that she is doing with local street girls. I think we all felt a twist in our insides as she gave us some cultural background. She emanates a vivid purity and with olive skin, dark curly hair and lovely brown eyes she is alluringly attractive. I wonder how she is single. It isn't being talked about but I get the feeling that sacrifice is normal Christian living for those here.

Not that there is any sense of lack in the lives of those I have met so far but a kind of atmosphere, something that subtly communicates a heart and mind set on higher things. I can't describe it exactly but it's not in any sense exclusive, it's just present. I may be able to explain better when I have been here longer. As she talked to us Sara exuded passion underpinned by quiet strength.

Once born in this northern region a Mozambican child is strapped to their mother and breastfed until two years old. At this stage the child is put right away from their mother and may be cared for by an older sibling; 'older' could mean only five or six, or an aunt or grandmother. Either way, if you cry from this age you can expect to have your cheek pinched until you stop. You are expected to quietly go where you are taken.

Around puberty there are shocking initiation ceremonies planned for both boys and girls. National law in Mozambique does not establish a minimum age of consent for sexual intercourse. Iris cannot ban families from visiting the children on the base and it is understood that some of them will be taken to visit their village and inevitably subjected to these initiation ceremonies.

Women are not valued here as we understand it in the west and they

Saturday

learn when very young that their identity or worth is viewed in the context of their sexuality. So from an early age life is about gaining a man who will provide.

Pregnancy is viewed as indication of the fact that the girl has achieved a level of relationship, a status symbol, which implies support or at least the prospect of food on the table. Young women are encouraged to have more than one man on the go because men traditionally remain with a woman for on average two children, before moving on to pastures new. Typically a girl sells her body for the price of a can of Coke.

It was very quiet as Sara gently presented the picture of a cultural norm totally alien to us. Iris has a *barraca* that Sara uses every Friday night. She opens the *barraca* as a 'safe place' for girls to come one night a week. She explained she likes to wash the girls' feet and chat. She offers to paint toe and finger nails.

'Please can I ask you not to judge these girls? We don't use the word prostitute. Some of them will be very young. We are there to offer them some focused attention and demonstrate the love of Jesus. Feel free to pray or share anything God shows you.' Sara went on patiently, 'I need you men to stay outside, about three metres in front of the *barraca* for security. Please don't allow any men past you and please don't chat to any of the girls. We need to be very careful that what we are doing is not in any way misconstrued.'

Someone posed the question that several of us were pondering: 'What about the provision of contraception?' With a tinge of sadness Sara explained the issue had been raised with supporters but it had been made clear that provision of condoms would trigger controversy. She admitted that sexually transmitted disease is a huge issue.

I felt shocked Ma, about the possibility that 'fat cat Christians' in the west could be in the background making judgments about contraception and threatening to withdraw 'support' if the missionary on the ground stepped out of their preconceived appropriate 'church box'. Their opinions, presumably preconceived from a very comfortable distance, are influencing life on the front line. I wondered how many of these 'supporters' have actually been here and respect for Sara increased as she calmly pulled the focus back to how much we could offer, with Jesus, in the evening ahead.

Clara, not quite fully recovered though keen not to miss out, inquired about 'the rest-room facilities' but was not reassured by Sara's response. I think she is weighing up her options.

For almost a year Sara has been doing this every week. The missionary who shares the vision with her is currently away so for a while Sara has been dependent on willing visitors. (I think her friend needed surgery.) I imagine staff generally have to go 'home' for any serious medical attention but what a trek it must be if you are feeling unwell or in pain. Anyhow, Sara was pleased that this week there are enough of us willing to go with her. She asked us to eat as soon as supper is served and then meet her back here.

I am getting to know the rest of the team from America now. Joe is a young teacher about Sam's age so early thirties I guess. He lives in the States. A few years back he stopped on the highway to assist someone who had been involved in a crash and was mowed down by a vehicle moving at high speed. He made an unexpected and amazing recovery but is paraplegic, hence the freshly laid 'disability ramp!'

Joe is very upbeat and has a keen sense of humour; he told me God has told him he will be healed in the future. What pluck to come to this environment in a wheelchair and he is completely independent. He and Al were to be our 'security' for the evening.

As I got changed Ma (we have to wear long skirts and cover our shoulders whenever we are taking part in activities off the base out of respect for the strong Muslim culture), I felt strangely excited. Only Day 1 and I had the opportunity to really be involved. I chuckled about us offering pedicures because part of my 'being in the zone' agreement with myself was a 'no nail polish' decision, which as you know, is a sacrifice as I enjoy wearing it so much.

I felt to wear no jewellery, no nail polish, bringing only lipstick and mascara was a quiet agreement with the Lord that I want to just be present. I would feel uncomfortable anyway sporting rings and glossy nails in a context where survival is the challenge most face.

I wondered how dirty and dusty it would really be. I thought about the fact that, though I have given friends and Sis pedicures, washing the dirty feet of total strangers would be a new experience. I prayed, 'Lord, show me how to love these girls; let me honour you in this.'

As we clambered into the back of the Land Rover and squeezed in I counted twelve of us plus a wheelchair ... in three pieces. Sara, smaller than any of us, appeared unfazed and hopped into the driving seat oozing anticipation. (I thought briefly of that joke about people in a mini.) I am filled with admiration for Sara; it was dark, hot and uncomfortable on the bumpy track but it felt deliciously real. This was it. A genuine opportunity to engage with the poor. The authenticity of the moment was spiritually intoxicating and I felt humbled and twenty feet tall all at the same time ... I think you had to be there, sorry.

Pemba Pennings

We parked near the home of some other missionaries who live on what was the original base, not far away, and walked another sandy dirt track into the heart of what felt like the Pemba equivalent of Soho (before it became a glamour spot). Music blared and clusters of people drinking at tables glowed in the night. I heard the odd shriek, rough laughter and a dog barked.

The *barraca* is a flimsy bamboo construction in an uneven row just set back from the tarmac road (on a wide area of dirt, pavement style, space). We were tightly sandwiched between a barber's and the nearest thing I've seen to a corner shop. This is a *barraca* packed from floor to ceiling with shelves stuffed with Omo, fruit juice, toilet rolls, packets of sweets, Jiff and other sundries.

The cement floor of the Iris *barraca* is about 5 feet by 12 and there is a naked light bulb hanging from the roof. We swept the dust and twigs out with a basic brush and Sara produced three *kapalanas*. These are the brightly coloured pieces of fabric the women wrap around their lower bodies, much like sarongs. She draped one on each of the three two-seater cane 'sofas' in the *barraca*, dropped a couple of rush mats on the floor and we gathered outside to pray. As we held hands under the stars, inviting God to invade the evening, his presence was heavy.

The team from the US Harvest School has two leaders with them. Both are Mozambican and Zena speaks the language fluently. The national language here is Portuguese and the local language is Macua. (My middle-class French about as much use as a chocolate frog then.) We didn't have to wait any time before a trickle of humanity began arriving.

I couldn't help being envious as Zena chatted happily away. The first few customers were children, small children, who could have been sib-

Saturday

lings hanging around waiting for big sisters or in some cases even children of the older girls. They all knew Sara and smiled to see her. She speaks quite a lot of Portuguese (she told me today she is having lessons) and cheerily engaged various ones in conversation.

I was very conscious of being unable to communicate and as I sat in the dirt with a lapful of begrimed feet, I rejected thoughts about germs; I remembered where Heidi describes catching lice and scabies. I glanced down to check for any breaks in my skin (the eczema on my right hand got quite bad on the way here and I had prayed). I realised in that moment my skin was completely clear: no cracks, no dry itchy patches left. It's still good today, how fabulous is that?

I suppose some of the girls will be carrying Aids. Awed, I set to cleansing and massaging unfamiliar feet of every shape and size. It's rather freeing when nobody knows that tongues isn't your native language! It is heart-breaking that so many beautiful children are just cut and about long after dark with nobody even concerned as to their whereabouts or welfare.

I was impressed by several of the other visitors who had learned both how to say what their name was and ask the name of their client in Portuguese. I felt free to pray aloud in tongues and focused on doing the best job I could with sticky, often old nail polish. I wished I had known, as I would have brought every polish I own to give to Sara; I could have hidden them in my luggage, even bought some on the plane. Too late now.

We worked with a steady background of banter I couldn't understand. It was fantastic when Zena announced first one then a second girl had accepted the offer of prayer and would like to know Jesus. I painted and prayed and tried not to think about the backache that was setting in.

Pemba Pennings

I was glad someone had reminded me to apply insect repellent.

Jojo is one of the team from America. Long, flowing hair, a willowy physique and in her early twenties she is what I would call 'arty'. Just a few telltale signs; things like her kit from outreach is still in the spot she dropped it some hours ago. She wafts about not thinking to take her dirty cup from table to sink much less wash and wipe it up. Every now and again she will fold her body into some unusual stretch or can be seen conducting an invisible orchestra. You get my drift; anyway, she joined Zena to pray for one of the girls and as is her wont it seems, she gently swayed and prayed with her body.

Suddenly, it was as if a spirit of lust came on one of the street girls as she waited to have her nails painted and she moved right in front of Jojo (whose eyes were closed in oblivious rapture) and right close up to her began mimicking Jojo's movements in a sensual manner. I hardly had time to register the shift in atmosphere.

It was quickly over as Jojo knocked her knee on the side of the piece of furniture nearest to her, opened her eyes and stepped back taking authority in Jesus' name. It was sobering though Ma. It was confronting to be suddenly in the raw presence of a spirit so opposed to who we are. Many of the girls have the shadow of demons in their eyes.

People here often admit to feeling tormented when asked (this is information from other people at this stage). Apparently, severe headaches and disturbed nights are common indications of affliction. The supernatural is accepted as the norm with many powerful witch doctors.

Sara told us that three girls have become Christians in recent months and she holds a discipleship group for them on another evening. Towards nine o'clock as we were clearing up, one of them, Sonia (who is

Saturday

nineteen) arrived and Sara asked us to gather round and pray for her. She explained briefly that Sonia is still trying to finish her schooling but lives with an abusive mother and life is very hard for her. It was such a privilege to be able to pray and encourage her and some of us had pictures and a scripture to share. How easy our lives are by comparison.

Several of the smaller girls had nasty sores on their lower legs, I prayed healing as I washed feet. I didn't see any wounds closing right then but I totally expected I might! We cleared away and as we paused again to pray together before getting back into the vehicle, I felt so thankful, privileged somehow. I'm not a missionary but I did feel like a 'sent out one' last night.

There are millions of stars here and even poor Clara's sudden, desperate need to rush into the darkness of nearby scrub only seemed to illustrate truth. Being a 'sent out one' is not comfortable! I really felt I wanted us to pray for Sara but thought it may be presumptuous so soon after getting here and the moment passed accompanied by a low moan from our ailing sister. (I think it is worth keeping up with the anti-bac Ma ... imagine how challenging a tummy bug could be with only two toilets and then if the water goes off having to squat in the dark and aim and then nothing to vomit in if both ends are struggling; please pray health in Jesus' name. I do feel really well at the moment.)

Aya was in bed with the light off when I got back so I was glad of my headlamp. I had to manage my response when I found she had her computer plugged in instead of the fan but she was asleep so I just changed them over. It is pretty much like camping because everything is in my case under the bed and therefore at floor level. I keep trying to remember to bend from the knee but there isn't heaps of space between the bunks; anyway am praying my back holds out.

Had my first shower, yippee!! Not totally alone but 48 hours without makes one feel benevolent and I just gave my huge grasshopper/praying mantis type companion a wide berth. I padded along to my room and slipped under the net for another good sleep.

That brings me to now; it's late Saturday afternoon. As I said, Saturday is a rest day so no planned activities. Molly is feeling much better but not fully recovered and everyone else went off to a beach somewhere. Al and Molly planned to walk along the road to visit The Pemba Beach Hotel and they invited me.

I declined initially on the basis that a five-star hotel could hardly be considered to be 'in the zone'. But on reflection I decided I didn't need to eat and maybe there would be somewhere cool to sit and write. And there is! It is really hard in the centre to be alone at all and I am easily distracted when struggling to write. On my bunk isn't comfortable and the light is very poor.

The hotel, ten minutes along the road, is the weirdest contrast Ma. Ornate pillars, ceiling fans that efficiently create draft, exotic palms in enormous elegant pots and verdant lawns spreading down to a private beach. Clusters of white people are enjoying various snacks and drinks. The portico-adorned entrance puts Dallas in the shade and eager waiters in incongruous crisp, white jackets hover. Al kindly bought me a Coke (I declined ice and lemon just in case. I don't know what water they used to make the ice and who knows what germs could be on the skin of a lemon??) and I have left him and Molly to eat their meal.

I am ensconced in the corner of a deep brown leather sofa on the edge of a vast terrace with a sea breeze, which is just enough to cool me

Saturday

but not blow the pages while I write ... delicious! I've written rather a lot but you can always read in stages.

I was reading in 1 Kings this morning and it struck me that when ravens fed Elijah there is no record of them carefully applying anti-bacteria gel to their beaks; ravens eat carrion, don't they? Not that I have germs on the brain, just saying. Golly Ma, I'm *so* looking forward to church tomorrow; I can't imagine what it will really be like. I mean when I was in Nigeria years ago I was all psyched up for a wild, African experience of church and then devastated when the choir appeared in robes and dragged us through the same old Anglican liturgy we suffered each week in the local parish church; ghastly. I think there may even be dancing here.

I'm still stunned to think Heidi and Rolland are due to be here for the middle week of my stay. The sign outside the church reads: 'Church on Sunday 9ish till about 12.' I hope they practise worship beforehand and we can just linger. Church, *in Pemba* ... I can't wait.

I'm getting to know Mo a bit. She is one of the hospitality team who corresponded with me. She is young and fun. It's great to put a face to my emails! Mo confided in me that she is madly in love with one of the doctors here but he wants to speak to her parents before they make anything official. They are both South African.

Earlier today I helped her prepare one of the rooms for a family who are missionaries further north and coming (with their 4 children) to stock up from the local shops and then sleep over before doing the return drive of several hours. Imagine living literally hours drive, over tricky roads, from the nearest shopping place! Mo thought they were Australian so I am looking forward to meeting them tonight.

Pemba Pennings

Almost time to walk back to the base so will finish now; the driving doesn't inspire confidence and I need to prepare for the walk which will entail leaping out of the path of oncoming vehicles who approach from random directions at varying speeds and cannot be relied upon to avoid unsuspecting pedestrians.

More soon Ma, love you. I really am in Africa you know ... unbelievable!

P.S. Just before I finally sign off Ma. Now late Sat night and I met the missionary from Australia. Just the wife Rita is here with her 4 children. Rita and her husband have family back in Australia and are establishing a new Iris base in Mozambique some way further north. They lived and worked here in Pemba for a year first. I enjoyed chatting with her and asked her if they have always worked in Africa. She said with passion that previously she and her husband worked for some years with homeless Aboriginal people. 'I love the Aboriginal people; we started a church for them in Darwin but God spoke to me when I was 12, calling me to live and work in Africa. We loved doing that work at home and now I'm fulfilling my dream. I waited a long time to come to Africa.'

My heart began pounding so that I had a pulsing in my ears as she shared her love of Aboriginal people. She talked about God loving and transforming Aboriginal lives. The conversation, though apparently completely random, took on a significance I can't quantify. I can't help thinking, *homeless*. The very context that God used to make me desperate for more of him, whilst growing a deep yearning for Aboriginal people. First Nations people are the essence of Australia to me, the land I have come to love so much and now call home.

A distant chord seemed to be struck. That same sensation of Holy Spirit

Saturday

hovering I had back in Exeter, when I read 'sent out ones are needed to go to people still in darkness.' I'm heading off to bed now pondering ... Rita is here for one night; I could easily not have met her. She could have been from any country as multiple nationalities are represented here. She worked with homeless people: Aboriginal people. Something deeply familiar yet startlingly new shimmers on the skyline.

I feel as if God is just shifting on his throne, not speaking or gesticulating but communicating ... Oh, I don't know. I can't pin the feeling down. I know I am at one level holding my breath. I know people get passionate about Africa. It's as if the country reaches out to envelop them, getting right under their skin and I do not want that to happen to me. I can't conceive of feeling the affinity and deep connection I have with Australia, for another place. Passion for Africa is raw and palpable here but my heart is already given. I feel I just could not manage experiencing the depth of emotion I feel for Australia, for somewhere else at the same time ... it would be terrible if Africa 'gets me'.

Right, I hadn't recognised that in me so clearly till now ... I need to come into this experience with God 'no holds barred', don't I? I'll just take some time to deliberately abandon myself to HIS purpose for me here in Pemba, unreservedly and then trust him to make his way forward crystal clear.

'Night Ma, thanks for listening x

Sunday early morning

Hello Ma,

Hope all well with you and that you had a great weekend. I did struggle a bit last night. Imagine a person plugging in a computer rather than the fan, which cools the whole room, in this climate!?

The thing is that visiting the shower is less than relaxing. I work very hard not to let anything touch the floor. This means juggling toothbrush and paste in desperate attempt to ensure nothing that enters my mouth touches the basin. Then I have my other essentials: headlamp, clothes and wet towel. The floor is lethal when it is wet so even staying upright is a challenge in flip-flops. It all results in my being coated all over again in an attractive sheen of sweat long before I reach my bed, so the cool of the fan is crucial to alleviate the feeling of getting into bed sticky and grubby.

I can't tell if I'm being purist, selfish, tested or simply being given an opportunity to have grace for other cultural habits. It feels rather intrusive and even counter cultural to me to have technology in the room but

Sunday early morning

Aya has set up a little office on the empty bunk opposite her. Each day she sits chattering, in a language that sounds like Chinese, to all corners of the world (whilst blocking the fan socket).

I know we are all different; I'm just not used to someone who switches the light off without any regard for what roommates may be doing or reading, or who with gay abandon swings open the room door 'to let air in', then pins it wide open irrespective of the state of dress or otherwise of said roommate. Yesterday morning I sought out a quiet moment at the table near the kitchen area to sift my emotions but Aya came and said she had nothing to do so could I tell her my life story because she likes stories ... Lord, help me to celebrate diversity!

I slept well during the night till Aya padded out of the room sometime before 5am (shutting the door quietly isn't her thing) and then slept again till 7am. I'm not sure how I am going to manage the heat and humidity; my pen is sliding even though it is early. I've slipped across to the prayer hut in a bid to get some time alone. The sea looks totally inviting but I haven't found anyone who is keen enough to swim with me yet. Being on the top of a rise there is a whisper of air movement, which is very pleasant.

Oh ... Aya has just joined me and is lustily singing an old chorus, my vocal cords are in spasm and I really don't want a little service. She is now reading a psalm aloud. It's so tricky because I really need time alone but she means well.

I feel at risk of a personal drought in a whirlpool of God activity.

It is noise and people everywhere and I must find a way of connecting with God, listening for him even when others are around. Before I went to bed last night Jojo's copy of *Jesus Calling* was out on the kitchen table and I opened it. Yesterday's reading was that great promise, 'I will never leave you or forsake you.'

This is just a brief note (bet that's a relief?) but I am really looking forward to church this morning and will write you all about it tomorrow. I feel such a sense of anticipation. I'm sure it will be an eye-opener. Really looking forward to the worship. Sunday in Pemba! I can hardly get my head around the privilege but I am actually here.

All for now then, much love to you Ma x x

Monday

Good Golly Miss Molly Ma!! Day 4 ...

I woke extra early today feeling rested so decided I would get up. It was partly the sound of heavy rain on the tin roof that brought me to the surface and then the sound got nearer and I had to navigate a large puddle at the end of my bed as I crept out of the room and was in the prayer hut by 4.45am. (I'm sure the puddle will have evaporated by breakfast as it has stopped raining. I'm just glad I chose the bottom bunk and thankful my suitcase wasn't floating.)

In the prayer hut it was magical, quiet and a perfect temperature. I haven't worn anything more than thin cotton shirts yet. A soft breeze wafted through. The glassy ocean shimmered invitingly in the silver dawn light (gosh, I would have loved to slip under the surface and be really cool all over, weightless, but I think that longing is just something I need to manage).

As I sat enjoying God's presence, and waiting for enough light to read my Bible, I felt a wave of relief. Yes, it is beautiful here in its way and I can appreciate it; I was trying not to compare but the deep cord of my heart, that place that felt so fully alive on the big road trip in the outback, still resonates only with Australia. Strange, because the realisation just came unbidden but I am deeply relieved. It led me to ponder again my chat with Rita and the connection I felt.

The power and the water are off today Ma, which is tricky. I think the thing I miss most is not being able to boil the kettle. I have to use bleach on my utensils but will just trust it will be OK. I think it evaporates, doesn't it, so I won't actually be ingesting it. Faith woman! Brings a new slant on being 'clean from the inside out'.

Well, I have been to church in Pemba!!

It is huge and held in that cavernous cement-floored barn-like building I told you about where through the village feeding programme hundreds of children receive a meal each day in the week. I couldn't wait to get there. I didn't want to miss anything so I decided I would get over to the church soon after nine o'clock in hopes there would be worship playing.

Astonishingly, between the visitors' centre and church, just hanging about on the track between buildings, were two rather lovely horses! (Of all things.) They are clearly meant to be there, as apart from passers-by of all ages very deliberately giving them a pretty wide berth, they were being ignored. I followed suit.

I am guessing the horses have been given to the community or maybe they are part of a therapy plan for more traumatised children; I don't know but later in the evening I was in the prayer hut again and saw two boys cantering bareback up the track through the length of the base. I love the sound of hooves and the sun was just setting but I felt wistful. It's

Monday

a bit like being right by the sea but not free to swim. With no language, communicating my riding ability, discovering the horses' temperament, etc. could be a bit of a challenge. I haven't heard or seen any mention of horses in the context of visitors anyway. I hope they are really well cared for.

I wasn't disappointed; arriving early at church I mean. Between 9 and 9.50am people trickled in. Flimsy rush mats are strewn on the floor at the front butting up to the raised stone step, which is the edge of the platform and then chairs and benches behind. The first to arrive by a long while were the women. They came in and just prostrated themselves on the floor and over the front of the platform or 'altar'. I sat on a white plastic chair near the front not wanting to be too conspicuous. Vain hope.

It was some time before another white face appeared and in the meantime I was so touched by the humble longing for God in the women that I felt I just wanted to be among them. I wasn't sure if it would be all right to move forward and sit with them. I didn't want to presume so I quietly slipped along and sat at the back of the group of women on the mats. I wanted to take my flip-flops off but felt nervous someone may take them. I had been discouraged from bringing a bag so didn't have my Bible or notebook.

We had been told that Mozambicans dress up for church and asked to respect the tone set by not appearing in very casual dress. I wore my long skirt with a pretty loose white blouse. I felt vulnerable but in a good way. I was anxious not to show my legs as I tried to get comfy on the rush mats flung on the cement.

A visiting missionary, who was here when I arrived, told me Muslim men see knees as erogenous. He said he had been asked for prayer by men wrestling with inappropriate desire triggered by glimpses of this area of the body. Breasts are constantly on display as the milk bar is open 24/7 but the female body between naval and knees is never exposed. I had wondered why in these temperatures all the girls had returned from outreach sporting dark leggings beneath their long skirts, but I guess clambering in and out of vehicles and constantly being on the ground have too much lust potential to risk.

I never thought to bring leggings but am being very careful how I move. (I was deliberately *not* thinking about the time Heidi describes, when the Holy Spirit overwhelmed her in a meeting, tipping her on her head where she remained for some time as others prophesied over her. Well, really *trying* not to think about it. I'm not resisting; but Heidi did have trousers on.) One by one the women became aware of my presence and each gently greeted me, initially hands were shaken but I let it be known I was happy to hug (truth be told felt in *need* of hugs!) and they responded with huge smiles and warm embraces. I felt graciously included but hideously the odd one out.

I ached to be able to communicate. I hadn't anticipated how hard it would be not to have any Portuguese or Macua. How do you make any meaningful connection with people when you literally don't know a single word of their language? I let the warm-up of the worship band wash over me. I closed my eyes and tried to relax. I had my hands open in front of me just resting on my crossed legs.

A little body crept into my lap and tears came as a hunger for love reached inside me. Unkempt, grubby village children, mixing with Iris children in their Sunday best, milled quietly around, found a spot and settled. Anything seems to go — lying, sitting, kneeling. I became aware of a blind man seated just a couple of rows back from the front and wondered if he would go home seeing.

The service eventually began but God's presence was everywhere already as hearts and lives were just laid out for him to touch and transform. Everything was in Portuguese translated into Macua (the local language) and sometimes English as well so the morning was unhurried as everyone patiently waited to hear in their own language.

The worship had a rich depth, a clean simplicity that drew me in even though, apart from the word 'Allelujah' which is pretty universal, I didn't understand. I wanted to lie on my face and decided everyone had their own flip-flops so why would they need mine? I discreetly put mine among those of the other women thinking (in less than faith-filled mode) that maybe Mozambicans didn't steal from each other.

African voices have a unique resonance and harmony abounds. Rhythm? Is the Pope a Catholic? At one point in the morning a large group of young men went up onto the stage area and led the most vigorous, enthusiastic dance I have ever seen in worship, or anywhere else (though there are those who may say I should get out more). Guitar, drums and base blended with voices lifting us into God's presence; it felt like a touch of heaven.

I sensed God speaking to me and wished I had my notebook to hand. I know it was something specific about him letting me feel his heart for Aboriginal people and a promise that he will show me what to do with the growing burden I feel. At some point when I can get alone and tune in I will ask the Holy Spirit for specific words that I can record as I feel a weight on this that may have far-reaching consequences for me. I received a really vivid picture; I was somehow 'in it' so maybe it's a vision? So intense, to the point of scary ... I think in a holy way ... if that's a thing. Need to process but it's a 'something implanted' type of feeling.

Oh my goodness Ma, just writing that I feel something profound, somehow beyond me, is unfolding. I feel nervous, excited, awed, daunted ... I don't know ... this is just little old me we're talking about. Something I can't quantify is landing, shifting, I don't know, deep in the core of me. Have to let it germinate, settle. Can't say any more ...

After the vigorous worship, any visitors having their last Sunday here were invited to the front for prayer and I was caught up with thinking how special that will be when my turn comes. By the time a white South African lady gave the talk there was a splattering of white faces around the building. I spied Hans and one or two others I had encountered on my visits to the eating area.

During the talk there was a fair amount of coming and going. It was long, due to being translated, but many responded to the basic message of the cross and surged forward for prayer at the end. I could have sat there all day understanding or not, it was just delicious to be in the Presence and there is so much to absorb. It's church but also akin to visiting an alien planet and finding God's love even more tangible than at home.

Plus knowing that he does miracles here. Expectation is conspicuous. Raw. I think it is something to do with the gnawing, palpable need of everyday basics, that we just take for granted, as if that somehow fuels spiritual hunger; so desire for God is unfettered, rampant even. I can't really explain yet.

Lunch afterwards was ... you guessed it, rice and beans. It must have all we need in it because I have energy and am not hungry in between.

Monday

My challenge is to learn and pronounce the word for 'small' in comprehensible fashion because I am struggling to manage the portion size and feel guilty even contemplating wasting food in this environment.

For the first time I plucked up the courage to offer half my meal to a boy on the table with me. I noticed many other diners spooning rice onto each other's plates and was relieved when he accepted. I think I need to say something that sounds like 'porko' but thus far my efforts meet a blank stare and a generous plateful. The lads serving the food definitely haven't got time for language lessons and I feel so self-conscious being served food.

One of the other visitors joined me as we left church and I was embarrassed because she pushed to the front of the queue ordering me to do the same and then she demanded a banana. My understanding is that fruit and milk are only for the children. We are guests here so it feels just inappropriate to demand anything. I know, it's probably a 'cultural difference' but I'm struggling because it feels like the same spirit as drives the supermarket trolleys where Dave lives (you remember Park'n'shop in Hong Kong?), the spirit that would rather mow you down than say 'excuse me'.

When I returned to the centre there was a group discussion in flow. A visiting missionary (who leaves today) was explaining that whilst here last year, he had purchased two banana trees for a blind man in the village who also comes to church. I pricked up my ears at the mention of the blind man and he continued, 'I want to go and visit him, pray for him and see how the trees are coming along. Would anyone like to come with me?' I was uncertain. If the blind man that I had noticed in church was about to be healed and his eyes opened I wanted to be there.

Pemba Pennings

The missionary gentleman in question is quiet and mild mannered. I wondered ... How equipped was he really to escort a group of us into the uncharted territory (for me) of the village? He is male but from my perspective the 'alpha' part could do with a little attention.

He is on his way to evangelise an African nation hundreds of kilometres further north armed with a bicycle and some herbal tea. He has the air of someone who has never felt fully heard and probably had a dominant mother. That could be why he appears to feel just ever so slightly uncomfortable around me although I think he is nearer to me in age than anyone else so far. I digress.

Would it be OK with Iris for us to just strike off into the village I wondered? What was the 'form'? Is there such a thing here? Several of the others were keen. It was really hot but our fearless leader said he was pretty sure he would find the right hut straight away and from memory he didn't think it was too far.

It was an opportunity to go into the village and have another experience of this new world. If I let the opportunity go by and they returned with stories of healing and a blind man seeing, how would I feel then? I mean this missionary spoke as if he was experienced and he had clearly been around for a while because all the staff knew him. I hadn't come all this way in order to shrink back.

I caught Molly's eye. 'Yes,' I said, 'I would like to come.'

'Now,' said Molly, 'you do know where in the village this man lives?' She fixed the missionary in question with a beady stare leaving us all in no doubt that she was not up for a hike or any outing resembling a mystery tour.

'Look,' he replied, 'I know it's not too far and it will be pretty easy to find.'

Monday

'OK let's go. I'll just get sun screen and my water bottle.'

Clara went to use the rest room one more time 'just in case' and I quietly gave myself a little pep talk. I felt naked, 'uncovered', but I came here to cross thresholds and step over personal boundaries so what was the deep reluctance ... fear or intuition?

We set off, a strange hotchpotch of sandals, hats and assorted garments. Molly and Clara had invested in *kapalanas* and wore western tops. Clara had a massive floppy hat with a cream bow that would have been completely in keeping at a royal wedding. She said it had been given to her and I think she wore it because she was still feeling slightly under the weather.

I still had my long skirt on and had changed my blouse for a long-sleeved high-collared shirt. I'm wearing my black cap all the time to keep the sun off my face, which doesn't feel at all feminine. I only use it at home if I'm walking in shorts and trainers; it feels all wrong with a long skirt. We all wore sunglasses. As we made our way down the main track to leave the base I felt very hot, very sticky and about as appropriate as a pork chop at a Bar Mitzvah. We are talking uncomfortable.

We reached the road and turned left then pretty quickly left again. Immediately we were knee deep in people. Mainly children. Some just fell in with our step, others darted to touch an arm or feel a skirt. Garments were varied. One small boy was in a pair of scruffy jodhpurs, another in a tiny tweed sports jacket with bare chest inside; but all of them smiled. All of them were dirty. Three children on a corner were having a great game with a discarded bicycle tyre, an old, lidless tin and what looked like a broken piece of mudguard.

As we trudged past, smaller groups of adults were sitting on the ground in front of their huts and people gazed with open curiosity. It sounds odd Ma, but nobody actually seems to 'do' very much at all. I mean even on the base wherever you look there are men or boys draped over logs or benches or by a wall just lounging, waiting, but I don't know what for. I've never been anywhere where so many people appear to have no focus at all for their day. I'm not criticising, just commenting. It was mid-afternoon; maybe in the village it's a break from whatever they do the rest of the day.

Due to the rain overnight the terrain in the village was less dusty and more ... mud. Molly and I slotted in towards the rear sensing that Clara was zoning in for a power encounter. Our leader made his whimsical way forward.

We walked steadily up a sand track that was more like a gully in parts. There was a rough wall atop a bank to our left with the base the other side but to the right, every few moments there was a turning. To call them footpaths conjures up the wrong idea ... bluebells, primroses and fresh country air. These worn tracks are just wide enough for one person to walk and swing their arms; but not out to the side! The family plots are mostly bordered by head-height woven bamboo partitions strung together to form crude fencing. One panel is left open to make a basic gate and every now and then I had a glimpse into an enclosure: a pot outside a door, a circle of smouldering embers or black feet. Several times I saw chickens scratching around the roots of small trees.

We had been walking for about twenty minutes when Clara tackled the issue of direction by speaking her mind loudly, 'We have definitely been here before.' As we took yet another turn into another muddy laneway, hesitation hovered and Molly cleared her throat meaningfully.

Suddenly a cheery greeting floated over us. Tension lifted as two

Monday

young men recognised our illustrious leader and greeted him enthusiastically. It became clear that they both grew up on the base but now being eighteen they live in the village. It took a few moments but they appeared agreeable to the idea of leading us to the blind man's hut.

'Is it far?' from Molly.

'Quite far. Not too far. Medium far. I show you.' (A wonderful African answer.)

The pace seemed to pick up slightly and we rounded a corner to find the rain had formed a pool that stretched across the path. There were a few rocks strategically placed as stepping-stones and I studiously placed my feet exactly where the young helper in front of me trod. A splosh from behind indicated Molly had not been quite as precise but I didn't trust myself to turn around.

Clara and Molly are very different. Clara is clipped and lean and explained later that she has won prizes for 'Body Sculpt' or 'Body Form' or something like that which she says is big in America. She has been married twice and is on the lookout for the husband God has promised her (I have a sneaky feeling the man who headed up our little jaunt is quite safe). Molly is a comfortable size, enjoys her food and has no intention of falling into another relationship. God has rescued her from addiction and poverty. He saved her daughter who then married a lovely Christian man and Molly shares their home helping to care for her granddaughter whom she loves with a passion.

As we came out of the puddle a thin boy morphed out of the shadow and placed a small hand in mine. He was wearing half a t-shirt (one sleeve had come away and dropped off somewhere or perhaps been ripped off for another use), baggy trousers that wafted between knee and ankle and was barefoot. I squeezed the tiny hand gently as his bony digits curled round, hooking on to the edge of my hand and then I tried not to hold so tightly that the little person would feel trapped.

Gradually I became aware of a low humming. The tune was definitely coming from the small body beside me and it was so familiar I was completely disorientated. 'Joy, joy, joy, joy down in my heart ... ' an old chorus I learned when I was about the same age as my companion. I quietly began to sing in English and he sang in his own tongue. A sweet but bizarre moment. My mind was leaping about but I decided the little boy must be one of many who come to the base each day for a short time of 'children's church' and then food.

We took a few more turns, seemed to repeat two previous turnings and then came out into a small open clearing. Led between yet more high bamboo fences we finally veered left through an opening and there we were in a small sandy compound.

We stood in front of a low hut with a narrow cement plinth across the front, which acted as a sort of basic terrace. A man sat on it with his face upturned to the sky. He wore a dirty t-shirt, old, loose trousers and a pair of tatty trainers, one of which was held together with tape. He held his head on one side listening intently to our approach.

It was really good to have the two young men with us because of the language thing. They immediately explained who we were and reminded him about the gifts of the banana trees. He nodded enthusiastically and held out his hands to shake each of ours in greeting.

There was a plastic chair half under cover of the edge of the hut and I sank onto it as the others sat around the gentleman. My little singing shadow climbed onto my lap and snuggled in.

Monday

'Do you know Jesus?' I asked in an awed tone. A nod was my reply. 'Would you like me to pray for you?' Another nod then he reached open hands onto his legs, closed his eyes and peace descended just like that. His eyelids flickered at ninety miles a minute as I prayed in tongues. Then he opened his eyes, sat up and very soon reached his feet to the ground and melted away.

I remain fully aware Ma, that Heidi wrote 'children have the keys' and am determined to be alert to any small ... well, I don't really know what could happen or what I may learn or see but alert and teachable is the posture I am aiming for. In a way that I can't find words for, this little encounter felt divine, in a sense that is completely new to me.

Clara was in full flow: 'Is your wife here? Is she a Christian? How many children do you have?' Honestly Ma, after all Sara had told us I felt these to be the most inappropriate questions. I mean why focus on potentially muddy waters? Surely these are 'western' questions?

My discomfort doubled as a lady entered the compound and I felt acutely aware that she was arriving in her own home to find an invasion. Her husband briefly acknowledged her but she quietly squatted in the corner and busied herself with a little fire and a pot of rice. No eye contact. I indicated she should have my chair and just sat on the ground in full sun wishing again that I had language to put us both at our ease.

It was taken out of my hands as Clara and the missionary insisted on her coming in closer and then prayed a prayer for the marriage with a cringing emphasis on 'monogamous relationship', which thankfully wasn't translated. I was preoccupied; I couldn't help wondering if, with her husband's disability, the wife had to sleep with other men to get food on their table.

Then the crunch question: 'Could we pray for your healing?' With translation from one of the young men with us, it became apparent that the man had had a bad pain in his head (stroke?) a few years back and since then only had limited use of his right side and had also lost his sight. We prayed for a while for his eyes. Nothing appeared to change but my mouth filled with saliva and I had this fleeting thought about spit and eyelids, which I squashed and swallowed.

As they prayed on, my mouth filled up again. Now some may say it was a nervous response but I know it hasn't happened to me before and I have plenty of moments with 'nervous potential'. I opened my eyes to glance at the young men who had joined us and was almost undone on the spot to see one of them had tears of compassion coursing down his cheeks. I quickly shut my eyes again and wrestled with the urge to offer to lick my fingers and place them on eyelids.

I'm not proud of myself. I absolutely succumbed to the fear of man. I could hear Randy Clark in my head from the conference in Cardiff, 'How many of you think you have missed a miracle because you didn't obey?' but still I couldn't get the words out. He points out *we* can't actually heal anyone, we only 'deliver the cheque' of healing as it were, so WHY is it so hard to step out? Disappointed in myself.

Clara moved to praying for strength to return to the man's affected side and for the back pain he had mentioned, both of which seemed to improve. After the prayer his wife was a little more relaxed and would look at us but I was feeling hot, confused, disappointed, awkward, out of my depth.

All these feelings were compounded as discussion began around the clearly worn condition of the blind man's footwear. One of the young men translated that the man was asking for new shoes. I felt sick and wanted to run as I heard Clara promising to get some and return tomorrow with them.

On Saturday one of the other long-term missionaries on the base patiently explained to me that many visitors have ignored the request of Iris (the organisation) to involve a staff member in the giving of things to local people or those on the base. Consequently young men in the local community have learned that they can ask for and receive a considerable amount of stuff from visitors. Over time they formed a network, which enabled them to in effect 'milk' the hundreds of visitors who come through Pemba each year.

Over years many Christians have misguidedly persisted in giving watches, tents, shoes and other goods, which can be sold here. A tent is particularly prized. Sadly, money gained has not been given to hungry families but increasingly spent on alcohol and drugs. Many stories are told to persuade visitors to give; these range from illness, meaning money for medications is needed, to fire destroying a home, to shoes breaking. What Christians don't understand is they have been propagating crime.

After one Harvest School, which happens twice a year for nine weeks at a time, students were invited to confess if they had 'given' independently during their stay in Pemba. It was discovered that many thousands of dollars that could have gone into the organisation and put to good use, had been squandered.

I'm struggling with it Ma, because it is surely obvious, a no-brainer. If I visit the home of friends or an acquaintance and their child sidles up to me, 'Mum and Dad say I can't have an iPad but would you please get me one?' no way am I going behind my friends' backs and providing one; it's unthinkable. But folk that visit here seem to be taken over by some frenetic need to give stuff away. I'm wondering if a form of guilt drives it because we have so much in the west, but then the giving isn't even from a good motive, is it?

It's rather sad and it has facilitated these young men being lured into blatant dishonesty. This means rather than developing into healthy role models, the younger children need to be protected from their influence. Also the parents of older boys are disappointed with their sons' choices and blame a negative influence, which they attribute to Iris. Imagine how that feels for those who have given their lives to live and work here. They are so gracious in including so many visitors when there is such risk.

All this was churning in my head as the discussion about shoes continued and then someone said, 'His wife would like new flip-flops too.' I was so embarrassed; all this in front of the two young 'village men' who may have initiated the situation but I couldn't follow. I saw the missionary give the wife a wad of notes and then, to top it off, he suggested, of all things, a photo shoot. (You know how I love the camera!!)

We were embarrassingly arrayed beside two leaves and a dry stick that was the alleged surviving banana tree. I just wanted the ground to swallow me. Molly had at one point challenged Clara, 'How are you going to ever find the way back here tomorrow then? You should not be making these promises.' She was ignored and one of the young men enthusiastically declared he could make himself available to show Clara the way.

The return walk was slightly shorter but no more comfortable and the whole 'shoe promise' hung in the atmosphere. I can't shake the memory

Monday

of a little boy squatting in the dirt chewing what initially appeared to behave like bubble gum. He blew a bubble as our eyes met and the 'bubble' had a small knot in it, which combined with colour and shape brought a whole new perspective on recycling. (Someone in the area has access to contraceptives then?) My tummy lurched when I realised but snatching it would be completely inappropriate, a lesson on hygiene not an option and with no language, all I could do was swallow and try not to gape.

Returning to the safety and relative comfort of the visitors' centre I felt relief, it already represents a haven to which I can return, re-group and attempt to process the enormity of each outing. Each foray into the 'world of the poor' is challenging familiar parameters but it's an arena that increasingly feels to be synonymous with God's heart.

As dusk fell I crept to the prayer hut to just sit. I would've given my flip-flops to float in the ocean, to swim away the heaviness but instead I did some deep breathing, decided to give supper a miss and had a shower. (Water on yippee!)

Early evening the others were all going to the 'prayer room' for a while and invited me to join them. This is a tiny building behind the big open prayer hut and it is kept locked. Only about twelve feet by ten, it is snug. Three mattresses with assorted cushions and pillows take most of the floor space and there is a plastic chair, which is handy if, as in this case, someone wants to sit and play the guitar. There are small windows with grids but no glass, with bright fabric draped over a rail. The walls are blue and painted with swirling waves. There is a large map of Mozambique on one wall and a small board with some scriptures printed out and pinned up.

As we settled to pray Zena (who grew up in Mozambique but is here with the team having been a leader in the school in America) told us, 'This is where Heidi does her intercession,' and suddenly I felt as if I was on holy ground.

The fruit of Heidi's life of prayer and sacrificial obedience surrounded us as we knelt or lay in the sticky evening and I felt humbled, excited and in the right place at the right time as we worshipped and waited in God's presence. It was a truly special time Ma. How awesome really to be kneeling on the floor where exchanges between heaven and earth have impacted this nation for eternity.

It was a huge day and getting horizontal felt good. It was very humid but I slept well until midnight when the power and therefore the fan went off. The air gets immediately so sticky it hits you (like coming out of the airport in the tropics).

I had one of my prickly episodes. I think it must be a side effect of the antimalarial tablets, but it is a weird sensation as if someone is sticking pins very rapidly into a patch of my upper body. It doesn't last too long but feels uncomfortable. I am being careful to stay fully covered up so it's not related to exposure to the sun. Anyway, it went off and I drifted back to sleep. The fan was still off when I got up this morning but it was early and slightly cooler. I met with Al and a few of the others and we went to the beach to watch the sunrise over the sea at close quarters. It was special.

Right, am finishing here. There is hospital visiting today and then the chance to be part of the homegroup evening Sara runs for the teenage girls who live on the base here. You guessed it. A pamper night where we will paint nails and spoil them!

I want to catch Mo and buy a second box of water so I can use it like

Monday

a small bedside table and keep a few things off the ground as my back is feeling the strain of everything at ground level. Still wondering how Clara will get the trainers to the blind man …

Love for now, big hug x x x

Tuesday

Morning Ma,

5.15am and I'm in the prayer hut. Aya was up rather a lot in the night but asleep when I came out. (I wonder if she suffers with cystitis? The nurse in me never off duty!)

Phew! Things feel a bit calmer today. Rita and her 4 children left yesterday afternoon. The children loved fondling and playing with the cats which means the small kitchen/eating area has felt overcrowded for a few days. The challenge now is to dissuade the cats from jumping onto all the surfaces, swiping bare legs under the table and generally thinking they own the place. It's a bit tricky because the more 'sensitive' among us insist on feeding them but the whisper is that if they are fed they won't do their 'job'.

Can cats live solely on bugs and small scampering creatures that none of us want to talk about for fear of speaking them into being?? They look really scrawny and I imagine worms are the norm; Molly lets them lick her limbs and her plate. Aya gets het up and is anxious about hygiene.

Tuesday

This morning before I went to the prayer hut I thought I would boil the kettle ready for later and was startled to find the night guard had locked one of the cats *inside* the kitchen. I suppose it would be a deterrent. Anyway, so long as I don't have to see anything vaguely rodent-like I can cope. I think. Talking about creatures, yesterday evening I saw my first lizard; well it's in the lizard family. Quite attractive for a reptile with the top half of its body, including the head, boldly striped in yellow and black and then the lower half of its body an electric blue. It was about 10 inches long so not tiny. It was enjoying the evening sunshine on the warm stone path. Another one this morning was on the wall outside our room so hopefully, like at home in Australia they eat any bug or insect smaller than themselves and will keep our room clear of mozzies!

I felt quite drained yesterday morning, after the trip to the village. Why in his wisdom do you think God set things up so that we are a key? Why does he choose to work through us so often? I didn't obey the prompt and pray for that blind man. How ineffectual and weak I feel. What is it that triggers this conversation inside just as I am about to step out in some way and if I don't jump quickly (like that time on the train when God gave me the word of knowledge about a big decision for that gentleman) I'm scuppered and the 'what ifs' become more real than anything else?

I feel pathetic Ma. I mean, miles from home, hardly know the people involved and *still* I manage a supreme fluff-up, basically to do with what others may think. What if I had obeyed the prompt and now the man would be seeing?

I am choosing to give the weight of it back to God, say sorry and receive forgiveness. It was disobedience, no excuses, I feel rotten about it. I am praying God will do whatever he needs to in me so that if he gives me a second opportunity (maybe at church next week?) I will obey the prompting immediately. I know he knew it was going to happen and I know it doesn't diminish his love for me but golly I wish I could have taken the leap and thrilled him. I've got a feeling I will have other chances ...

I'm really appreciating the freedom to pace myself with having three full weeks ahead of me. It's a good length of time. Knowing I have at least three opportunities to join in with activities (and some even happen more than once a week), means I don't feel the pressure of needing to rush at any and every opportunity that presents itself but can take time to ask the Holy Spirit each evening about how to plan the next day. I think that's the only way I can do it; then I can build in rest and processing time as well. The hospitality staff are very good about encouraging sensible rest. I imagine they have seen people take on too much too soon and just get swamped.

The team visiting from the Harvest School has a number of things planned for them and they all set off straight after breakfast today for a morning in the school which is built on the edge of the Iris base. It's attended by hundreds of children both from the base and the surrounding region.

They reappeared an hour later rather crestfallen as hundreds of pupils in uniform had turned up but because no teachers arrived, the children had to be sent away. Last week was a school holiday so perhaps today was an extra day but for some reason the pupils hadn't been informed. Undeterred, the team decided they would use the time to go into the local 'town centre' but were waiting ages for the person who was to take them.

Tuesday

Old habits die hard and I decided Monday morning was a good time to do some laundry. I found it rather therapeutic, completely different to any previous 'washing day' experience! At the far end of the open section in the middle of the centre there are four deep cement troughs or bins all joined together. Two of them have plug holes for drainage and a tap and two are just cement pits, not quite as deep as a wheelie bin because I can lean in and touch the bottom to fish out items I drop. A couple of scrubbing brushes (almost a full set of bristles if you use them together), a plastic beaker, a bucket and a plastic bowl with a large crack in it, perch on the stone edge and there is one large plastic dustbin that can be used for rinsing or soaking. I brought a small bottle of liquid laundry detergent with me so I need to make it last. The therapeutic part was scrubbing garments on the small rippled cement ramps that are part of the edge of the troughs with the taps.

All my garments have a fine coating of red dust but it's amazing how quickly the worst of the grime comes off even white collars and cuffs and then everything is dry in a couple of hours. With no 'quick rinse' button the whole rinsing thing is a bit more of a challenge because as soon as one garment is rinsed in the clean water bin the water is soapy, isn't it? The whole sloppy process took me some time but to be honest, having wet limbs and damp clothes is no hardship.

We're encouraged not to leave things on the line too long as items do disappear from time to time. Maybe people from the village climb over the high stone wall even though there are glass bits stuck in the top to deter them. I don't know … it must be very hard if you have so little and just a few feet away people have such wealth.

I just saw the base director and his wife going into the prayer room behind me so perhaps they have regular sessions together in there. Their

Pemba Pennings

days must be chock-a-block so how encouraging is that? It certainly feels as if prayer underpins the whole set-up here.

On my way back from the washing lines I noticed the storeroom door was wide open. This is a small room or large cupboard next door to my dormitory. It's only about 6 feet wide but goes back just over twice that, so is very long and narrow. The shelves are packed with blue bed linen (which all visitors are requested to bring and then invited to leave for the common good) and the piles reach way above my head. Furry wriggles towards the back of a shelf caught my eye, and naturally a cat with newborn kittens is settled among the clean sheets. Toilet rolls and a few basic cleaning materials, a broom with four and a half bristles and a kind of stringy mop thing … more 'thing' than 'mop'.

I was slightly disappointed the first couple of days to find the two Mozambican mamas, who are in effect the housekeepers, spend all their time just outside the store room on a solid wooden bench which is right under my window. They appear to chat and listen to the radio most of the day and initially, (no glass in the window hole remember) I felt that spending time in my room would always be noisy. But as it happens I'm not spending time in there so it doesn't matter. I just step over the languid limbs and bits of broom that linger outside my door.

They respond to my cheery greetings with big smiles but I'm finding names here so difficult to remember, as most of them are completely unfamiliar. Their days give the impression of being one long picnic and sometimes a gentleman joins them for rice and beans at lunchtime; maybe he is a husband, I have no idea.

I was careful to put everything back in my suitcase under the bed this morning wondering if the floor would be swept. Also we have been

Tuesday

asked to be careful not to leave things about that may prompt temptation. (I don't know if we do our own housekeeping or not yet.)

I was aware of a shadow flitting to the dark corner of the room beneath the bunks as I moved my case, and presume one of those lizards was catching flies. They seem pretty shy so I'm not worried about it coming near me. The mozzie net seems to be doing its job as I have no bites and have not heard any ominous buzzing. Someone did mention that it is only the ones that don't buzz that carry malaria but what do I know? Anyway, I'm conscious you and several others promised specific prayer for my health and I'm feeling well so thanks.

Once they returned from their sortie into town the American team assembled in the communal area by the kitchen and I passed them on my way to lunch. They had eaten in a café somewhere in 'town,' which I consider to be an act of bravery!

I would have loved the company of another visitor really but I took a deep breath, clutched my plate and headed for rice and beans. As I mounted the concrete steps to enter the eating hall, a young man, sitting amongst several on the low stone wall that runs the length of the veranda, leapt into my path. 'Have you got the trainers?' My tummy turned over in the face of naked expectancy. It took me a moment to place him and then he announced, 'Me Jason Mama, you promised to bring shoes, yesterday, in the village.' The penny dropped.

My appetite scurried to a far-off corner and held its breath. Jason was smiling broadly but I felt intimidated and out of my depth (for a change!). Hastily I denied it was me who had made any promise and explained I would get Clara.

Heartily thankful that I knew where Clara was at that moment and willing her to have remained in the kitchen hut I hastily retraced my steps. Phew! There she was. I vaguely wondered if she had indeed bought shoes on the trip into town as I informed her that Jason requested the pleasure of her company.

Aware we had an audience I struggled to keep tension out of my voice. 'I made no promises,' she insisted whilst studiously avoiding Molly's piercing gaze. Molly made it quite clear that it was her opinion that in fact, despite encouragement to the contrary, Clara had done just that.

I looked from one to the other feeling increasingly damp and experiencing a discomforting tightness as if all my clothes just shrunk a size. I could feel if it meant running the gauntlet of Jason I wouldn't manage lunch ...

'Please Clara, I think you need to speak with him,' I managed. Mentally, I rummaged desperately for the paragraph on 'tricky situations between guests' in the visitors manual but drew a blank. Clara uncurled like a reluctant feline and rose from her position on the stone bench.

I had seen Ben (who met me at the airport) through an open office door and suddenly had the idea that Clara could maybe involve him, as a staff member, in explaining whatever she was going to say to Jason. Gratefully she hurried to find him. I left it about fifteen minutes and then I tentatively made my way back to the food hall and was heartily relieved to slip in and join the tail end of the queue.

The trainer incident provoked a fairly heated discussion about the whole 'giving' thing and I apologised to Clara later for speaking to her in front of the others and explained how nervous the incident had made me feel. By then she was readily admitting she may have overstepped the mark and with Ben's assistance she had agreed to provide money for Jason to purchase and deliver the promised trainers.

Tuesday

I didn't inquire about the detail of this working out and how the man may feel being given (or not, I couldn't help thinking) the shoes via a middleman and not the promised second visit to his village. It just occurs to me now Ma, that perhaps Jason is even planning not to pass on the money or trainers at all ... It is horrid to have suspicion prowling.

I felt desperate for some time alone with God in the afternoon and headed for the prayer hut really hoping to find it empty. I was disappointed. Children were playing and chatting. I went and sat on the ground outside the little prayer room we had used the night before. I sank onto the cool stone in the shade of a wall wondering if I could concentrate with the children nearby. Suddenly a young man appeared with a key.

Unlocking the prayer room he retrieved an instrument. Without hesitating I leapt up and asked him if I could use the room to pray until he returned to lock up the instrument. I think he was a bit surprised ... I may have had an air of desperation but he nodded and slipped away. I could hardly believe the timing and sank into delicious solitude. I felt in need of 'processing time' and just sat savouring God's presence for a while, enjoying the breeze that blew through due to neither window having glass. After a while I felt quieted and the anxiety over the new footwear incident dissipated.

It still feels very special to have been able to pray at all in the spot where Heidi encounters God. What might God do in me in this environment? Like a bubble coming to the surface, the memory that I had heard God speaking to me in the worship at church, when I had no means of recording it, became clear. I got out my notebook and pen and sat quietly.

I asked God to bring to my mind anything he wanted to say or particularly had said in church. Straightaway I was back in that space I found so hard to talk about when describing church to you. God has often spoken to me through pictures but this was different, more vivid. Rather than looking at a picture and sensing a meaning or message for someone this was a different experience. Maybe like the difference between looking at a scene in a picture in a gallery and being dropped onto a theatre stage where the scene is being acted out: except this 'scene' was situated outdoors.

I describe it like that because I experienced the harsh, dry heat of the outback. I was squinting in the searing sunlight. I could taste the dust of the outback. I also experienced a sense of horror because about ten feet away from me there was an Aboriginal woman lying in the dirt. Motionless. She wore a bridal gown. It was obvious the gown had once been beautiful but in this encounter it was ripped and blood stained. Her face had been bashed and was also bleeding.

Words came and I wrote,

> *Yes Haze, it's the Aboriginal people, I bleed for them and you have caught my heart. Don't fret about training or 'the way to reach them'. Trust me, I will make a way. I'm reminding you about Elijah and Elisha – impartation is part of my plan. Be mindful of 'the key'. As you press in and immerse yourself in my heart, there will be an unlocking to release me in POWER.*

I felt awed Ma and could only sit for some time. Clearly this speaks about restoration for his Aboriginal bride but what is God unfolding?

I did feel a surprising connection with Rita; maybe it is God teaching me more about his heart? Perhaps I will have opportunity to get to know some homeless Aboriginal people and serve food when I get home or

Tuesday

find a church that is reaching out. I told you how I've reached a stage where I'm feeling I will self-combust if God doesn't move in power to break addiction and save those he brings into my life who have lost hope.

God did speak about a 'key' and 'experiencing his heart for the poor' before I left. He said to spend time 'in Heidi's shadow' so maybe that links with 'impartation?' I want to be sensitive to his heart more and more. I feel encouraged that he is going to teach me. I'm reassured that some of the emotion I am experiencing is God letting me feel his heart; that is what I have been praying, but only tentatively as I am unsure. I mean, what could that look and feel like in an ordinary life like mine?

Apart from the map I told you about there is a pin board on one wall, opposite where I sat, with two scriptures typed out. I read,

'Now, Lord … enable your servants to speak your word with great boldness. Stretch out your hand to heal and perform miraculous signs and wonders through the name of your holy servant Jesus' (Acts 4:29,30). Also Psalm 91 with promises of 'shelter' and 'refuge' and 'covering with feathers'. I felt peaceful and aware of his presence so I worshipped for a while.

After a couple of hours I began to wonder when the young man may return but I had no appointments so decided to relax and pray some more.

After three and a half hours I began to feel a bit bothered. The prayer room is kept locked and if he didn't return I would have to leave it unlocked to search for him. I hovered for another twenty-five minutes then decided to make a break for it and trust nobody came and removed the CD player. Hopefully anyone passing by would just assume it was locked as usual. I exited and pretended to lock the door, in case I was observed, then scuttled back to the visitors' centre in hopes of finding a staff member with a key.

Zena was near the kitchen and fortunately had her keys with her. I returned to the prayer room, with the gong for tea now being hammered, to find the door securely locked. I had a strange feeling that someone had been watching and waiting for me to emerge — maybe that poor young man had waited ages.

That is the sort of thing I mean about extra 'strain' because if I was black I'm sure he would have just come when he was ready and I feel awkward that I am treated differently. I thought he had understood I would leave as soon as he needed to return the instrument and lock up again.

As I made my way back along the path to then cross the main track and return to the centre I became aware of a rhythmic, swishing noise. Looking away to my right, in front of the row of cottages where some of the missionaries live, there was a lone woman vigorously scything grass from around the base of a small tree. Something about her stance caused me to wonder if her day had been laced with frustration.

A starkly solitary worker, I wondered if I could encourage her. I called out,

'Hello, do you like to work alone or would you like some help?'

'Are you a visitor?'

'Yes, I'm Hazel.'

'When did you arrive?'

'On Thursday.'

'How long are you here for?' I had the distinct impression that insincere short-term offers of help were not appreciated.

Tuesday

'Three weeks.'

She stopped working and with one hand on her hip laid down the challenge,

'Can you be here at four-thirty tomorrow and meet me up there?' gesticulating behind her where I could see the gate to one of the little dwellings. (A number of the full time missionaries have rooms and basic kitchens in a row of simple hut-style buildings.)

I answered in the affirmative and continued on my way pondering what it might feel like to give yourself to a project and find casual observers trailing through week after week. I can imagine that reaching out to make new friends when they don't linger long enough to understand the vision that keeps your heart beating could be draining in the extreme. 'Lord, let me be a blessing.' I felt someone who is familiar with being let down had set me a test.

I had saved some rice and beans, from the generous portion at lunch, in a small bowl in the fridge and felt slightly guilty for taking the easy way out and skipping the evening mêlée in the food hall.

I'm struggling a bit Ma, in the visitors' centre, with people wearing earplugs and listening to music and sermons on their devices … only because I feel we miss out on communicating with each other. I suppose I am more aware because of my decision to be 'in the zone' and technology free. It didn't occur to me I might be the odd one out. Still, I think I am and in more ways than one!

After eating there wasn't long between carefully cleaning my utensils and getting ready to go to the homegroup pedicure evening. I just had time to pour boiling water, for the third time, onto the coffee bag (what a treat) that the generous Al had given me at breakfast. If I didn't feel quite so vulnerable I would make a joke about 'missionary material'. (Never far from the surface is the memory of the experience of loyal relatives, laying their lives down for the kingdom in Nigeria, being gifted recycled tea bags. How gracious was Jeannie...commenting they must have been very good quality and only previously used once!! Horrors. Surely Ma even heaven shudders...)

Sara was hosting her normal home group for the girls who live on the base (Iris girls) and (don't laugh) she had a pedicure pamper night planned so invited any visitors who would like to, to be involved in spoiling the girls. The little dwelling where she lives with another missionary shares a wall with the visitors' centre. As with Rahab Sara encouraged us to be praying as we painted nails and to share any pictures or words God gave us.

The atmosphere was quite different to the Rahab night. These girls are on their own turf and I suspect familiar with well-meaning visitors wanting to connect. I didn't feel fully at ease. The girls chatted and laughed together in their own language. It was much like being with a bunch of streetwise teenage girls at home but not being able to join in the banter. Clammily uncomfortable, I couldn't be certain that I wasn't the butt of the joke.

Two of the girls I spoke to were wearing pretty silver rings and when I commented Bea explained that they were 'ceremony rings'. My stomach turned over and her face blurred as I tried to hide the horrific mind pictures I was seeing. Bea's features slowly regained focus as relief dawned ... it was a different ceremony. She explained that Mama Heidi had given some of the girls rings as a sign of the promise they were making. I presumed to 'keep themselves pure' although more detail was not volunteered.

Tuesday

I concentrated on remembering the names and faces of just three girls and will pray and ask God if he has anything specific for them. They did speak some English when encouraged by Sara but I felt foolish most of the time and wondered if the girls were quietly making fun of our stumbling efforts to demonstrate ... well, that we care I suppose.

During the evening Sara mentioned that the missionary she lives with is off to the UK for some leave on Wednesday so I may be able to get this to you via her; I know you would love to have something in the post and I feel ever so slightly like a person who has suddenly seen an opportunity to get something 'out' from behind enemy lines!

Just before switching off the light at bedtime I noticed Aya fiddling with her foot. When I asked if she was all right she showed me what looked like huge blisters. One is on the side and the other on the top of her foot. She was clutching a piece of foliage with some reverence and as she broke it and applied glutinous gel to the swellings I recognised it as a succulent, fleshy piece from the aloe vera plant.

Aya said she thought she must have been bitten by something when she went out on bush outreach last week. Both areas were looking pretty red and I explained that aloe vera is soothing but has no healing properties I know of to directly combat established infection. I had a short wrestle with myself (what if I need to give her the dressings I brought for myself for possible use at a later date?) and then offered two of the special dressing plasters I brought for emergencies. I explained they are designed to remain in place to cover the area for a few days whilst healing takes place underneath. (Vital here to protect from infection where our feet are in the dirt all the time.) She said she has used aloe all her life and it is marvellous stuff but gratefully received the dressings.

Pemba Pennings

Aya looked at me and then said, 'I keep needing go toilet, very much.'

'Did you have to keep getting up in the night? Do you suffer with cystitis? Do you know what that is?'

'Yes. I feel not too well. I keep must go toilet. You pray?'

I prayed Ma, and she slept through the night. Poor girl must feel rotten. I did explain about the need to drink plenty, especially water. I hope she feels better today. Her foot looks very uncomfortable.

I did notice Jojo returned from the outreach with her leggings tightly tucked into socks that were well pulled up over ankles that were sturdily encased in closed sneakers. Her feet made rather an unusual spectacle in the heat, protruding from the folds of a thin cotton skirt but perhaps there was method …

So today I hope to be a blessing in the clinic; I feel in a strange kind of way that I want to put my nursing to the test and I am mindful that any experience gained can contribute to my retaining my registration. The clinic is open every day here on the base. Anya who is the nurse who appears to head it all up was speaking at church on Sunday (she is South African and reminds me of my GP in Canberra, you remember Rhianna?) I was able to have a brief word with her and she told me to arrive and 'play it by ear' so I am hoping I can be of some use. Thinking I will go later this morning.

It's 6.45am and I am already sticky with perspiration so I'm going to shoot off for my bread roll, have a quick wash and then head for the clinic in hopes of being able to contribute today.

More tomorrow Ma. Hard to imagine so much can go on in any one day, isn't it? Hope all is well your end.

All my love x

Wednesday

Darling Ma,

So, Day 6 in Pemba has already dawned and how exciting ... Aya is completely healed of her cystitis!!

Yesterday didn't quite go as planned.

I got to the clinic to find they don't have a normal day on Tuesdays as they are closed to patients for staff meetings, admin, etc. It took me a short while to even locate the clinic. It is in a separate compound and small huts, all quite close together, surround it.

As I pushed through the large wooden gates I greeted a guard who was sitting on a chair reading a children's book with colourful pictures. I am practising some basic phrases now I am getting my bearings a little more and I was delighted; my greeting gained a response, though sadly all I could do was smile and nod my head since '*Bom dic*' meaning 'Good day' and pronounced 'Bong dee-ya' provoked a whole string of words that were incomprehensible to me.

There was a slight 'ghost town' feel about the area and I have since

Pemba Pennings

learned that this part of the base is the compound used as accommodation for students who attend the bi-annual Harvest School here in Pemba. Up to 300 students descend on the base and part of the whole experience is living 12 to a dwelling, with a tiny kitchen/dining area and a very basic bathroom in each. They are all a few minutes' walk from the sheds and huts that serve as classrooms.

As I approached the small hut, which is the clinic, a young man armed with a hose was busy washing out a couple of the by now familiar plastic bins. He greeted me, shook my hand and introduced himself as Juma. There was a strong smell of bleach causing me to wonder just what had been in the bins previously. 'Nobody here Tuesday,' he stated with a wide smile.

He clearly wanted to chat. I am consciously trying to practise 'stopping for the person in front of me' as I have heard people here talking about, and being 'in the moment'. (Both quite hard when you constantly feel uncomfortable and anxious about the possibility of causing cultural offence.) I tried to adopt a posture that would communicate my willingness to linger.

A jet of water drenched my feet as, launching into an account of his role as cook on bush outreaches, Juma overshot the bin he was spraying. I suddenly remembered I hadn't put sun block on my feet and began to look for a way of excusing myself as the sun beat down. 'Where can we meet to talk some more?' he pressed me, a knot of anxiety pushed against my ribs. I jauntily exclaimed I was here for three weeks, had to go now but was sure to see him around.

How can I tell if he genuinely wants to practise his English (which seemed pretty good to me)? Maybe he is a 'village boy' hoping I am a

Wednesday

soft touch. Perhaps he is a Christian and would just like to chat about what God is doing in our lives but my pulse was up and I was acutely aware there was nobody else in sight.

I made my excuses, hurried past the guard at the gate and headed back to the centre. I'm still having those odd prickly episodes so I think if he is not rushed off his feet and there is an easy opportunity, I will ask the doctor tomorrow if its normal or if he thinks I should stop taking the doxycycline. Maybe I should have gone for the expensive option that you take less often but £75 seemed a lot of money. (I'll let you know what he says.)

It was such a relief to feel a bit more relaxed at lunchtime (nothing prepared me for the underlying grinding anxiety that being in such an alien environment has provoked) and I enjoyed my rice and beans (still too much!). I had an easy chat with several children who I joined on the long table.

Passing the admin offices, the bamboo door in the fence was ajar and I glimpsed a group of staff eating lunch together around a table in a small courtyard area. Don't get me wrong, we're not talking landscaped patio just an area of hard-packed mud. There was a family atmosphere about the group, which blessed me even though I don't know any of them; I suppose it was the lovely al fresco ambiance, reminiscent of Mediterranean holidays as they laughed together with their children.

Each mealtime I walk the same way around the office building and just a few yards on there is a particularly unsavoury smell. A suspicious looking damp trickle, that is sometimes a small stream, has to be navigated but nobody seems unduly concerned. We all simply step over it.

It was mentioned that there may be a group visiting the hospital to pray for the sick but I didn't feel up to another raw encounter with gaping need, plus several people had stated they had become unwell after visiting the previous week, which did little to enhance the appeal. Maybe I will be ready next week …

I decided to join a number of the team who seemed to have thoroughly enjoyed being part of the 'Feeding Village Children' programme, which takes place daily in the church. Children who hope to eat have to arrive by one o'clock or the gate is closed. There is a time of 'children's church' and then a van reverses up to the entrance of the church building.

A group of strong young men (who I learned have all grown up through the programme themselves and are in effect 'giving something back') heave the inevitable plastic bins brimming with rice and beans into the building. After some singing and a short talk the children are instructed to line up. As they file up they are handed generous platefuls of rice and beans and slopping is common. Pretty soon the ground was awash with spilt food and I struggled to keep my balance on the wet cement. The noise was incredible and it got hotter and stickier as we served.

As several of the Harvest team were on hand I soon felt surplus to requirements and stepped outside for air. I struggled when I saw one of the bigger boys being quite rough and brandishing a stick to make the smaller village children move into the area where he wanted them to sit and eat. Herding them really. I suppose he was anxious; there are many children pressing to find a spot to sit and eat their food and it could easily be chaos. I was relieved when one of the other older lads retrieved the stick and I hope explained to him that there was a different way.

Wednesday

Most of the children had threadbare garments, bare feet and many had toddlers in tow. A number could be seen tipping the larger part of their meal into grubby containers of various description, mostly looking like they had been fished out of the gutter, to take home for their family. The children themselves must be hungry but many of them eat less than half the portion.

I felt hot, bothered and deflated, Ma. I didn't linger. Such a large number of families represented; all having to subsist on part of one child's lunch. It's too much to take in, rows and rows of hungry brown eyes, yards and yards of stick arms and legs. Heart-wrenching. The other visitors returned to the centre saying how much they loved it. I don't think I'll go again.

We've been told that children and young men who live on the base are not to be in the visitors' centre to ensure the area offers a level of calm and rest for visitors. As I reached the entrance gates a young Mozambican man was hovering. He introduced himself as Mikel and asked if he could please talk with Joe. He spoke of having been with Joe on outreach with such warmth and enthusiasm it felt as if they were old friends.

Joe rests in the afternoons which is obviously important for his body otherwise he would be sitting on his bottom all day long and at risk of pressure sores. I went to the far end of the centre and called quietly outside his window in case he was sleeping. He does all the activities with the team as if his legs worked and is always in amazingly good spirits. I admire his fortitude and he is easy to talk to. He answered and appeared a few minutes later wheeling himself out towards the gate.

It came to light that in a generous act Joe had agreed to give the tent he had brought with him from America to use for the overnight bush outreach, and Mikel had come to claim his 'gift'. Tents are a highly sought-after commodity here so he will likely have sold it on for a princely sum. This may cause all sorts of issues with his peers and family.

For those growing up here and then working on the base there must be constant temptation, being confronted by westerners who relatively speaking, are all exceedingly wealthy. I think that's part of the strict 'no giving' policy that we are told about in orientation and is also explained in the written info before folk arrive.

Honestly Ma, my respect for the people who are living here full time just grows every day as they warmly welcome visitors and graciously manage our blunders. I mean they *live* here; we are in *their* home.

(Talking of growing respect for those serving here full time, did I mention I went to offer to help Christy again this morning in the pre-school, when other plans went awry, only to be told she was at home unwell in bed. The girl who told me explained it was probably worms and that Christy was fine although had had a broken night due to a nocturnal visit by a certain rodent, which seemed under the impression that a bed share was on the cards! See what I mean? And she is here long term!)

Equipment is not easily available here so any tents, sleeping bags, bed linen, etc. that visitors donate go into a central pool that helps to continue facilitating outreach and equipping the next round of visitors. I have found it quite upsetting that it is Christians who are making life harder in this area. I suspect the subject will come up at the meal table and I hope to help the others to really see the value of respecting the way Iris wants giving to happen.

Wednesday

UTTER BLISS as we have power and running water today! I was chatting with a full-timer who mentioned there have been others who had problems with the antimalarial I'm on. Apparently none of those who live here are on medication because longer term it can cause liver damage and although we are not in a high-risk area I can quite see that Iris haven't the resources for caring for sick visitors. I was shocked to learn some of the students from America are not taking anything (even though it states clearly in the info pack that it is compulsory, along with health insurance, for all visitors).

Several of the students wanted to watch the sunrise over the ocean so I was up with them and on the sand by 4.45 this morning. It was cloudy so although I always love that stillness before dawn plus being by the water, it wasn't the most spectacular sunrise.

I was interested to see one of the full-time girls from the base out jogging along the waterfront alone. I guess over time and with language skills, going out as a girl is easier but it seemed incongruous somehow: lycra and cushioned Nike against a backdrop of skinny silhouettes crouching over a fishing net on the beach and an elderly lady tottering along the road under the weight of bananas.

I was intrigued to see a line of people at the gate to the base. It was only just after four in the morning and some of them appeared to have been there for quite a while. Several were settled down with sleeping children draped over a limb or propping a basket between themselves and the wall.

I asked Ben about it later when I bumped into him. He explained that the clinic is able to see thirty patients daily. The first thirty at the gate each morning are let in to see the doctor. Folk walk from miles around for the free medical care and it is easy to see the need for the new hospital that is being built on the base. Iris plan to offer daily outpatient clinics, plus dentistry and obstetric care. Eventually operating theatres and the whole works will be available on site. The clinic section of the project is in the finishing stages and I will help move bits of furniture, dressing packs, etc. into the new building tomorrow.

When I questioned Hannes about the doxycycline reaction he explained it is not uncommon to experience these weird prickly episodes. I just need to keep the sun off my skin (easier said than done!). He also shared the information that my drug is only 50-70% effective whilst the more expensive option is 70-90%. But it tends to be those who travel out of this region that get hit by malaria. He advises to definitely keep on taking it and it is likely the reaction will pass. I like him and am thrilled there is romance in the air with M!

I kept my appointment with Tina (of solitary scything fame) and we set to, pulling weeds in what she told me is to be the prayer garden. Bethel Church in California donated funds for plants and paths so a beautiful place for prayer can be established.

Tina is forthright and is very specific about her requirements and how the weeds are to be pulled. The most voracious are a plant with an incredibly long taproot, which has to be teased out of the ground lest it break off and then multiply.

With the obvious connotations about things needing to be rooted from lives and communities we used this act of weeding as fuel for prayer and passed a peaceful, productive hour together. I'm not saying Tina is looking for new friends or even particularly welcoming but I want to be a blessing on God's terms. She has a determination about her, is obviously

Wednesday

a pioneer spirit and looking for new friends is hardly going to be high on the list of a person sold out to God in a foreign land where going without is a way of life, is it? We share a passion for prayer and I have made it clear I am happy to pick up rubbish, join her in a night of prayer or serve her in any way and I was really pleased she suggested going to supper together.

I have so much to learn Ma, from a young woman who has laid her life down. I must have done something right as I'm invited back to weed for another hour before sunset tomorrow. Bringing rubber gloves out here with me was definitely divine inspiration. Tina dives into the undergrowth and grabs these tenacious plants with her bare hands but I cannot block visions of creeping, slithery possibilities so am opting for the Mrs Mop look, regardless of curious stares from passers-by. What is one more curious look? Tina has been here years and so knows many of the children well and I loved hearing them chat over supper. (Particularly wonderful for me to have someone to teach me the word for 'small', as in portion; if I can only remember it.) What a relief. *Pouco.*

Can hardly believe I've been here a full week tomorrow. A third into my visit; but who's counting?!

More soon Ma.

Huge hug from me and thanks so much for ongoing prayers x x x

Thursday

Here I am again Ma, and another 24-hour roller coaster to report!

I hope you are faithfully meditating on 'Do not be anxious … ' and not fretting about me. All will be well. I am on a great God adventure and so out of my depth that it is 'God or sink' so years of prayer are being answered. I am increasingly aware life as I have hitherto known it is unlikely to continue. How exciting is that … Oh my word … or as our beloved Holger would say, 'Oh my shorts!' (Not that shorts can feature here.)

I am increasingly conscious of keeping my legs covered since learning that thing about the knee-to-thigh zone being considered highly erogenous. Covering up is to do with respecting the Muslim perception of knee to thigh being the gateway to the birth canal from which emanates life, or something along those lines.

Anyhow, in spite of the heat I can see why wearing leggings under our long skirts when clambering in and out of trucks is a good idea. Hard to imagine a flash of my knobbly offerings igniting unholy passion but there we go.

Thursday

I am not reassured by the knowledge shared by one of the white male staff here that it is likely that prior to meeting me, a Mozambican male is only acquainted with white females through the dubious vehicle of porn movies. It's obvious many of the males around the base are familiar with the western female staff and he is making a generalisation but the gist is enough to make me think socks, leggings and trainers would be the order of the day if I do at some stage 'go bush'.

Last evening was rather interesting. There is a desire to meet need and connect with those in this area who could be viewed as more 'middle-class'. These are local Mozambicans who are established and comfortably off. Iris has a strong emphasis on engaging with the poor in the region but it is recognised the more affluent also need Jesus. Some of them have become Christians and would benefit from teaching and fellowship so with this in mind a second opportunity to attend church in the week has been created.

My understanding is this is only the second time this meeting has happened but Tina suggested we go. I was pleased because sometimes it is slightly tricky to know if it is appropriate for visitors to attend something. I want to take all opportunity to put myself in God's way and experience life here, so welcomed this invitation.

I suppose with Iris working from the beginning with the destitute and outcast in Pemba, it could be that those Mozambicans who are professional, have travelled and are comfortably off have never considered being associated with what is happening here on the base.

The concept is to offer a more westernised style of church to this section of the local population in hopes they too can hear about Jesus and grow in their faith. The same musicians and singers led the worship as on Sunday and God's presence was just as tangible although there were only about thirty-five of us there. I didn't notice any well-dressed middle-class looking locals but it is a small beginning. Me? I just lay on the floor on my face soaking up God's presence and experienced a deep peace.

Hard to register I have been here a whole week. I am having a quiet afternoon attempting to digest, process and get this latest letter written. I'm living at the edge of a vast ocean of experience Ma, and if I don't get down the speed, height and temperature of the last wave, I have a sense it will be lost to me forever as the following wave comes swiftly in its wake to pound, engulf and crash onto the shore of me.

I really wasn't sure where to be yesterday morning. I think my inner churn was partly due to knowing that prison visiting was in the afternoon. Whilst it did sound like an adventure, I avoid, as you know, any movie or novel involving incarceration. I just can't bear to see people caged. It makes me feel physically constrained and the bestial behaviour that such places seem to induce in human beings plays on my mind. But I have sensed all week this is one thing I would do. I am accepting that the words 'comfort' and 'zone' are not even in sight of each other here much less uttered in the same sentence.

Back to this morning: I joined the girls from the visiting American team who were running an activity for a group of women from the village. Local women, many of whom are already widowed, come each week and after worshiping together they do some craft or have opportunity to have a go at something like painting. In the past things like jewellery making has then enabled them to have something to sell at the shop on the base.

Thursday

On this particular day a young woman (I think one of the full-time Iris staff) came to say the usual missionary was away and she was stepping in as 'helper'. She explained she had hoped to do some kind of creative art class but due to lack of materials it was not going to be possible. I felt sorry for the local ladies who had walked a distance, waited for quite some time sitting on the ground under the trees nursing anticipation and who were now going to be let down.

Our helper/leader turned brightly to the group of us and inquired as to our 'artistic talents'. She was suggesting that improvisation on our part could still produce a fulfilling morning for the women. I shivered and realised I was in totally the wrong place.

Wonderfully, Jojo took this as her cue and morphed into full creative flow. She began to sway around the large piece of wood that represented a craft work bench and on coming out of a particularly flamboyant twirl collected a paint brush and a blunt crayon that were lying there. She smiled serenely at the helper, requested paper, whereupon a large sheet (that looked as if it had held at least one person's fish and chip supper in some distant past) was produced and pinned to the stock cupboard door.

A child's paint box appeared and as discussion around the design of a style of poster swelled to a crescendo (I can't remember the context or what the topic was to be), I melted to the end of the hut and out into the compound where I willed the shadows of the big trees to absorb me so the waiting women would not wonder why I was abandoning ship.

I had peeked into the stock cupboard and honestly the shelves were just bare. The helper muttered about stock being low but I was mortified. Surely if Christians in the west knew of the need, the whole hut could've been stuffed with resources? I felt so tiny thinking again about the amazing staff here pressing on year upon year regardless of any impediment that life throws at them.

Later in the day I heard from the team that a special time of worship evolved with these amazing women and they had a fascinating morning where Jojo taught them all sorts of things about different ways and styles of creating pictures. It is fantastic how something from nothing appears to be consistently created here. Absorbed with my own feelings again I had mind pictures of mountains of crayons, paints, paper and card that has passed carelessly through my hands and felt ... I don't know, guilt, frustration, longing. I was left feeling perturbed and acutely aware of my own lack of resourcefulness where the younger girls had just plunged in to tackle the task.

My feet seemed to take me towards the clinic and I hoped for some menial activity to present itself. I wanted to be occupied, useful and to stop thinking. No such luck! Or should I say, blessing? Tricky thing 'luck' isn't it? We don't really believe such a thing exists, do we? Anyway it was still only just after 8 in the morning and there was a complete lack of activity or personnel at the clinic. Nothing for it then but to retreat to the visitors' centre and have some quiet time with God. As it turns out this proved to be good preparation.

On my return our room was empty. I wasn't sorry. I thought I would do a bit of housekeeping and then have a read and pray. As the set of bunks opposite mine are unoccupied I have made good use of the piece of string a previous visitor left and have now pegged several bags up off the floor at waist height between the beds.

If our room were full there would be seven of us living in this small space and we would have to take turns in getting our cases out so I am thankful I

Thursday

seem to have hit a quiet patch for the visitors' centre. I can reduce dramatically the number of times I need to bend and haul my suitcase out from under the bed in a day by keeping things such as bug repellent, sun screen, my cap, tissues, etc. all in a bag pegged up.

I have three bags on my line. I was sorting the one in which I have my wash bag and a few other bits and bobs when I came across a pile of dusty grit in the bottom corner. On tipping the contents onto my bed you can imagine how I felt to discover nothing was torn but there were obvious *teeth marks* (horrors!!) neatly along the edge of a precious coffee sachet. One that I had been kindly given and was saving. (For what? I don't know and it's a bit of a lesson about hoarding, isn't it? Is it my heart posture that God wouldn't bless me with another sachet of coffee if need arose? Why hadn't I just enjoyed it as it was given? Maggots in my manna, I know!)

I experienced a mental kaleidoscope of the sight of a darting shadow under the door, the impression of shadow again behind my suitcase and then a rustling sound, which it now seemed likely was not the breeze on Aya's book pages. I had to leave the room and sink onto the bench outside as realisation hit me. A third occupant had joined us. We had a rat! I know … the stuff of nightmares!

All too swiftly the story of Christy (the young teacher I met earlier in the week) in her bed ill, and the mental graphic of her awaking to face a whiskered rodent on her pillow came to mind. Then the voice of my dear friend Morna peeled between my ears. Her parting pearl to me had been, 'Always remember Haze, whatever challenge you face, vocalising it only compounds it, gives it greater reality.'

You would be proud of me Ma. I took a deep breath, re-entered the room and pinning the door wide open to allow as much light in as possible, I set about removing any trace of the littered coffee sachet and double checked my bags for anything vaguely edible. I did make as much noise as possible and prayed in tongues out loud. I sealed up soap and toothpaste, anything that could deceive a starving rodent on a mission into thinking a titbit lurked.

To the casual observer I looked like a happy camper just having a tidy but knowing me so well you would have noted the wet upper lip and furtive glances to all four corners of the room. As I write I have not breathed a word to anyone and am desperately hoping that is the end of this particular story. Thank you Jesus.

It was still only 10am when I was done so I took myself back to the clinic and found a hum of activity. There was much moving of boxes and packages as furniture and supplies were transferred into the new facility. The long-term staff here truly are amazing and seem to calmly walk through huge frustrations. Various pieces of equipment have been donated.

I really struggled with feelings of anger as it appeared as if certain churches viewed the clinic as more like a dumping ground. (What looked like a Victorian birthing chair turned out to be a donated dentist's couch but why didn't the dentist concerned send a modern chair? One we could lift without a crane?) I felt a sense of shame that this much needed and fervently prayed over clinic was graciously receiving totally out-dated cast-off equipment from the affluent west. Something feels out of kilter.

It was humbling and exciting to be assembling shelves and filling cabinets with supplies that will undoubtedly influence the course of many lives here in Pemba. Anya is in charge. What a dynamic lady. She

Thursday

preached on Sunday, oversees the healthcare of all and sundry for miles and is now occupied with the building project of the new hospital. Any one of these roles could overwhelm an average person. She has a great sense of humour and deals respectfully with local workmen and staff alike.

Local carpenters and builders have done all the work. You could be forgiven for expecting, as I was, to see crates of plastic storage units, work benches and easy clean surfaces bearing the familiar words 'Made in China' or 'Ikea', to be lined up and awaiting unpacking. Nothing could be further from the reality that met me.

The doctor's desk, crafted from local materials by local men, arrived with the drawers on the wrong side. (Meaning that in order for the doctor to put his legs under his desk it had to be positioned where the door was behind him and the approaching patient would be greeted by a great view of the doctor's back!) The drawers under the treatment room work surface, which would be opened and closed all day long for access to dressings, syringes and suture packs, were ill fitting and took all my strength to open. In spite of all this it is obvious that the commitment to honour and bless the local community is paramount.

The carpenter was invited to observe and comment upon a suspicious looking mould that was present in several pieces of furniture and it was graciously pointed out to him by Anya that it was a problem that would inevitably inhibit final payment. No criticism was levelled and no accusation made.

He left the site with his pride intact and spoke positively of resolving the issue. I got the impression it would be in his own good time but the unspoken message from the team is that we are here to serve, love and give of our best because we honour God by loving the poor and respecting those who do things in a different way to us. We are guests in this country.

Having skilfully negotiated with the carpenter, Anya announced she was off to the hospital with one of the children who was due for surgery. She moves with an air of confident focus and a certain twinkle from one task to the next. Even with the inevitable challenges of having been out here a number of years, laughter is never far from her eyes. It's clear she gets things done and I sense staff willingly rise to her expectations. Her whole person is inspiring and capable, making me feel I would love to be on her team. (What am I saying?!)

Outside, clusters of men were lounging around all across the building site. Here and there odd pieces of structure protrude from the dirt. They could be construed as the small beginnings of foundations but I observed nothing that could be considered 'work' or construction. The others made no comment as we beavered away moving furniture and fixing things in the scorching heat; just cheery conversation as use of the new facility was anticipated.

Two Mozambican lads who had been recruited by Hannes assembled some flat-packed shelves. True to form the shelves were uneven and there appeared to be three bolts that had not made the journey. Patience and perseverance came to the fore as the unit was disassembled and the building process begun all over again. Ultimately six of us pondered and re-positioned with no joy until it was spotted that one of the supporting struts had to be inserted a different way up. Everything here feels as if it takes much longer and acceptance of a different way of doing even what may be familiar, mundane tasks is crucial.

Thursday

I can only respect the genuine commitment to keep everything indigenous. It must surely be tempting to recruit a construction team from Europe and get the hospital up and running, but the authentic approach taken by Iris means local families are fed as the men work for wages.

Local men are learning skills and are given opportunity to see a project through to completion whilst knowing a sense of ownership. I think this determination must come from Heidi and Rolland because I have not experienced any muttering or questioning among the team. How embarrassing when you think about the uproar at home when some brave vicar wants to remove pews or change the hymn book. I realise I am gaining only a snapshot and that bribery and corruption are the norm but that doesn't seem to undermine the decision by Iris to honour and bless.

Just after lunch Dan, who is an Australian working here for a couple of years, arrived in the centre with Sol who was born here. I don't know if he grew up on the base. They oversee the prison visiting and come to give visitors preparation before each visit. (More evidence of gracious patience; just like Sara with the Rahab ministry. It's great they take time to patiently explain and prepare us and each activity is bathed in prayer.)

I quietly yearned for the safety and anonymity of being part of a large group but the American team had an activity planned. Several of them had been to the prison the previous week and were enthusiastic about the experience. Aya appeared and I was grateful I was not to be the only visitor on this excursion.

Dan began to explain about the prison; it is known as 'the jail' and the men can be incarcerated for up to six months whilst they await sentencing. After that, serious offenders are sent to the 'big prison' that is some distance out of town. He said murder, armed assault and robbery warrant very long sentences here. If wrongly accused, I can't imagine how it works because nobody seems to have any money; I guess things we take for granted like appealing your sentence, even if you are innocent, are probably not an option.

Aya seemed a bit restless and as soon as Dan finished speaking she spoke quickly explaining she wanted to buy bananas and give one to each prisoner. Dan had said it isn't a big jail and there would likely be up to 60 prisoners. I struggled with the concept of a supermarket sweep en route as the idea of tossing bananas to men in captivity seemed rather shocking.

I was stunned that Aya could be thinking of anything except getting on with the mission (now with hindsight I see it was a generous thought) but Dan seemed unfazed and patiently explained this may not be practical. Demonstrating amazing grace and tact he patiently commended Aya for the desire to give then he and Sol talked around options with Aya until a plan was agreed.

It was decided we would stop and purchase sachets of fruit juice powder as this could be distributed by the prison guards and would be put into the prisoners' water, which would be available from a communal pot. I felt awkward when Aya went on to state that she also needed to buy an adaptor. What was going on in her head? Here we were about to take our lives in our hands, taking a step of faith akin, in my book, to that of walking on water, and all she could think about was her shopping! (I realise now that was *my* perspective but I can't write honestly from someone else's can I?)

I had donned the requested adornment of a long skirt and felt un-

Thursday

comfortable that Aya was in her usual three-quarter length trousers the shape and style of which mean it's impossible to tell if they are cast-off shorts from a rotund husband or trousers that her son has grown out of. Let's just say they are clearly not made to measure and give her a rather waiflike look. (Again this is only how I was seeing things and clearly demonstrates the level of anxiety I was experiencing.)

I tend to feel that Aya is quite a bit older than me but it's hard to tell. She stands just above the height of my elbow and sports a different baseball cap each day. I felt conspicuous and awkward, unsure of what her next move or statement may be but still very glad not to be the only visitor going. She had told me in terms that did not invite debate that I definitely ought to go to the jail, so at least I wasn't in trouble. But she has pretty strong ideas about what I should be doing and isn't afraid to voice them.

We made our way along the sandy track to the vehicle compound to await the arrival of our driver. Time (apart from the gong that sounds when the meals are served) is an ethereal concept that inhabited a former life and nobody here appears conscious of it. Days consist of sunrise, morning, afternoon and sunset and I haven't encountered urgency in any form. Dan had booked a driver and truck but it is obviously normal for the two to appear … when they appear.

We were blessed in that less than half an hour's wait found us aboard a middle-sized truck. Behind the three-seater cab was a large flatbed tray with shallow sides and a torn canvas canopy stretched over a rusty metal frame. Someone had obviously found a better use for the planks that normally would serve as bench seats. Dan indicated we girls should climb into the cab and, remembering to clutch my skirt around me, I obeyed, thankful not to have to perch in the back although very glad Dan was not far away.

Our driver was a particularly small Mozambican gentleman sporting a lop-sided smile, which endured through even the deepest of potholes as we lumbered towards I knew not what. We approached a muddled kind of junction which offered a choice of routes, one being the broken tarmac we were on, another was a dirt road measuring just about a car's width and a third appearing to be little more than a rutted cart track. Dan tapped Abdul on the shoulder. Abdul grunted and plunged the truck straight at the track, which appeared to lead into the heart of the village that surrounds the base.

We trundled on amongst simple dwellings, narrowly avoiding staring children below and overhanging boughs above. Hesitating each time there was a fork in the track Abdul eventually drove into a dead end and pulled up. Dan jumped out calling that he wouldn't be long. I felt vulnerable and conspicuous perched above the raggle taggle children who gathered to stare.

A sense of aloneness engulfed me. Recognising my usual coping mechanism of humour was unavailable (no chance either of my companions would 'get me') I closed my eyes and focused on my breathing. Dan had encouraged us to bring water and had explained the prisoners would most likely ask to drink from our bottles. I had a number of reasons to be distressed. What if I

a) Want to say no and shock them by breaking custom or
b) Agree to offer my water bottle but am then unable to explain that I don't require it back without causing offence (let's not overlook that it's unlikely a man will be in prison for seeing an old lady across the road) or

Thursday

c) Be expected to pass my bottle around and drink myself between other users?

This intrepid woman of faith and power had decided not to take any water.

We should only be gone a couple of hours and I could manage that long. I felt I wanted my hands free so I took nothing, just tucking a tissue into my bra for good measure. Dan emerged clutching a piece of paper which turned out to be some kind of form the driver required and which his boss had omitted to leave ready for him to collect at the office.

Thinking about it Ma, I can't remember if it was Dan or the driver who left us but I managed to keep breathing and repel the encroaching panic because there are literally thousands of local people crammed into the village, and if we couldn't reverse out of the corner we were in it was as if a huge black ocean may swallow us up. Golly I felt so nervous! Sounds rather ridiculous now but I think you may relate. It is all so alien.

'Shay zoosh tay arr-ma' (*Jesus te ama*). Aya made me jump as she made these sounds like a giant insect in my left ear. 'You try, you say now,' she leaned over me to the driver and said again loudly and slowly, 'Shay zoosh tay arr-ma'. Abdul nodded and looked at me expectantly. I willed him to return his focus to the oncoming traffic, which was mostly on its own side of the road but quickly understood that I was required to repeat the sounds. He seemed satisfied with my stumbling effort and Aya beamingly announced we had said 'Jesus loves you', explaining to me that it is very important we communicate with the prisoners.

I am learning that journeys here tend to be multi-purpose in nature and true to form we pulled up outside a small corner shop. The two men hopped out of the truck and reappeared with a plastic bag bulging with sachets of fruit flavoured powder and a bottle of water each.

I honestly was trying to just go with the flow and embrace the whole experience but I clearly failed miserably as Dan (who I had known for almost all of two hours at this stage!) leaned over from the back of the truck and kindly said, 'You can relax. Just try and relax.' He is a rare man attuned to the feminine pitch or my acting skills need honing. Next stop was the jail.

I can't remember much about the outside of it Ma, but the road leading to the jail seemed to suddenly have rather smart homes with gardens exhibiting various succulents and even a few interesting if incongruous sculptures. This was a sharp contrast as most of the buildings we passed were in need of repair and appeared weary. We left the truck and an arrangement was made for a pick-up later.

I prayed that God would help me represent him well whilst thinking it was a pretty tall order in a context in which I had no idea how to behave or relate. Abdul drove off down the road ensconced in the safety of the small cab and I experienced a clamping sensation in my chest as the mother ship disappeared in a dusty swerve.

Feeling vulnerable in the extreme I was grateful there was no suggestion of pausing for a time of prayer on the steps. In a swift, firm movement we found ourselves as one ushered into a small office.

Two guards appeared to be sporting almost a complete uniform between them. The one who had the upper half greeted Dan warmly whilst his eyes roved over Aya and myself. It felt a bit like being on a stage set with a few pieces of furniture positioned to give the impression of an office but there was no computer or piles of documents in evidence.

The more senior person was behind the desk and a younger man had

Thursday

his back to a window that was beside a door so we were really in a short corridor leading from the front porch to … what? I wondered if it would be rows of cells behind the door? Or maybe we would be in a small room set out like a chapel? Perhaps a communal lounge-style room, basic but where prisoners could relax.

I had no idea where the 'visit' would take place. Through the murky glass it looked like it could be daylight beyond. Maybe the men were in another building then? The younger guard was grinning broadly and was asking Dan if he'd 'brought it'. The 'it' turned out to be bleach and a broom and I heard Dan say he would try for next time. Then he held out the sachets of juice powder and the guard just took them nodding. Aya leant over and nudging Dan pointedly said, 'For the prisoners, for the prisoners.'

Dan indicated we should move through the room and out of the door, which the young guard opened. He stood aside as we exited the office and we found ourselves at the top of a flight of metal steps, like a fire escape. Dan in front and Sol behind we walked in a line down the steps.

We were in a yard, an expanse of scorched dirt enclosed by a high wall. A longer narrow building was opposite and at the end that protruded into the yard a group of men gathered, right there, in the open. They were in rows of about twenty and stood three or four men deep. A solid, black, wall of intimidating, begrimed testosterone.

Dan showed us to stand in a line facing the men and with our backs to the wall. I struggled to banish thoughts of firing squads. What I'd been told about men here viewing porn and making assumptions about white women skipped into my head.

Growling at fear I swatted such thoughts and focused on pressing myself against the wall as if I could magically morph into bricks. It felt like having a giant x-ray as fifty plus pairs of eyes bored into me. My feet found a little ledge that marked the rim of a small gulley about the width of my foot size and I thankfully wriggled my feet into it so I could wedge myself in position and lean on the wall for support.

As I focused on continuing to breathe I was intrigued that Aya appeared quite at home. She showed no visible sign of being in the least uncomfortable or nervous but I didn't have opportunity to dwell on the thought as two things happened simultaneously.

One of the prisoners, conspicuous by his spontaneous gyrations and bouncing dreadlocks, suddenly leapt from the ranks and began singing lustily. As he sang he encouraged the other men to join in various refrains and with no inhibition he began leaping and dancing up and down the length of the assembled group. Every eye was on him and as he reached the end of the first line in the group on his third pass, my eye caught movement.

There was a solitary prisoner at the far end of the yard. He was using the gulley, in which I had my feet firmly planted, for a whole other purpose — as only boys do. Hastily averting my eyes I sought to appear engrossed in the exhibition in front of me whilst willing my legs to hold me up long enough to wriggle my feet up at least on to the outer lip of the gulley.

To be truthful Ma, I was completely transfixed by this man's gyrating (the one singing not the other …) and as he continued leaping and cavorting I began to wonder if this was demon possession. A sideways glance at Dan showed him to be looking pretty relaxed. Sol, who was standing reassuringly a few feet in front and between the men and us, suddenly exclaimed something, raised an arm in the air and then shout-

Thursday

ed, 'Hallelujah'.

All the men responded with a loud 'Amen'. The dancing individual then began a new song and all the men joined in. With no warning, in a blink, there was a spirit of worship present. The rich sound of harmonies filled the air and reverberated off the walls and buildings. It went right through me and I couldn't stop the tears Ma, they just rolled down my face (and are again now just writing to you about it). Right there in the dirt and brokenness the sweetest offering of worship you can imagine: raw, unrestrained adoration ripped the atmosphere, mysteriously exposing something of heaven.

One after the other the songs rolled on. Initially, dreading the pain of emptiness, I avoided making eye contact but as we worshipped I felt bolder. Something in me wanted to reach out. How many of these men have mothers?

I couldn't help noticing a young man who had one eye so swollen it was protruding from the side of his face, squashed closed. I tried not to think about how he got his injury. Another prisoner had a swelling the size of a cricket ball on the side of his head. It was just behind and slightly above his left ear but so huge you couldn't miss it from the front. My tummy churned to think that their already tough lives include violence. How could victims do that to each other?

The men continued worshipping so I just put my hands out in front of me asking God to carry these feelings that are too heavy for me to bear. Dan explained later that the leaping man was called Jordan. He had been very sick and on a previous visit was healed and gave his life to Jesus. Now he is teaching and supporting the men and there are a number of Christians in the jail with him.

As the singing ended I decided against rummaging in my bra for aforementioned tissue (for obvious reasons!) and used the sleeve of my shirt for mopping. I am being careful to wear long-sleeved tops and always a hat. The sun was beating down.

Sol said a few words, which we couldn't understand and then suddenly Dan stepped forward. Turning to Aya and me (looking at this stage rather like a half-baked episode of *Little and Large*), he cheerfully said, 'It would be great if you would just introduce yourselves. Sol will translate and if you can share something that would be good; anything the Lord is showing you to encourage the men. Just a few minutes.'

'Put on the spot' nowhere near covers it but in that moment Jesus offered me his arm and I stepped away from the wall. I smiled at the expectant faces and wanted more than anything to communicate love and encouragement. I began with my name, told them that I am a nurse and thanked the men for hosting us explaining it is my first time in their country.

One thing about having a translator is I find the pause as they speak a helpful moment to plan what comes next. Amazingly, in the moment of stepping forward I knew instantly that I was going to simply share what God has been showing me about that familiar verse Nehemiah 8:10, 'The joy of the Lord is your strength.'

I explained that this joy is not as I thought for years, as in 'your joy' meaning my being determined, that because I have God's love in my life I have no excuse not to be joyful. I believe that my joy is not about happiness, which depends on what is actually going on in my life. I shared the mind-blowing revelation that the joy this verse speaks of is the Lord's joy ... *the joy that he takes in me!* This joy is not influenced in any way by circumstance and will never change. The Lord finds joy and pleasure in

Thursday

knowing me. I am the apple of his eye, which gives me joy. Knowing that his heart throbs with delight over me is what gives me strength.

How can I not be strengthened and filled with hope when I understand I give him joy just by being myself? I encouraged the men to take heart and receive strength through the knowledge that God is delighted and celebrates over each of them.

Then I gratefully sank back against the wall, happy to let Aya have her turn. She spoke animatedly for a few minutes about Jesus having come to 'set you free'. I felt awkward Ma because the 'free' was delivered in a high, piercing tone as if her voice could push the men out into freedom and I couldn't help thinking … I mean, I know the freedom we have in Jesus is without walls but these poor chaps are totally confined behind the walls of the prison.

I had a few unchristian thoughts. I don't know. Maybe it's just cultural differences and who am I? God knows I'm totally out of anything remotely resembling a comfort zone! I just studied Aya's back as she stood delivering her message and marvelled that a person can just make a decision and 'do it', no nerves, no hesitation. I felt overwhelmed by the plight of these men. I was staggered by the way they humbly listened but Ma that was just the start!

Aya finished and conducted by Jordan the men applauded with enthusiastic 'Amens' and 'Hallelujahs'. Then Dan stepped forward and gave a simple gospel message inviting any who didn't know Jesus to raise a hand and be prayed for. One man stepped forward in response; it was clear as we worshipped that many of them already know Jesus. Next Dan invited any who would like prayer or who were sick to come forward announcing we would pray for them now.

Almost as one the men moved towards us, a giant wall of need. Suddenly Aya's voice was heard speaking to Dan, 'I think they must kneel down; the men need to kneel down. It's important, it's submission.' I was mortified. I already felt very small in the face of such courage and life-saving faith. The last thing I wanted was anyone kneeling at my feet. She turned to the men and said it again indicating with her hands they should all kneel.

Graciously Dan let it happen and then he said, 'Pray for as many as you can,' and got busy laying his hands on the men in front of him, blessing them. The hunger threatened to swallow me up as desperate men pressed against me wanting me to place my hands on their heads and bless them. Out of my depth? Yes! Hot, sticky, nervous? Yes! But resourceless? No. In a moment I knew if I deliberately stepped to one side and invited the rushing torrent of God's love to flood through me and out into these men, he would.

In a flash, thoughts came, 'You brought me here, Lord, you have a purpose in everything, you are the resource that never runs out; let your love come now to meet need in your children.' And then the profound longing to see God move took over. As I reached out and laid my hands on the first head, my fingers met the unfamiliar sensation of coarsely textured, matted hair; I sensed blessing pouring over the man and a peace descend. What do you pray for someone who is in prison; you don't know what for, how long he will remain or if he understands the four spiritual laws?

What I found is that none of that matters because as God allowed me to see the men as he sees them, compassion propelled me and I couldn't touch, bless, pray for or encourage enough of them. As if Jesus was liter-

Thursday

ally pouring love over them and I had only to move out of the way and let the wave pass. I prayed in tongues and trusted the Holy Spirit to minister to needs I will never comprehend. I felt humbled and also perplexed Ma. Just because I am white they believe I have something to offer.

I was acutely aware of the swollen eye as I moved along the line gently blessing and touching bowed heads ... was God going to heal the eye? Would the man's face go back to normal with sight restored? As I got nearer I could see redness and inflammation indicative of infection; surely God would move to heal this poor man. Maybe that is just why I am here, I thought. I have been longing for God to heal through me. I laid hands on him and prayed as fervently as I have ever prayed. Nothing changed.

No time to ponder as Jordan thrust another man towards me, both on their feet now and Jordan gesticulating whilst in broken English telling about a bash on the head that produced the massive lump I had seen earlier. He also mimed that the man was deaf in that ear since the injury. Wouldn't it be great for the swelling to disappear and God restore hearing right then as I prayed? That must be his intention.

More men were rising to their feet, some pushing in to get another blessing. I was jostled but pushed down panic with one hand and reached out to touch the hurting man in front of me with the other.

I prayed on in tongues and longed for God to move so much it was a clenched fist in my chest. Nothing had been said about a time limit but suddenly Dan called that our time was up and we needed to leave the yard. Time up, just like that! (It was disorientating having taken so long to focus and I thought things were just getting going.) The swelling remained and Jordan began to ask Dan about some eye drops, which

Pemba Pennings

I gather have been helping the other man's condition. But Dan said it could take two weeks to get some more as he ushered us steadily through the thronging bodies.

I was aware of hands reaching to touch me. I don't mean grope or anything but just as if they believed something may 'rub off'. Reality kicked in with a jolt when one of the men grabbed my wrist and pointing at my watch, at me, then at his chest made it clear he would like me to give it to him. Mentally berating myself for not leaving it behind I smiled as kindly as I could whilst shaking my head to indicate that I was not going to part with it.

I fleetingly thought how awful it would be for only one person in that context to receive such a gift. There is a general expectation that if one of us has something and a local person wants it we should just freely give it to them. It is taking me some time to adjust.

As the bottom of the steps came into view I raised my head and observed three women, way over in the far corner of the yard. They hovered in the shadows appearing fearful, uncertain, fragile. It appears there is a small facility for women prisoners also. Oh my goodness, I wondered what kind of treatment they receive. How could they be with so many men? Were they being abused? Faces hollow with longing. I ached to reach out and to be able to hug them but it wasn't possible. Sol was our shield in front with Aya behind him and then Dan behind me.

Just as we got to the first rung (the steps were iron with lots of gaps rather like our fire escapes) our 'shield' suddenly veered off to greet a prison worker who he recognised. The man Sol greeted had a hose and was filling a large bin beside which was a stack of assorted plastic beakers. I couldn't have felt more vulnerable if a high wind had rushed

Thursday

through the yard whipping all my clothes from my body!

Looking straight ahead and willing Sol to return to us I followed Aya up the steps. The prisoners surged around the steps, reaching out to us through the iron struts and moving beside us as we walked then pressing in under and around the open metal struts.

Suddenly above us an arm appeared through a hatch in the door at the top of the steps. At the end of the arm the guard's hand was clutching a number of the sachets of fruit powder. Aya reached for them (to be fair to her it seemed exactly what the guard intended). Unsuspecting she turned them over in her hand and then as black hands pressed around her a sound began to rise as men thought she may have something for them. Aya began giving out the sachets randomly placing them in the nearest open hands. They were clutched and instantly swallowed in the seething mass of shimmering limbs. Other empty hands immediately crammed the small space. The noise began to swell and the men pressed in closer. Clutching the stair rail I knew a whiff of fear. The last sachet was gone.

Uproar broke out as men realised they had missed out. The door above us flew open and I pressed myself into the wall as guards bearing large sticks rushed down past us into the yard. It was a riot. Men were fighting with each other to get hold of a sachet. Sol reappeared and he and Dan ushered us with determined stride to the top of the steps and back out through the office. A brief apology in Portuguese to the man still seated at the desk, a promise of bleach next week and we were whisked into the open space outside the front of the building.

I was literally holding my breath and let out the air with relief as we stepped on to the road. It was only a few minutes till we would be back in the refuge of the cab under Abdul's smiling gaze. Dan directed us to walk to the gates and turn left to arrive at the truck. (He didn't actually say 'walk and keep on walking, do not look back' but it was that kind of moment.) We turned the corner and there at last ... was a huge empty space where the truck should have been. I couldn't believe it.

It wasn't Aya's fault that we went to bless prisoners and started a riot. Both men said they had thought the juice powder to be a good plan because they anticipated the guards emptying them all into the communal water bin thus enabling every prisoner to sample the fruit juice.

I lost interest in the discussion about how the sachets should have been distributed. I was just grateful my heart hadn't actually stopped beating. Aya shrugged and seemed untroubled. I've got goose bumps again just writing about it Ma and am having to rebuke vivid mind pictures of pasty white limbs that were once attached to my body being tossed above the heaving throng... I think it was a bit of a close shave!

The men seemed relatively unperturbed and decided to call Abdul. This was a great idea till they both found their phones were out of credit. Overhearing the words 'walking' and 'base' in the same sentence did nothing for my frayed nerves. 'We'll start walking and we'll buy some phone credit,' Dan announced cheerfully. I don't know how far it really is but it was hot, dusty and what if Abdul never returned? The base must be several kilometres away.

I took a deep breath. OK here we are in downtown Pemba. I have no idea how to return to the base. I have no language. I didn't bring water. I am white and therefore represent wealth to those here that have so little. Plus I am a woman. (Don't panic Captain Mainwaring!)

Dan and Sol were striding with purpose towards the nearest street

Thursday

corner and I hastened to catch up with them. Aya was quite a way behind and I suddenly remembered her sore foot. When I turned she was chatting away to a woman clutching a babe in arms and vigorously practicing her 'shay-zoosh te aa-ma'. I called to the men to slow down which they did.

Some dishevelled-looking teenage boys approached Dan clutching handfuls of what looked like credit cards and were in fact phone cards of multiple companies. After shuffling through dozens, with me wondering where on earth they came from, it was discovered none were compatible for either phone. Happily the next seller of phone credit did have what was needed. Dan duly called Abdul then told us he was on his way and would meet us as we walked. We continued on with poor Aya now limping along.

As we turned a corner into what is described as the main street, a man was walking towards us. He had fabulous skin Ma with stunning deep, deep eyes and beautiful smooth limbs. I think he is the blackest man I have ever seen. He was elderly and looked like some kind of peddler as he had a framework across his shoulders with multiple pairs of sandals suspended from it. The sandals were securely tied in pairs to the frame with random bits of thread and twine and the frame was tied to his body. Presumably as a precaution to prevent others helping themselves to his livelihood? I moved out to the edge of the road to accommodate his extended width and kept my head down.

The speedy flow of perspiration running down my back went up a few knots as I heard Aya say she wanted to know the price of the sandals. Dan slowed the pace and turned to face us. I felt awkward as the peddler excitedly began his sales pitch and painstakingly commenced untying his load. Dan engaged him in conversation and then turned to us explaining this man was Tanzanian (hence the darker skin). He asked Aya which sandals she would like to try? 'I want to know the price,' she said as yet another pair was released and placed temptingly on the ground at her feet. She looked at Dan then back at the man then at Dan again, 'I want to know how much he is wanting to charge.'

I looked longingly at the nearest pothole and wondered how deep it was as a small group of passers-by gathered to witness the grand sale. Dan told Aya a number and she shrugged and squealed (I guess cultural shopping differences are inevitable) exclaiming it was far too much and that she would expect two pairs for that price. She looked the man in the eye and waggled her forefinger under his nose, 'Too much. You charge too high price,' she chided.

If you were blind you would have been convinced she was addressing a recalcitrant schoolboy. The man shrugged in disgust and began retying his neatly lined up wares to the weary frame. Dan sounded as though he was apologising and thanked the man profusely for showing his goods whilst I did my best to melt behind Sol.

I was relieved to hear the grumbling of Abdul's approach at last as the truck lumbered into view. I sighed deeply as I squeezed into my spot between Aya and the driver, thankful to be four feet above the tarmac and savouring the thought of being back in the centre and reunited with my water bottle very soon.

At this point Aya reminded Dan that she required an adaptor. We turned into a street where stalls displayed stacks of fresh produce under flimsy canvas. Some booths were a bit set back from the road and were more like tiny shops with shelves crammed with packets and tins right

Thursday

up to the ceiling. It was noisy and the smell of rotting vegetable matter hovered. Abdul pulled in and Dan and Sol disappeared into one of the set-back booths clutching the adaptor Aya had brought along to show what she wanted.

I felt less vulnerable now we were seated at shoulder height should anyone approach the vehicle but still suggested Aya lock the door, as the window was wide open for air. A man came to the door and lifted a plastic bucket full of apples up to Aya. She picked up one or two and examined them then she waved her hand dismissively and declared she wanted bananas. The man's face lit up and he put the apples under a rickety table before moving off down the street.

Moving quickly, given the temperature and the fact that time is of no consequence, he soon reappeared and moved towards Aya's window cunningly disguised as a banana tree. He had a huge hand of the ripe fruit, several kilos worth, in his arms. Aya again went through the ritual of picking over one or two then hesitated. At this point the atmosphere changed.

The man was uttering something I couldn't understand but didn't sound complimentary as the huge hand of bananas came at speed through the window and landed on the ample dash shelf below the truck windscreen. Tension flooded my middle as I wondered if the gentleman selling them was considering joining his wares but Aya saved the day by tut-tutting and shaking her head. She reached forward and tore two bananas from the hand. 'I only want two,' she said waving them in his face. 'How much?' He simply leaned in, grabbed his goods and flounced off muttering and gesticulating to vent his disgust.

As Dan and Sol clambered into the back, new adaptor in hand, I pon-

Pemba Pennings

dered how a potentially life-changing few hours for me could be a glorified shopping trip for another and unbidden, the old insecurity was in full frame. Am I too intense? We once more set off for the base. I was musing that absolutely nothing else could be crammed into one little afternoon ... even in Mozambique. I wondered how I would ever get all this down on paper to tell you. But ...

My thoughts were rudely interrupted by a scuffling sound followed closely by a cry from the back of the truck. Looking around was a shock. There were now three men in the back. What's more, the third man was clearly unhappy about something and raising his voice as he shook his fist at Dan. Dan indicated to the stranger that he must leave the truck (which was still moving mind you!) and Sol leaned over to ask Abdul to pull over.

I don't know how long the man had been there and it was some minutes before he and Dan stood at the back of the truck each with a few coins in hand. More heated words whilst Dan patiently shook his head holding out the coins in his open palm. They were counted again whilst the inevitable cluster of interested onlookers gathered. Ultimately the stranger shrugged his shoulders, smiled at Dan and went off happily in the direction we had come from.

Dan explained when we got back to base that there had been a misunderstanding over the change given when they bought the adaptor and the stranger had mistakenly thought Dan had not paid enough. The back of the truck is open and we hadn't been moving at speed so the man had just sprinted and leaped into the back of the truck to retrieve what he thought he was owed.

As we turned into the familiar sandy transport area I felt on total

Thursday

emotional overload, unable to process one more experience. I gulped as Dan explained that the injuries we had seen were most often the result of beatings by the guards when they required information about other prisoners. (I was thinking, just let me get to my room.) And then Sol gently told us how he himself had been in prison. That was where through Christians visiting he discovered God's love and the truth of Jesus loving him enough to die for him.

I didn't hear the story because my heart was an open wound and a lemon just squeezed into it. This gentle, loving man in that place? His tender heart in all that brutality and deprivation? Aya said, 'Yes, yes. It is always better, much better if those who have experienced it do the work.' I couldn't look at Sol and felt the need for distance from Aya. I mumbled my goodbyes and fled.

So that is why I am taking time out today to rest my heart and process with God. I know God heals. I desperately wanted him to heal the men I prayed for. It was so humbling because their expectation was just that and also that God would do it through us. I know he heals and I know he wants to through my prayers so what needs to change in me? I wonder if I was a bit too focused on wanting to see God 'do it' and not concerned enough about the men's hearts and situations? It is a subtle change of emphasis but crucial I think.

It's challenging, especially here in this environment where we have all come expecting miracles and knowing they do happen regularly. I know compassion is a key. It's the old thing of loving the giver for who he is and not just for his gifts. As I lay on my face in the church service in the evening, I invited God to do whatever he wants in me so he can love through me more fully. His presence was so heavy I couldn't walk in a straight line when it came time to return to the centre but I didn't mind. He is moving.

Before all that happened I was up early in the morning and went as usual to the prayer hut. I was reading about Jesus being baptised and thinking about where it says 'the Holy Spirit remained on him'. Bill Johnson (from that church I visited, Bethel) teaches about living a life as if the Holy Spirit were a dove on my shoulder. I would move carefully, always with the dove in mind, never wanting to startle it. That's what I want ... for my life to be a resting place that the Holy Spirit inhabits and then for him to bless the lives of all I meet.

Golly, this is a bit of a marathon Ma, you deserve a medal if you've made it this far! I decided not to join those going to visit the high-security prison today. I really need this space to process and regroup plus there is always next week.

Sadly there was a rustling by my head last night so rat problem not solved. Thinking I will go and support Christy in pre-school again tomorrow. I love taking opportunities to bless and encourage the staff here. I'll take Christy some of the hand cream I brought. Maybe it would be OK to vocalise the rodent issue with her since I know she will understand. I wonder if the blind man from the village will be in church on Sunday?

More soon but sending all love for now. My thanks to all who are praying for my health and well-being. What an amazing adventure!

I love you Ma x x x

week two

A skeleton had been laid out on the raffia.

Friday

Dearest Ma,

Here I am again at the page. I've been here a full week.

Last night, sometime after supper, Joe came wheeling into the kitchen area to ask for help. When we got back to his room he showed me a small (but very real!) scorpion above his doorframe. We procured a piece of wood much like a broom handle. While I stood by offering moral support Joe managed to reach up and balance the scorpion on it. Then propelling his chair with one hand he deposited it outside in the undergrowth. I felt intrepid just observing the procedure.

Not so intrepid however at 3.50am when I was awoken by munching, although I surprised myself by having the courage to switch on my head torch. The chewing and rustling seemed to be coming from nearer to Aya's area this time. I did warn her a couple of days ago that rats can be a problem here so we mustn't have any food in our room that isn't in airtight tubs. She scolded me, told me not to be fearful and suggested I pray more.

Friday

When I got up this morning I found an old dressing from Aya's foot wound in the bin and then noticed a packet of open crackers in the line of things on her bed. As I mentioned Aya has the only single bed, the others are all bunks; she lines all her possessions up under the window along the side of her bed. Although it's only a single she is so petite that there is ample room for her to sleep beside them. I bet rats would love the sugar-loaded juice powder that she drinks all the time. But I can't seem to help her to understand that they will be attracted.

I think I am learning more grace. Every couple of hours yesterday Aya was lifting the plaster (the one I carefully explained needed to be left in place to allow healing) to poke aloe vera gel into the wound. Her foot is looking more red and swollen now.

Then still on the topic of wildlife, poor Molly took a swig of her morning coffee only to come eyeball to eyeball with a baby reptile of some description. The sight of Molly's tonsils was sufficient to stir it into overdrive. We all just froze open-mouthed as fear propelled the petrified creature out of her mug at high speed and across the table before it disappeared into a crack in the wall. Very exciting way to start the day and this encounter led quite naturally to a chat about who may or may not be going on outreach this week.

Bush outreach happens every week. This is what I have gleaned about it so far. It commences on Thursday afternoon when those taking part leave the base. The outreach is routinely over a twenty-four hour period but sometimes the destination can be so remote it could be many hours' drive. These more remote places are referred to as the 'bushbush' and the outreach will then normally extend over two nights.

It is a massive commitment with all that is needed having to be packed up to travel. This means all food and a considerable amount of water are taken by the cooks who are usually young men who work on the base here. Add to that the large utensils needed to produce rice and something (?) over an open fire a long way from home. The team can be quite sizeable and cooking for up to twenty-five (sometimes more) hungry travellers is no mean feat.

Team members and any visitors or students who are available all bundle into trucks with a bedroll, tent, sleeping bag, basic wash kit, their plate and eating utensils plus adequate drinking water. There is no corner store in the bush villages so insect repellent, tissues, etc. if forgotten simply have to be done without!

The basic format is that the vehicles arrive in the village (I think some kind of message is sent in advance and permission granted by the local chief, so if there is an Iris church in the village they will be expecting the visitors and word is spread over a vast area inviting people to come), and then the team offload and set up camp wherever the village chief or the church pastor has allotted space.

Once night falls the Jesus film, projected onto a makeshift screen (large sheet) fixed onto the side of the truck, is used as a tool for introducing the gospel message. After this, one of the Iris team gives a talk. Then people are invited to give their lives to Jesus before all those who have gone to 'reach out' are called upon to pray for the sick. A late supper is served around a fire (it is pitch dark by this time — has to be to see the movie — but you remember how quickly night falls in Africa) after which everyone crawls into his or her tent.

The following morning those who pray for the sick, which is all visitors plus team, are invited to visit huts and pray for those in their homes

Friday

who were too ill to come to the meeting the night before. It has been made clear already that any food offered is to be accepted and gratefully consumed. This will be a great honour and involve sacrifice on the part of the family making the gesture. Molly made it clear she has 'done Bush Outreach' and is not planning on repeating it. It feels as if it is a significant part of the Pemba Experience.

I was feeling that I would inevitably need to go. As Thursday approached the anticipation mounted but then I was chatting with Joe and he shared that the Lord had told him not to go this week. I was challenged because I hadn't specifically asked God for myself. The general feeling is that to see miracles you need to go on this expedition so I was assuming I need to put myself out there however unappealing the idea of sleeping on the African dirt with only a hole in the ground as en suite.

There would also be the small matter of fasting or trusting for supernatural preservation when offered local delicacies. (And what might they be?) I took some time to ask God and felt that I too was to stay behind this week. As I sat alone quietly listening to God and welcoming his presence I realised something. I am hungry to see God act but my heart is not breaking for the villagers to receive Jesus. I think it's part of that ugly old thing when self rears its head; I slip into being preoccupied with the stuff that God can do and lose sight of who he actually is and what he wants to do in me. It's too easy to get preoccupied with the 'gift' and then my focus is no longer on 'The Giver'. It's a subtle shift Ma but it's huge.

I know from Heidi's writing that there is a level of compassion that unlocks powerful love. I think the Holy Spirit is showing me that I need God to melt me inside; to change me so I long for people to know truth and freedom with the same passion I long for my own flesh and blood to live in blessing and health.

It feels a bit scary, like volunteering for surgery, but I can't do it for myself. Be mad to come all the way out here and then erect barriers. I know I need a 'no holds barred' lifestyle. I know he has to work in me on his terms alone. I just never understood before that 'depths of love' could really mean I'm not meant to see, feel or even remember when my feet last touched the bottom!

Please remember to pray for me this week. This process feels very scary, I feel churny as I recognise after this I may be less than comfortable with life as I have known it, may not quite 'fit in'. I don't know … it's just swirlings for now but whatever it looks like, I know it's HIM and that for me there is no going back.

Heidi writes about this aligning of our own emotions and passions with those of God. I understand God's supernatural love made the ultimate sacrifice of his son. I think there is a condition or spiritual space where a person is so utterly desperate for more of God that his love collides with the natural wilfulness of our humanity causing a profound yielding of spirit and will.

I think this may be what is described (in Iris, or it may be American Christian speak) as being 'wrecked'. (I have certainly never heard this expression in mainstream/normal church.) This is presumably in the context of the total annihilation of the old, human effort of trying to love in the right way in order to make way for the new, supernatural love to flood in and through a life.

I admit I feel daunted by the thought of such a fundamental encounter with the Almighty but I am desperate for more and it looks increasingly as if this is the only way. I can't believe it Ma, for decades I have

Friday

understood and read that Jesus told us to 'pray for the sick' but now I find what is actually written is *'heal* the sick' ... and then there is the small matter of casting out demons, raising the dead and cleansing lepers, all of which I seem to have conveniently overlooked.

Thinking about the experience in the jail I felt in a way disconnected, as though I were watching myself have the experience. It may be that it was because it is all so alien but I'm wondering if I'm doing that emotional control thing ... I mean I can't not think about all the big things I am experiencing but at some level of emotion (or is it spiritual?) am I still 'in control' in an unhelpful way?

Anyhow, I am as open as I know how to be and am determined to cultivate intimacy by spending as much time alone with God as I can. His presence is totally addictive because I feel so loved and accepted. I love it when he whispers and shows me things. He really cares.

Poor Aya, by mid-morning yesterday her foot was full-blown cellulitis and infection has got a hold. I had to be a bit firm and admit to my nursing qualification but eventually she agreed to come to the clinic with me. Hannes prescribed antibiotics and rest for the ankle, which was by then very swollen and painful. He dressed the wound explaining the dressing should be left intact. We walked slowly back to the centre and I made us a drink and prayed for healing again.

Aya doesn't grumble but it must really hurt. I hope it recovers in double quick time. Whilst at the clinic Hannes invited me to spend the day with him next Monday in a nearby village where he holds a weekly clinic. I will look forward to it although I feel apprehensive about what I may encounter ...

So Thursday afternoon, if one doesn't go on outreach, is a quieter afternoon as most of the emphasis is on getting everyone who is going assembled in one place with the necessary gear. Then a flurry of activity as departure occurs after which all is quiet for a bit.

I took the opportunity to blitz our room. I hoisted my mattress outside and was mortified when I lifted the pillow on the bunk above mine to come eyeball to eyeball with the rat himself. I think he was as stunned as I was because he shot out of hiding and into the far corner of the room. I feel so desperate about it I am seriously contemplating shutting a cat in the room and simply trust about my allergy.

I discreetly put Aya's crackers in a sealed bag and have hung them on the back of the door but I think rats can smell through bags. She doesn't believe me. Pretty amazing Ma, I am sharing my bedroom with a rat and … I don't feel panic stricken. I do want to sort it though.

I'm enjoying having a go with the language. It feels so much better to be able to say, 'Good morning, how are you, I'm fine thanks,' and know the other person understands. The guards in the centre are game for a bit of practice and I love their throaty chortles at my stumbling efforts. The ladies who clean are happy to exchange greetings too but the younger one has asked me for my lipstick so I feel rather self-conscious whenever I wear it now. I suppose it may be alright to leave it for her when I go. I'll ask one of the staff but then I would want to give the other lady something too. It feels disrespectful to give a half-used lipstick but she acts as if she really wants it.

I have bumped into one of the girls from Sara's Monday night homegroup several times and I think God is whispering a word of encouragement to me, about the aroma or fragrance of her life being a pleasing offering to him. Holy Spirit prompted me, to bring some of those min-

Friday

iature perfumes I buy duty free, so if Sara thinks it is OK maybe I can encourage her, by writing the word in a card and give her the gift of a bottle of perfume. I am praying for her anyway and if the urge doesn't go away I will speak to Sara.

I am practising tuning my ear to any prompting from God and in the prayer hut this morning a man appeared and sat opposite me. I felt God dropped a word into my mind; it was a scripture. I waited a while then plucked up my courage and approached him but he immediately said 'no English' so that was a bit of a flop. I will press on.

I was thinking about the key thing; you remember about the blouse just before I left England? I'm not fretting but mindful of the 'unlocking' I felt God speaking about. I am wondering if it's me that needs unlocking? I mean I do care very much about all the stuff happening around me but caring in itself doesn't release answers, does it? I feel God has done preparation work in me but I sense there is more. Then I think, am I just being true to my 'frightfully British' roots? Or am I simply thinking too much (again).

From the odd comments I have heard I think Heidi may arrive in Mozambique today. I still can hardly believe she will actually be home whilst I am here as one of the staff said her normal schedule for this time of year is to be overseas. I am longing to be in her company but also know trepidation.

The tangible sense of God's presence was awesome, in the truest sense of the word, on the one occasion I have heard her speak. The work established here and the evidence of heaven invading a nation is mind-boggling and Heidi's laid down life and vision ignited the fire. How can I not feel apprehensive and very small?

Pemba Pennings

Most of the other visitors staying in the centre went on the outreach. I wonder what stories they will have to share when they get back? I had a pleasant hour making myself useful picking up rubbish (rubber gloves again to the fore Ma!). You wouldn't believe it really. The concept of putting rubbish in bins is alien and 'environmentally friendly' would be less understood than tongues.

I find it difficult but I suppose it could be argued that non-biodegradable rubbish only stems from western imports. I don't know. In a culture where whatever you have is to be shared then how does personal responsibility or respect for the property of others fit? Literally anything and everything is just discarded on the spot where it is no longer required. It is such a basic in regard to health and hygiene it's hard to be shuffling through litter. I am happy to serve in picking it up and filling black bin bags. I am mystified that it is just accepted as the norm. (But then you couldn't get much more 'westernised' than Hong Kong and look at the rubbish washed up in front of Dave's place.)

As I worked I enjoyed praying in the garden around the building where I think Heidi has her office. I thought about leaving a card on the door to welcome her home and maybe thank her for all the travelling. It must be a sacrifice to leave this place, these people who fill her heart; but the fact remains, if she didn't I wouldn't be here and I'm sure it's the same for countless others.

And the group of us who attended that conference in Birmingham? We are all really pressing into God. We are desperate to know more of his heart and see him bless lives through us. That's all as a direct result of Heidi being in the UK.

I think next week will feel very different. The team from America

Friday

returns home on Sunday and they create a lovely buzz just by being around. Some new guests have arrived but I'll tell you about them when I have got to know them. They are older and one of them, a Korean gentleman, is here for an appointment with Heidi so maybe he is the reason her schedule changed. I don't know. I just know this is a really significant experience in my relationship with God and I need the courage to remain open. I wonder if Heidi is here for long enough to go on outreach next Thursday?

I realise part of my hesitation about bush outreach is launching out into wildest Africa, with a group of young Mozambican men I have only just met, in charge. (There speaks a woman of faith and power!) But having read about Heidi's experiences on outreach it would be incredible to actually go with her. I can't say the word 'safe' springs to mind but I'm sure the experience as a whole has the potential to be very 'formative' on the faith front. I feel especially blessed having come with no expectation of her being here at all.

Saturday tomorrow and it's the staff's day off here on the base. Many take children out for an ice cream or to their homes for a meal and visitors are invited to do the same. I'm not sure how I'll spend the day but I'm off to help Christy with the children now and am looking forward to taking them all to the beach.

I love you Ma. Isn't God just so amazing? I've known him all my life and yet the adventure of there always being more is totally exhilarating. I hope I'm able to share what I'm learning with you and Sis. Feeling rather smug as I am now managing the whole loo thing much better. One tissue can launch a thousand ... well anyway ... remembering to not drop the tissue in the toilet means no fishing expeditions and I still haven't begun my initial loo roll yet!

I've cleaned the communal shower area a couple of times and will have it nice for the girls returning from outreach. Having been here a week I feel completely ridiculous having wondered about 'housekeeping service'. Visitors are responsible for all the areas we use. Hopefully the water will be on for them but I will fill the standby bins so they will be able to have a good wash down whatever. I'm aware the team leaves on Sunday so I hope it won't feel too lonely next week.

If Heidi is here maybe she will speak in church on Sunday. That would make for a special day. I'll let you know but all love for now, keep warm, a pleasant 30 degrees here! x x

Saturday

Dearest Ma,

So, it's Saturday and I can't seem to find peace this morning.

I enjoyed the time on the beach yesterday with the children and really gave myself to playing with them. I sat on the shore and they loved pouring water all over me. I was completely dressed because we have to fully cover up even if we are swimming and it's so warm I knew I would be dry very quickly. We collected starfish and generally had fun at the water's edge.

I had a special moment with a little girl who is new to the group and is exhibiting challenging behaviours. My heart feels torn for these little tots, Ma. The traumas they come through before coming to Iris; unimaginable things. In a quiet moment this vulnerable little girl climbed onto my lap and snuggled in. As I held her I prayed healing love would soak into every part of her and a white feather just floated down out of nowhere. The tangible warmth of Presence enveloped us in that moment and it felt ... sacred, holy.

Pemba Pennings

I think I got a bit too much sun but it was good to have the rat conversation with someone who understands and has overcome! I was trying hard to stick with Morna's advice but I admit it was something of a relief to share with Christy. I think I have done well not to share with the girls in the visitors' centre, tempting though it has been to see what response the news of nightly rodent visitations would provoke from some of the less acclimatised younger girls. (Naughty I know.) I am choosing not to dwell on the fact that there are those who receive visitations of a wholly angelic kind whilst mine all have incisors and long tails.

Walking up the beach I managed to tread on some marine life and collect a load of really fine spines in the sole of my foot but I prayed and after wielding tweezers and some antiseptic cream the foot is fine. Thank you Jesus! There are urchins with vicious spines all over the beach but maybe this was a baby (I didn't see) or something else altogether. Anyhow, I am just so thankful my foot is comfortable. Infection can be a real challenge here.

I don't think I mentioned to you that one of the younger single full-timers here was bitten in her bed by a spider and the bite is angry and red with infection. Her leg is badly swollen, it looks awful and walking is very painful. She is so brave and will obviously have had prayer but she currently has to live with the challenge. At least all the rat is doing is snuffling around.

I wasn't very hungry for beans and rice at lunchtime and felt queasy probably due to a bit too much sun. In the little kitchen area Aya was happily frying onions whilst sharing her elation about finding out that I am a nurse. She insists on announcing to all and sundry that God sent her a 'private nurse'. I am trying not to mind but it feels awkward.

Saturday

Mid-afternoon the others returned from outreach all fired up and excited with stories of hundreds coming for prayer after the showing of the Jesus film. They were very tired and dishevelled. Jojo, the rather wispy, creative dancer in the group, dumped all her outreach paraphernalia (her bag lay slumped where she dropped it in the communal area, like a weary stray dog) and disappeared to sleep leaving me wondering about which planet she hails from and all of us needing to clamber over the abandoned heap. She is delightful, just not very earthed.

I felt a bit unsettled by all the stories, wondering briefly if I had missed out in some way but I enjoyed chatting and sharing the afterglow of it all. I headed to the prayer hut for an hour to re-centre myself but was frustrated as a group of boys chose to come into the hut and were amusing themselves by breaking up stones and dismantling a banner of some description. I made the mistake of suggesting they not destroy the banner for the sake of it and got short shrift from a particularly belligerent boy who informed me in no uncertain terms, 'This is Mozambique, not America.' I was firmly put in my place.

It must be hard for the children growing up here to have a constant stream of visitors. I do find what appears to be a complete lack of respect for property and the ocean of rubbish we are living in puzzling but am much aware of the need to have my L plates firmly in place. Strictly speaking, we westerners could easily be viewed as uninvited guests. Need more grace.

In the evening I really wanted to support Sara in the Rahab ministry but was still feeling rather woozy so held back. I did at the last minute think maybe I could manage it but by then she had enough volunteers, which was a bit of a relief. It is part of the journey of being here I think, learning when to engage in activities and when not to. I can see some visitors running themselves ragged in their determination not to miss anything but then if they get ill or are grumpy it would seem to defeat the object of being here to serve and learn.

Aya keeps saying 'go for it' as I ponder the activities of the day and I feel a bit judged to be honest, but perhaps it's just her way of not wanting me to miss out on anything. I do feel rather the odd one out when I hold back and possibly appear to be slacking, but the Holy Spirit is whispering each day and being sensitive to him is one of the crucial areas I am growing in so whatever it looks like I will hold my course.

Every now and again I am having a meaningful conversation or prayer opportunity with someone during the times when most visitors are out. I'm trusting that is part of God's intention for me here. One of the girls on the American team has been feeling unwell and dehydration is obviously a common problem. I struggle to see how drinking water can be hard but she admitted she didn't even drink one whole bottle yesterday. She was feeling a bit better in the evening but languishing was definitely the order of the day. I had a quiet evening reading over my journal and trying to digest things.

Mid-evening Dan arrived in the centre to invite us to join him in Muslim outreach in the morning. It's in the mosque! Oh my goodness, Ma, 'burqa', 'jihad', 'Koran' and visions of swarthy men with dark, penetrating eyes. Words and pictures rushed to suck me into fear. What is that about? Ignorance obviously! But also what has attached itself to my psyche through media? I don't at this moment have a single Muslim friend so no fear, opinion or apprehension is based on first-hand knowledge or relational experience. But the urge to run was strong.

Saturday

Thoughts swirled. I am a woman. I am white. I have no language. I am Christian. How could I possibly wander into a 'Muslim men only' zone and survive? What was Dan thinking? 'Just go for it,' Aya echoed in my brain ... still a way to go then in the 'God's woman of faith and power' stakes! I really am not feeling to 'grab every opportunity for the sake of it' is the right way for me.

I want to be fully sensitive to discerning the right place, right time for my personal journey with the Holy Spirit so will embrace the discomfort as part of the learning to walk humbly with God that the Bible talks about. Uncomfortable though, Ma.

I am disappointed after yet more nocturnal rustling and nibbling in the night. I am so desperate I am now seriously on the lookout for an opportunity to shut the cat in the room to solve the problem. I woke at 4am again and at 5 went to the prayer hut to try and calm my spirit. I was thwarted by the bright spotlight that had been left on, peace evaded me, there was music playing and boys seemed to be everywhere; well they are everywhere of course, they live here, many of them.

I need to manage my attitude as more cultural differences emerge with the only functioning socket in our room constantly in use. Aya is phoning and skyping in what sounds like high-speed Chinese (though could be tongues for all I know) for long periods each day. It just doesn't feel at all in the spirit of suffering for Jesus in Africa! It's day 3 of her antibiotics today so hopefully her foot will be better.

A few other visitors also spend a fair amount of time and energy being completely frustrated by the lack of internet. I feel I am on total overload and the thought of attempting to juggle my 'other' life from this environment is just not an option.

Pemba Pennings

The truth is for me it's a no brainer Holy Spirit thing since he spoke clearly about 'putting life down for a season' in order to gain the maximum from this experience. I know I need to release others to do their Pemba visit their own way but it is somehow jarring to the whole atmosphere when those who manage a connection stride about the centre speaking loudly into their particular device. Bit bugging too, if I'm honest, with the fan socket blocked I feel … I don't know, disregarded somehow. More learning opportunity! Nobody said this mission thing was ever going to be easy.

You remember Clara (who was unwell last week). She is rather more 'fiery' than some and when they arrived back from outreach she passionately announced that God had clearly spoken to her in the bush saying, 'Stay.'

I presumed she meant in Pemba (not actually where she was situated in that moment) but her description made it sound like an encounter with a divine puppy trainer! I struggled to find the appropriate response. I found myself wondering what 'stay' might look like and how the permanent staff here, many of whom have travelled a painstaking spiritual and practical journey to be here full time, cope with a constant stream of (possibly misguided?) well-intentioned visitors announcing all manner of random God thoughts.

There is a beautiful acceptance and such humility in the atmosphere. The full-time Iris staff who live out here deliberately invite encouragement from visitors. They even seem to anticipate that God has brought us in carrying blessing for them. I find this totally humbling but am incredibly blessed when there is opportunity to encourage. I am emboldened to think the Holy Spirit can strengthen lives through me in this phenomenal place.

Saturday

Not sure how Clara's 'call' will work out as she reappeared some while after her announcement to say she had checked her bank balance and has only $100 to her name. She promptly accosted the dreamily drowsy Jojo who was unsuspectingly emerging from her post-outreach slumber. 'Jojo, God is saying I should stay on here. I think he means you too. Have you prayed about it?'

Blinking owlishly Jojo donned her spectacles and stared dumbfounded. Mumbling that she wasn't sure, she dutifully bolted for the prayer house. She left, navigating her pile of camping gear, which was still strewn abroad. But not before she asked me for my watch. Trusting that I would see it again I handed it over. (If you know you use a watch why wouldn't you bring one?)

Shortly after this most of the group left for the shops; such as they are ('shops' is rather a generous name for the tiny *barracas* I told you about) and some beach time. There was talk of ending up in one of the cafés along the waterfront later. They are a generous spirited bunch and I was kindly invited. I have been thoroughly blessed by their spontaneous offers to include me in things but am happy mostly staying on base.

The Korean couple I mentioned were expecting to meet Heidi yesterday evening and had been told to expect a pick-up by a driver. They were duly dressed rather more smartly than the rest of us that evening and sat waiting. And waiting. (Welcome to Africa!) And waiting. No driver appeared but they received a message a couple of hours in to say pick-up would be after breakfast today.

A lovely American lady called Nina has arrived in the visitors' centre. She told me she has been coming each year for a while. I am impressed, not least because I learned she can't eat the food here due to its monosodium glutamate content (that flavour enhancer we read about being plentiful in Chinese takeaway food at home) and brings all her own supplies.

I wonder if MSG has addictive properties as I am finding I am increasingly enjoying my rice and beans. Another opportunity to trust. It's definitely out of my control anyway. What the American visitors seem to fit in their luggage is a constant source of amazement as all manner of condiments and supplies appear.

Nina sacrifices annual leave from her job in the US and comes here to work each year. She has written this fantastic material, a discipleship programme really. She comes to teach young adults who travel in each day for various courses. It is a clever way of addressing characteristics of the Christian life, things like honesty, faithfulness and loyalty. Each module of the course is based around the life of a Bible character. Mozambicans love stories so weaving truth around the life journeys of people in the Bible is a brilliant teaching tool.

In a culture where most have nothing, looking after number one is the name of the game. It's survival using any tool available so kingdom principles are far more alien than to the average westerner. Nina has a friend with her this year. She and Karlie work together in the States. I am going to enjoy getting to know them and they've kindly invited me to go off base with them today.

I haven't heard of hostage-takers operating in the area so have decided to brave the outing. I feel nervous and apprehensive but Nina, having been here several times, is very confident so I will trust her. I am hoping the beach she plans to visit may be cleaner than the local one here as I don't think I will want to swim with so much rubbish in the water.

Better go now as don't want to keep Nina waiting and need to pack my bits for the beach. More soon x

Saturday evening

(Today went well Ma but will just finish Friday's news before bed and start on today in my next letter.)

By the time I left you and went to get organised this morning there was still no show for the driver of the Koreans but they seem to be set to continue waiting patiently. I think the husband had or has some political role in his country and I gather he is here to discuss the issue of the water supply to Pemba. He spoke as if he played a key role in a successful scheme in Korea so that could be very exciting for this whole region.

I left to return to the room and received a pep talk from Aya who was between calls. She chided me again that I should just forget about the rat and do like her (putting all my bits at the foot of my bed). The few bits I have I keep in sealed containers hanging by my bunk; anyway I would have to sleep in a ball, I don't want stuff all over my bed. She told me again I need to 'pray and trust' (like I am not!) I suddenly felt in need of alone time.

There was dialogue at volume in the communal area. Dear Molly had kindly leant Jojo her precious toilet roll (trusting her with the whole roll rather than administering a few sheets which was definitely going the extra mile in this context) and I emerged from our room just in time to see a completely soggy toilet roll being returned to a crestfallen Molly.

Clearly Jojo's thoughts had been elsewhere at the crucial moment. (You may be impressed to know I have successfully mastered the art of using half of one of the Kleenex tissues I brought which are double thick and then I wash my hands thoroughly; yeah, possibly too much information? Well, Sam is unlikely to ever read this and he is the most sensitive in the family. Although…there is Sis!)

The Koreans, still patiently waiting as I passed a final time with Nina and Karlie, received a message that a driver would collect them in thirty minutes. They did eventually get to have the meeting they came for but coming from their culture I think it was a fairly stretching visit.

Since I last wrote I took a tumble. The floor tiles in the toilet and shower area are so slippery when wet. I take the minimum in with me, as there isn't really anywhere that feels clean enough to put things down. I had toothpaste on my brush in one hand and some water in my beaker in the other with my flannel over my shoulder. I slipped and fell quite heavily, grazing my knee.

However, thank you Jesus, I somehow managed to keep my toothbrush off the ground and lost no water. Impressive but also goes to show the level of desperation about germs coming into contact with my toothbrush.

Clara happened to be at one of the basins and took the opportunity to utter what seems to be her trademark. A loud 'Sharma' bounced off the walls as she turned to face me. (I think this may be tongues or it

Saturday evening

could be some warfare tool I have yet to learn about. She is heard to be exclaiming at regular intervals.) I staggered to my feet taking care to keep my toothbrush aloft as she delivered advice.

'Hazel, you need to look out, be on your guard. The enemy would just love you to break something!' I think I managed a benign smile or maybe an 'Mmmm, thanks for that Clara' before she swept out.

I am trying to make sure I greet the guards and the ladies who work around the centre each day. This morning the security guard indicated he had pain and in broken English, with sign language, I understood him to be saying he has a hernia in his groin. He seemed to be explaining that whilst he has had one side operated on he needs the current hernia to be treated in hospital. I wasn't quite sure but wanted to pray for him so asked one of the Mozambican young men who is here.

I know this young man has spent time in the US so I felt a bit more comfortable to ask his help in understanding. He spoke with the guard and then simply said, 'He needs money for the hospital. The operation costs money and he doesn't have enough. He is on a waiting list but without money it is no good.'

I felt sick because I was trying to offer to pray, not give money. It made me feel uncomfortable and the familiar feeling of sadness that I may be misguidedly thinking I am offering friendship when others are solely motivated by the hope of getting money from me. Anyway, the same guard was back this evening and I felt to offer to pray. He said again that it would only be any good if he can go to hospital. I prayed asking God to heal him or provide finance for the hospital.

Tell you all about our outing next time. (Want to be up fresh tomorrow for church.)

Love you very much,

Hazel x x

Sunday evening

Dearest Ma,

I was just telling you last time about Saturday being a 'day off' so Nina and Karlie were keen to get to a beach just along the coast. Nina knows a number of the young adults in her classes quite well and one of them on hearing of her plan helpfully offered to book a taxi. We waited a while at the front gate at the appointed time and were not surprised as the minutes stretched.

I had initially felt optimistic about getting a fair deal and a normal ride but said 'taxi' inevitably arrived looking like a cross between a battered saloon and a ute with an open back. No great surprise as it became apparent that the driver turned out to be a mate of the 'helpful' young man and already had several cheerful passengers all hanging on to various parts of the vehicle. I hopped into the back and hunkered down.

We were only going the short distance to Kauri Beach. This is an area just along the coast with a restaurant overlooking the beach that welcomes all and has terrace areas where a number of base staff like to

Sunday evening

escape and relax. The owner is a garrulous South African gentleman and the house specialty is curry. A hotel is nearby, set just back from the road it is separate.

The others decided to take a long walk out to meet the receding tide so they deposited me at the hotel pool assuring me swimming was permitted. I was intrigued as Karlie spoke about never having been in a place where the water is tidal. She couldn't get over the idea that the sand would soon be underwater.

Thankfully I slipped into the cool water of the luxurious pool albeit clad in modest baggy shorts and tee shirt. I had a delicious swim and a rare moment of shady solitude before, just as the others returned, we were 'moved on' by a slightly harassed man who I presume worked at the hotel. Swimming by non-guests is not encouraged. Oops! It was gorgeous Ma, as the pool was slightly higher than beach level with lush palms and a view out to sea. I felt kissed by heaven.

We ambled over nearer to the restaurant and I recognised various Iris folk unwinding and enjoying their time off. I felt a bit sorry for them if they were trying to unwind from life on the base and visitors' faces constantly appear.

I guess not having multiple places to escape to must be part of the sacrificial lifestyle they live. I would find that very demanding. One thing to never be able to get alone for 3 weeks but as a lifestyle? Sacrifice of gigantic proportion in my book.

It was lovely to see two of the girls on staff chuckling together over a card game and obviously enjoying one another's company. That must be a huge blessing. Sharing the dramas and challenges of everyday here could forge lifelong friendships. Those who have said 'yes' to serving here Ma, have all my admiration.

We lingered in an area overlooking the beach and the ocean. The available seating area was akin to a very wide stone wall with a flat top sporting basic wooden tables and chairs. It was built right on the sand and butting up to the sandy bank on which the restaurant was built. The sun is relentless and I knew that for me to walk out across the vast expanse of sand would have been a mistake.

As we waited for our drinks I took the opportunity to ask the Lord if he was saying anything to me in that moment. I so often hear him on the beach at home. I gazed out towards the ocean.

There had been an assortment of people passing along the beach but at that moment the vista in front of where I sat was empty. Except for one small boy clearly visible as he played in the waves far away at the water's edge. He was conspicuous because he was alone and I felt the Lord saying that I am clearly visible to him, his eye is on me. He spoke about 'focused attention'. Totally reassuring!

Later in the evening back at the base I was thrilled to be invited by Zena to pray. She is the beautiful young Mozambican woman with a great voice who has been in leadership at the US Harvest School but is originally from here. Zena leads worship on the base and asked me if I would like to join her for a night of prayer. I am enjoying getting to know her a bit and we have had opportunity to chat and pray together. She shared with me how desperately challenging she found it leaving home and family and moving here from Maputo.

Her story has given me insight Ma, as she spoke about the heartache of living for eight months in the village. How ignorant we must seem. The profound loneliness of rejection by regional tribes, a different local

Sunday evening

language and a single girl living alone are all well recognised elements of 'the sacrificial call' where most western visitors come from. But we see black skin and unspoken assumptions join the dots to form a grossly distorted picture. Zena is every bit as much a missionary, a 'sent out one' as a person going from home to share Jesus in Spain or Romania. Zena now lives with other Iris staff and things are easier but the price has been high.

We spent several hours together worshipping and praying. I took time to read my Bible and was drawn to Isaiah 48:6-7

> *From now on I will tell you of new things, of hidden things unknown to you. They are created now, and not long ago; you have not heard of them before today. So you cannot say, 'Yes, I knew of them.'*

Also verse 21.

> *They did not thirst when he led them through the deserts; he made water flow for them from the rock; he split the rock and water gushed out.*

I found myself praying that God would split the rock of my heart so the life-giving water which is him gushes out, bringing LIFE. Earlier in the week I came across a promise about him bringing water in the desert.

It's strange Ma ... in worship times I am having vivid pictures, seeing myself in the outback and sometimes there are Aboriginal people too. All these scriptures about water coming to the desert; a strange excitement is percolating. It happens completely unbidden when I am absorbed in worship and not thinking about anything. Presence is so heavy sometimes I lose all sense of place and time. It's mysterious ... in a good way.

Sorry to go on about it but ... so much for Aya exhorting me to 'just forget about the rat'. After swimming and being out in the sun, plus the emotional energy it takes me to be brave on an excursion like yesterday, I slept particularly deeply. As you know we pretty much go by the sun here and I get up around 4.30-5 having got to bed by 9 quite often. That said, midnight is akin to the 2-3am deep-sleep slot in the real world. So when the night was pierced by a shattering squeal around midnight I was slumbering blissfully. With my ears ringing painfully I re-entered earth's orbit with a rude jolt and struggled through groggy palpitations to orientate myself.

Suffice it to say, it swiftly became clear that on this particular rampage crackers had not satiated rat's hunger and he decided it was time meat appeared on the menu. Unfortunately for Aya his meat of choice was toe shaped. Also unfortunate for her unsuspecting roommate (*moi!*) since this meant it proved to be a shared experience. Horrors Ma ... an actual bite on her foot.

Of the three of us in the room I don't know who was more terrified but the rat disappeared at high speed; presumably his ears were also ringing. Famous last words then, 'trust and pray'. Not wanting to be uncharitable Ma but I have never been so grateful not to be chosen!

I made a decision to talk to the powers that be in the morning and fell back to sleep, naming and claiming preservation of life and limb, as if my entire future depended on it. (Now I think about it, I wonder where the security guard was because if Aya's scream had been for a more ominous reason, help did not come running. Thank goodness for angels.)

Back to this morning, I have just been reading in Isaiah again now and feel Ch.42:6-10 is being highlighted to me:

Sunday evening

'I, the LORD, *have called you in righteousness; I will take hold of your hand. I will keep you and will make you to be a covenant for the people and a light for the Gentiles, to open eyes that are blind, to free captives from prison and to release from the dungeon those who sit in darkness. I am the* LORD; *that is my name! I will not give my glory to another or my praise to idols. See, the former things have taken place, and new things I declare; before they come into being I announce them to you.'*

Honestly Ma, I have this strange urge to read 'Aboriginal people' instead of 'Gentiles'. It's as if I hear a voice in my head as I read. I remember a prophet signing his new book for me with a verse about 'moving from a kingdom of darkness into light' and this scripture feels somehow weighty in a holy sense.

I know in a way the Aboriginal people in Australia have been held in a darkness but 'outrageous', 'incredible', 'impossible' are words that don't even begin to touch the idea that Almighty God could be entertaining any thought of my being somehow involved in the re-writing of history ...

OH MY GOODNESS Ma, just as I am thinking how totally supernatural any such jaunt would need to be ... you'll never believe it ... a solitary white feather has just floated down out of the space above my head inside the prayer hut and landed gently on the ground at my feet. Feeling overwhelmed.

Oh Ma, it really is as if God is saying, 'Yes Haze, you are right. This is to be a supernatural undertaking but it's OK, that's who I am. Here, have a feather out of nowhere as a little sign; I can do anything.' As if he is promising to keep me safe by reminding me about that psalm where it speaks about him 'covering me with his feathers'.

Feel almost breathless with the weight of love in the atmosphere; deeply apprehensive, daunted even but not afraid. What am I getting into? Will fill you in about church but just going to take a little break to try and absorb, well, I don't know what really but need to just sit awhile...

Had a break Ma, and a big drink of water. Still feel strange (I think in a good way) but I think it may linger so will try to continue. I was so excited about church and there was an air of expectation as people wondered if Heidi would speak. I felt strangely nervous about being in her physical company. Especially coming from what felt like an out-of-body experience but I think is a proper divine encounter. I felt sure I must look different because of feeling so odd.

I told you about the 'atmosphere' that emanated from Heidi in that meeting in Birmingham. Intangible; really hard to put into words. As if some kind of incredibly strong, muscled superhero (like a cartoon character) were wearing a heavy-duty boiler suit made of a beautiful fabric that is love. But every seam and all the buttons were straining as the energy within sought to find a way out without blasting us all out of the building.

At that same event in England I experienced something like a deep craving, I didn't want to take my eyes off Heidi, wanting to watch her greeting and hugging people close up but needing the safety of distance. I know, I'm not making much sense but that's just it. I can't fathom what it is in the atmosphere around her life that sets her apart.

Maybe that's why I'm here? To discover more, possibly a whole new aspect of this following Jesus adventure I signed up for. I mean, I've

Sunday evening

known Jesus all my life but that raw energy, power dynamic, the new thing that was at work was completely unfamiliar. Whilst I felt drawn in (and I have also sensed it in her writing) it is totally unnerving.

Oh Ma ... what have I got myself into? And then ... Oh yes (Phew!) I remember I am only here because I said 'yes'. All the rest I can trust to God. I've known for a while Ma, that there *has* to be more so I keep trusting and inviting whatever the *'new thing'* is. Am already praying I have the courage to receive, to step into whatever it is.

Back to Sunday morning church. I was also preoccupied about the blind man we had prayed for in the village (I found out his name is Seyth) and wondered if he would turn up and if he did should I pray again and expect a miracle? As I entered the church building (remember it's a large open-sided shed-type construct) nothing in me wanted to resist the vortex of holy hunger that sucked me straight in.

Many women were already kneeling with their upper bodies prostrate over the edge of the stone stage (altar) long before the service began. Some wept, some were quiet and others prayed fervently. Children of all sizes ran around barefoot or in flip-flops often clearly the wrong size.

The worship was again exuberant with dance featuring and Heidi was indeed with us. She wore a vibrant floor-length two-piece with matching headband. Her outfit was the colours of fire and it did seem as if the fire of God was present. She was obviously delighted to be home and preached a great talk from Colossians 1 focusing particularly on verse 9 where Paul writes, '... *asking God to fill you with the knowledge of his will through all spiritual wisdom and understanding.*'

It could have been just for me Ma, speaking to exactly where I am. The thing is, unlike any other talk I've heard on 'finding the will of God for your life', that mysterious, magnetic dynamic was at work again and divine will was presented like a mouth-watering banquet of everything you love to eat. Divine purpose offered like an invitation to an incredible feast where every craving, hunger and desire would be fully satiated. My whole being was energised with the anticipation of what God might do next. I could have listened all day.

Mid-morning the whole US team were called up to sit on the edge of the stage. It is tradition that on the last Sunday of their time here visitors are prayed for, prophesied over and presented with a gift of a string of beads made by the women here. I didn't notice if the guys had something different because that was the moment in the proceedings when with knees like jelly I spotted the blind man, Seyth in the throng.

I decided to approach Tina, requesting her company if she thought it was OK for a female visitor to pray for a village man.

I really felt I should step out and I fully expected his eyes to be healed Ma. He accepted my offer to pray and put his hands out in front of him with his eyes closed. I felt compelled to place my fingertips on his eyelids and mouthed a request for permission from Tina (I don't know what she thought about this perspiring request or the fact that I couldn't stop my arms trembling violently). The tremor in my arm was so strong I was worried about poking him in the face but couldn't stop the movement and was convinced God was about to do the impossible.

I prayed intensely in tongues for some time. No idea how long exactly but every muscle in my body was tense and somehow my legs didn't seem to belong to the rest of me. Sensations like shooting electricity came in waves through my arms and legs. After some time he opened his eyes and smiled benignly. He still couldn't see. I was so grateful Tina

Sunday evening

was with me. Afterwards she encouraged me to keep praying and expect to see God move.

I didn't know what to feel but many hours later I still ache in my arms and legs from the intensity of the event. We know God does open blind eyes but are there particular keys? After church, Seyth sent the lad who was with him to ask me if I could give him a rucksack but I think the one I brought is rather large. I wonder if he ever got the money for trainers from Clara?

As we went back into worship I sat on the floor and a small girl in a threadbare cotton dress wriggled onto my lap and snuggled in. Tears rolled down Ma, as a little heart hungry for love pressed into me. Dirty, hot and sticky, squashed, but Jesus is here in a whole new raw kind of way. I had another picture of myself with a camper van in the desert. You know I have been wondering about getting a new vehicle: I sense it may be something I can sleep in.

Maybe I will go to rural communities and make friends ... What is love going to look like for people who I long to connect with but with whom I have so little in common? Something important is unfolding. Thanks so much for praying.

Once church was over I thoroughly enjoyed my beans and rice at lunch time and have decided not to worry about the fact I seem to be the odd one out. It is unusual to bump into a missionary or another visitor eating with the community.

The visitors' centre was eerily quiet after the team left and I was in the kitchen area chatting quietly with Aya and Karlie. We were joined by a new arrival who is a middle-aged lady called Sophie. Sophie is a very in-your-face sort of person and appears to be of Latin American origin.

Pemba Pennings

Her son Wilf is with her. He comes over as rather quiet, subdued even. Sophie arrived in the kitchen area and without preamble began wielding bleach and clattering about.

Aya had just said to me, 'I cook. You tell me story.' (She had seen me writing and I reluctantly admitted to having had a few things published and, when pressed, explained I mainly write God stories to encourage others.) She was wearing one of the multiple caps I mentioned and playing for time I asked her why it had the letters P U S H written on it. Her face lit up and she explained in a tone of voice that suggested that if I had any spiritual intuition at all I would surely know that 'PUSH' to even the most newborn of Christians reads as 'pray until something happens'. Animated now she continued, 'Juss like my W O W cap I tell you!'

I must have been looking as blank as I felt as Aya left the kitchen space and the two fish she was preparing on a plate, to come and stand in front of me. Leaning in she enunciated slowly, 'Walk on water!' then hurried on enthusiastically, 'I from Tai Wan. I even commission tartan cap, it say, "rejoice evermore, pray without ceasing, everyday give thanks". You soon see.'

I hardly had time to wonder how so many letters could be fitted on one small cap because as Aya returned to the kitchen area a piercing shriek splintered the sleepy Sunday afternoon quiet. This was immediately followed by a desperate wail, 'Waaagh, are you believe it? Are you see it?'

In that moment a scrawny cat streaked past me, with a fish half its size in its mouth, and bolted into the gents' toilets. Aya grabbed a broom and then hovered (we all knew there were no males around but it's strange how the mysterious, invisible barrier around the gents makes it a 'no go

Sunday evening

area' as though urinals have an aura that repels oestrogen! Never mind aura, the distinctive aroma does it for me!).

Not so Sophie; still brandishing her bleach she overtook Aya in a whoosh, emerging triumphant two minutes later. Jubilant she carried the fish at shoulder height but well away from her body, the cat having yielded its prize. Sophie began showing Aya how to rinse the fish in a weak solution of bleach. It did eventually get cooked and I declined the kind offer to share.

Sophie wasn't impressed, announcing she would like us all to eat together ... every day. Organised meals? Watch this space!

After church the highlight of my day was one of the hospitality staff approaching me to say that as a number of rooms are now vacant would I care to move? 'Is the Pope a Catholic?' I hear you say. I know. All joy Ma. And what's more, I have a little two-bed room all to myself, no bunks. I may need to share later in the visit but that's fine. Oh my goodness, I feel like royalty.

Aya had shared her nocturnal visitation with staff and was also offered a move but she is still insisting that rats do not climb *and* is keeping her crackers hanging on the door. She said she prefers to be alone and then launched into a story about sharing a room with one of her sons and his aftershave choking her, which I didn't think was very subtle. I am using a scented body spray but Lavender Mist can hardly be compared to a boy product and I am only spraying it under my clothes. No offence taken.

Learning lots Ma, big hug, off to finish setting up my new room. Tomorrow is the day I am invited to work with the doctor so need a good night's kip!

Love you x x

Monday evening

Whoa Ma,

Where to begin?

I had a HUGE day with Hannes the doctor. He goes each week to the nearby village of Mieze. Iris has a farm there and missionaries who live with them are loving yet more children into life. I think they have a small school and other things happen there like a milk clinic for breastfeeding mums. I don't know how often this is held. I heard someone speaking about goats but I didn't see any, and I know 'crops' are a feature. To be honest Ma, it was such a huge experience that checking out the livestock didn't enter my head. I'm not at all sure I will be able to convey on paper all the day held for me but, well, begin at the beginning I suppose and see how we go.

I do feel I need to write whilst it's all fresh because the waves of both emotion and experience are intensifying. The swell is gathering momentum and so much of the time I am only just still afloat; just able to bob over the next wave trusting I can ride the oncoming tide. I can't tell if I

Monday evening

am being steadily sucked out into the deep or am about to be unceremoniously spewed up onto the beach. All I can do is cling to the certainty that my being here at all is God's doing.

This sense of being totally out of control makes it all the harder to comprehend the apparent trend among other visitors for 'mission trips'. I can't conceive of being in this context just 'for the experience' or in order to 'tick Pemba off the list'. Anyway, the Holy Spirit is carrying me and I have prayed for years to 'go deeper' in my life with God so if this is what it looks like in his purpose for me I want to do it well.

There is something significant here, about learning to *see* Jesus, finding his image, something that reflects him, in everyone. Mysteriously, I think this has the potential to transform how I relate to people, even those with whom it would seem I have nothing in common.

Heidi speaks graphically about seeing Jesus, particularly in the children. I am a complete beginner. Where might all this be leading?

I was up early as usual this morning and then made my way to the little clinic hut on the base. Hannes arrived in a white jeep-style vehicle with a red cross on the door. He gathered various things into the truck. After a short wait a young Mozambican joined us and I was introduced to Ivan whom I presume lives in the village.

Hannes explained Ivan is his general assistant and is a great help, particularly with translation. Ivan didn't give me the warmest of greetings but by now I realise the effort it must be engaging with new faces each week.

A younger boy hobbled into view in obvious discomfort though smiling broadly. He must have been in pain but still exuded the buoyant cheerfulness that pervades among the children here. However poor they are smiles abound.

Pemba Pennings

As he packed various packets and bottles into plastic crates, Hannes asked me if I could be ready to do the medicines at the clinic. He explained we needed to go via the hospital to drop off the younger boy for an x-ray. He suspects the ankle is fractured. I travelled in the front and the boys clambered amongst the paraphernalia in the back.

I couldn't help wondering how a really sick person would ever survive the drive to the hospital. The vehicle shook and all our joints were jarred, the piece of road directly leading to the hospital is the worst maintained piece of road so far, Ma. It looked just as if a dinosaur had blundered drunkenly down the roadway leaving small craters wherever he trod. Hannes did his best to avoid those he could and we crawled through the others mindful of our young patient and the vehicle. On arriving I was relieved when it was suggested I wait in the vehicle.

The hospital is one place I am dreading visiting. Images of bloated babies and dismembered bodies from the news broadcasts at home are distressing enough and I really feel apprehensive. I know prison is daunting and the bush villages totally unknown but something hovers in the atmosphere around the hospital. How will I manage the trauma? Multiple things we blithely treat, sending patients happily on their way, are shortening life and causing hopelessness here.

I realise that sounds self-absorbed and a far cry from being filled with faith to see God heal but ... I am just taking one step at a time as I feel the Holy Spirit nudging. This whole experience is enormous Ma. I'm still waking up and attempting to digest that I am in Africa, never mind a tiny corner of Mozambique where the miraculous is expected. Deep breathing again!

Others last week returned to the centre excited to have had opportunity to pray for the sick in hospital but nobody leapt out of bed and went

Monday evening

home. How can I walk into a ward where, unless your relatives bring it, no food is offered, looking well-fed, opulent, 'fat cat comfortable'? Imagine hungry, pain-filled eyes everywhere ...

I don't know how Jesus did it. But then the people he encountered were all healed, weren't they? It's crucial, Ma. I need to learn all the lessons. He definitely said to us, 'go and heal the sick'. (Stark contrast to hopeful prayers ...) Sometimes I can see why so many Christians haven't pursued supernatural stuff because life is undoubtedly more comfortable before you gain understanding; no going back for me.

Hannes re-joined Ivan and me, having accompanied the boy inside and requested an x-ray. We set off for Mieze. It was great to be feeling I may be able to contribute in a useful way but as we got out onto the smoother tarmac of a more main road, I also knew more than a frisson of apprehension about the unknown.

I had no idea really what to expect but the word 'clinic' obviously conjures up a certain picture. The one at the Pemba base is very small but well ordered with a good flow system, two consulting rooms, large waiting deck area, a locked drugs cupboard, a tidy treatment room and a basic kitchen area meaning some semblance of familiarity with work at the hospital.

Oh my goodness, Ma. Nothing had prepared me.

The views on the journey there are pretty amazing with vast expanses of what appears to be deserted scrubby bush, then forest wildly rolling to meet blue-grey hills in the distance. But dotted all through will be unseen clusters of simple huts with people scraping an existence, giving birth, raising children, burying their dead and desperately trying to grow food for their families. Knowing of the poverty and struggle somehow mars the beauty for me ... imagine if every person hidden from view had enough, had clean water, health care and felt valued as a human being.

In contrast with 'Village of Joy' (that is the given name of the Pemba base) which nudges up to the main road and is enclosed with guarded gates, Mieze feels wide open. Bald scrubland is split by a dirt track, which we turn left into. I had the impression of a few simple buildings and children gathered further back from the road.

Clearly visible immediately and on our right as we approached was a busy well. Women with various receptacles were pumping a long handle that appeared double ended. Many had babies strapped to their backs. There were large banana trees already giving welcome shade to those waiting in the early morning. The well was clearly a hub and chatter filled the air. People had been gathering since long before dawn knowing the doctor would be coming, all keen to gain their place in the line.

There was a small building behind the well. The walls looked like whitewashed cement, chipped. A basic construction looking rather like a well used lock-up, possibly a stable or storage area. Hannes pulled up whilst I was still wondering where exactly the clinic would be. A few men lingered together some distance from the busy women and watched silently as we alighted from the vehicle.

There was a low wall of rough stone off to one side with a wide top on which were piled assorted roles of fabric that could have been rolled up garments. I fleetingly wondered if this was an impromptu haberdashery, conveniently sited by the well, where women could shop for *kapalana* fabric.

Ivan began unloading and not wanting to stare (as I already felt totally conspicuous) I got busy with a crate of drugs, and head down, fol-

Monday evening

lowed Hannes. He headed straight for the cement stable and I followed him through the doorway into the dark. As my eyes grew accustomed to the gloom I could make out a weary looking plastic table and a couple of chairs.

Think ... the old cheap flimsy patio sets at home. This one has definitely seen better days and the table is so encrusted with years of red dust I couldn't tell you if it was originally white or green. But it still has 4 legs and Hannes put the box he carried onto it. Meanwhile my brain struggled to recognise this space as anything vaguely related to health care.

As I gazed around, words like 'hygiene', 'sterile' and 'antibacterial' wafted between my ears jostling for a landing spot and finding none. Honestly Ma, by comparison, the ponies at home had luxury in our most basic stall! The floor was more dirt than floor. Just inside the door against the wall was a rickety raffia daybed (about the height of a poolside sun lounger in a different life). A wall divided the room with a doorway in the middle. No door. A short rickety looking bench sat against the wall on the other side of the opening.

I stuck my head through the empty archway to see an old bucket and what looked like a pile of earth with a flat top in the corner, a kind of shelf but wider. (Aghast I wondered, examination couch?) There appeared to be an open cubicle in the far corner of this second room. Sluice, I wondered? Back in the main room there was one window (hole cut in the wall) in the same wall as the door.

Ivan seemed anything but delighted to find himself here but I was too busy managing myself to think of trying to tease him into good humour. As my eyes got used to the light I could see that the chairs were actually stacked in pairs. Placing a chair on his side of the table with another about four feet slightly to his left in front of him and a third under the window in between, Hannes indicated the fourth. He asked me to set myself up to his right facing the doorway.

The table was roughly between us and covered in things he had brought so I deduced that 'set myself up' meant sit with the plastic boxes containing drugs arrayed at my feet, ready to do as he asked.

In that moment, completely unbidden, I had a mental picture of myself hearing the familiar instruction from a doctor at work where I would be sterilising an already clean area and donning sterile gloves and mask in preparation for opening a totally bacteria-free dressing pack or procedure kit. The situation in the hut clinic was so real, I was so present in order to cope, the fleeting recollection of my normal life was the one that felt, quite simply, like an out-of-body experience.

I attempted to familiarise myself with where things were in the crate, having very roughly assembled antibiotics in one corner. Hannes warned me a number of blood pressure meds would be called for so I put them in a different corner but it still looked a chaotic jumble.

The surrealism I experienced felt akin to that weird thing that happens when you badly need to find something and you anxiously open the drawer that you know it is kept in but can't see it; then returning later, when the pressure of the moment is passed, you find the thing just where you knew you kept it. I was looking at a large volume of medication but so out of familiar context it was a struggle to see specific items.

The occurrence of a small boy of around seven or eight materialising on the chair under the window opposite me was a welcome jolt. As I focused, Ivan was bending over the boy's lower leg. The patient appeared to be alone and his wide, dark eyes held pain. He was sporting a large

Monday evening

blister presumably from a burn.

Ivan didn't speak a word. With no explanation or attempt to allay fear he unceremoniously stuck a needle in the blister then dressed the shin before sending the boy on his way. (Bedside manner and patient satisfaction plans to be addressed at the next Departmental Restructure meeting!)

The wire mesh nailed over the window-shaped space in the wall, freely allowed the echoes of well chatter to be heard over the background noises of scooters, trucks and various traffic. Sound travelled straight across the scrub to bounce off the walls of the small building. The chirruping of children at play also wafted in.

Into this cacophony walked a tall, upright man in full military uniform of some description complete with trousers sporting newly pressed creases. Two well-dressed gentlemen flanked him wearing smart long trousers, formal shirts and shoes. (Everyone here wears flip-flops.) This was so jarringly incongruous I fear I literally gawped. Recovering quickly it became apparent that they were formally welcoming Hannes.

I am not sure if they were government officials, traditional tribal owners or local chiefs but they exchanged greetings with Hannes then disappeared. This ritual seemed to be a green light for the waiting people as immediately an elderly Mama shuffled though the doorway grinning broadly.

She knew she was 'number one' in the queue so I guess the little boy with the burn had slipped in under the radar! She indicated that a cough is troubling her and Hannes explains that the cough is a common side effect of her blood pressure tablets and will improve. But then after checking her blood pressure he decides she needs an extra half-tablet a day for

28 days. Enter the drugs nurse! I was slightly flummoxed as I hadn't got the tablet cutter ready to hand (and it's pretty unlikely the patient would have one in a medicine cabinet back in her hut).

Ivan comes into his own in this context as he translates. I can't say enthusiasm was evident and I began to wonder if his presence was not entirely optional; maybe young men connected to the base rotate to help Hannes.

During this consultation and whilst bent double over the drug box in an attempt to operate the tablet cutter without the use of a flat surface to work on, I had been vaguely aware of movement and scuffling in the area of the daybed off to my right. But with damp palms I was checking and rechecking that I had the correct tablet and dosage so hadn't looked up. (Neoprenalol? Help! There are a number of ' –alols' in the drugs world.) As the elderly Mama left she passed an anxious young woman entering. She was clutching a sleeping baby.

The child had several lesions on its little face and clearly had a fever. Mum lifted the baby towards Hannes and then began indicating that she was suffering from backache. As she rose to mime her symptoms she clearly felt Ivan's translation needed clarity; she thrust the baby into my unsuspecting lap the better to demonstrate. Clutching her stomach and bending double for full effect she told Ivan she had been coughing for a year and was currently having morning and evening fevers.

The drama unfolding was gripping till somewhere between stomach and fever I became acutely aware we were in a 'nappy free zone' and held my breath. The little bub was burning up and I could hardly bear to look at what must be painful infected sores.

Such heartache Ma, when you think how easily sorted it would be

Monday evening

at home. Hannes asked mum her age. She didn't know. He listened to her chest; no crepitus. He prescribed Panadol and antacid and then an antibiotic suspension for the baby. Phew! All found in my box and duly given with Ivan spelling out instructions; though how in a time and date-free culture you monitor regular medication I have no clue. I gratefully returned the baby to mum feeling I had had a narrow escape.

The background noise of well water sploshing and passing traffic continued outside. As I watched mum and baby leave I glimpsed the truck through the open doorway. Men leaning on every available surface now surrounded it. All that was visible was the cab roof.

In that moment I suddenly registered that in paddling to stay afloat in the sea of emotion that churned at the plight of the young mum, I had broken the golden rule of drug administration and completely omitted to check any expiry dates. In a flash of mental panic I saw all my previous nurse managers lined up firing-squad style. Not for the first time this trip I was aware of perspiration trickling down behind my knees. (Did I mention Ma, that I am already convinced I will never be the same; no idea exactly how or what God is purposing but so many of the things I am experiencing are just off any previous known scale.) And then I looked to my right.

As I stared my brain could not compute the picture my eyes were sending. I felt the universe freeze in shock. I heard nothing for several minutes and tears come even now as I revisit the scene. My chest was so tight I couldn't breathe or move as I attempted to comprehend.

A skeleton had been laid out on the raffia. The bones had sallow brown skin stretched taut over them. The head was bald except for a small tuft of course black hair just above the forehead. The face beneath had deep eye sockets and a sharp mound with cavernous nostrils. My eyes felt like the only part of my anatomy capable of movement as they slowly registered the dark tableau. Hollow eyes flicked open and stared unseeing around the room. Fear pranced deep in the sunken caverns. The woman was loosely wrapped in what was once a brightly coloured *kapalana*, now faded, grubby and worn thin.

An elderly lady crouched by the patient's head and pleadingly searched Hannes' face for answers. My spirit nudged my body back into the room as I struggled to absorb the words I could see Hannes was uttering. His lips moved but my ears were having difficulty connecting with the sounds. Gradually I identified words and felt my body take in air. I was thinking it must be cancer and how evil the disease is as it eats people up from the inside.

As Hannes continued explaining to the two women my inner self could take no more and ran screaming and wailing from the hut. Oh God! HIV? Aids? This is treatable!! How can this be happening on your planet?

'Here, we do have some treatment for you but it is only antibiotics, which fight infection. They cannot heal the sickness.' He gently leans over the patient, his hands travel up the flimsy string that was once neck and as purple lips part he looks at me, 'Severe dehydration is due to this tumour. It inhibits swallowing.'

I glimpse a huge, ugly growth mushrooming from the back of the tongue like a chunk of brown brain matter with uneven surface, the texture of bark on a very old tree.

He continued, 'These tumours are common in end-stage HIV. The system here is that suspected cases of HIV go to the hospital for a diag-

Monday evening

nostic blood test and then they receive an appointment for an Aids clinic. The wait is usually about a month. Too late in this case.'

Hannes copes incredibly, Ma. I still feel shell-shocked because if this lady were in the west she may have lived for ages. The heavy knowledge that she is just one of many will never leave; how does Papa carry all this pain and still lovingly oversee the earth? The prayer to 'know his heart' may have undreamed of implications for this little human.

Drawing in the patient's companion Hannes slowly went over the relevant facts again, stipulating we have no cure for the sickness. He gently explains the gospel through Ivan and says that all we can do is pray and then does. After 'Amen' a heated discussion breaks out as the old woman insists Hannes *do* something. Seeking clarification he turns to Ivan, 'What does she feel we can do to help?'

Ivan explained that she insists the patient (we think it is her daughter) needs to go to the clinic (the one the hospital route would lead to eventually where they do have drug programmes for HIV patients caught early enough). I don't know if she sees this as her last hope or has no grasp of how little life is left ... it becomes clear that the woman is not leaving till she feels need is met. Hannes (presumably aware of the line outside) finally tells me he will give them money for the taxi to go directly to the government clinic.

I have no idea how far away that is and my inquiry never found voice. Like the hundreds of other questions that come in a day here, it remains woven, open ended, into the rich, chaotic, stunning, gut-wrenching tapestry of events that are tumbling over me to make up my Pemba experience.

Someone from outside went to fetch a much older gentleman who

Pemba Pennings

came in visibly scared. He announced that the patient is his mother (which Hannes says is doubtful having examined the patient and in view of his obvious seniority). Probably a language issue but at this point it didn't seem important. Can you ever imagine a situation at home where patients have no idea of their own age and no next of kin can be accurately discerned!?

Hannes wades out to the vehicle that is now surrounded by men two and three deep, to see if he has any cash for the taxi fare. I don't know if this would be his own money or if Iris gives him a float and naturally too many other things happened for it to be appropriate to pursue the thought.

Desiring to encourage the mother that we were trying to help, Hannes decided we would also give the patient an antibiotic. Even the trickle of water I offered could not get past the tumour on the back of her tongue and the fit of painful, exhausting choking it precipitated was agony to watch. I offered the mother the tablet and indicated her daughter should try and swallow it.

I felt desperate to offer some form of comfort or reassurance and I reached out to gently place my hand on the bony shoulder of the mother. It was awful, Ma; she stiffened, rigid, like a person standing to attention and I knew I had done the wrong thing. I don't know if it was my whiteness, if I broke the wrong hand Muslim thing or what but I never felt more ineffectual. I immediately withdrew trying to ward off despair as the strangled sound of uncontrollable retching reverberated off the baked walls.

Once the sound subsided and she had dabbed her daughter's chin with a scrap of cloth that was even grubbier than the piece over the

Monday evening

patient, the old lady turned to Ivan. He had sat straight-faced patiently interpreting and now turned to Hannes expressionless. 'She has joint pains and wants medicine.' Hannes gave her some paracetamol.

As the next patient entered I pondered again how patient confidentiality was simply gobbled up by need. So, three hours into the day by now, we were seeing patient number four. The middle-aged gentleman in front of us was sporting a Muslim skullcap and flip-flops (obviously he also wore something in between but I was struck by his hat and then rummaging at floor level to tidy pill packets his knobbly feet and flip-flops were in my line of vision). Ivan stated, 'Urine pain.'

On cue the patient leaped to his feet and gave a groaning demonstration of pushing wee from his bladder. I only watched out of the corner of my eye since I was suddenly apprehensive of how detailed this mime would be (hence no recollection of garments). He gratefully accepted the proffered plastic cup and duly went to the far end of the second half of the hut to fill it.

He was hardly around the corner before a man wearing a cap, a spotless pink polo shirt, long trousers, shoes and socks strode in. He carried a small girl who could have been about six in his arms. Ivan listened then told Hannes, 'Cough and fevers.'

As this consultation was underway the elderly couple began painstakingly assisting the ill woman on the daybed to her feet. She didn't have the strength to support her head, which lolled as they moved her, much less stand up. The old man squatted right down and the old lady heaved and rolled her daughter onto his back. She whimpered, pain in every move as clutching a bunch of cloth he shunted her weight to centre his burden. The old lady strapped the fading body in place with the strip of material he offered. Then with fleshless limbs dangling, dejected mother trailing behind, I watched this little family stagger away into a chasm of suffering and loss. I felt totally wretched. Till that moment only numbers in a news bulletin. Now? I will never forget the emaciated face of Aids in Africa.

No time to process. Just as a teenage girl slips through the doorway sporting a rainbow-coloured headscarf, the man with the specimen returns, his precious liquid cargo held at arm's length. A collision with the next patient, a robust, alert female wearing a fluro-green t-shirt over an equally bright *kapalana* is happily averted (particularly since yours truly was bang in line of potential spillage).

The vibrant teenage girl slides on to the end of the little bench by the door and appears rapt by the exchange between Hannes and the man with his pot. I am distracted by an exchange between Ivan and the girl after which she skulks out looking daggers at Ivan.

I think she was indicating a sore foot and was attempting to jump the queue but the number system rolls on. Robust fluro-lady sits mute. I notice old nail polish and shocking-pink flip-flops. She appears transfixed by pot man's description of 'blocked pipes'. As Ivan deadpan translates, 'The patient is concerned that his penis is weak.' I dare not catch anyone's eye. Hannes does a dip test of the urine and pronounces prostate issues, which will require the patient's attendance at the hospital.

Moving forward to the patient's seat immediately in front of Hannes the brightly dressed mama states in English her problem is mycosis (this is a common fungal infection which thrives in the humid conditions here and loves the lack of ablution facilities). Hannes escorts her into the 'exam room'.

Monday evening

I am not sure which orifice he inspected but she was less than happy on her return because she wanted tablets and we only have the option of gentian violet, an oral suspension. I guess she must have had the problem before and found tablets work better. They would be much more convenient.

Ivan wonders aloud where our lunch is. I am unsure what he means. Wanting to be prepared and wary of suddenly needing to eat something of unknown origin (I know, not fully in keeping with true woman of faith and power mode BUT surely a girl has to work up to walking on water?) I squirreled half of last night's supper into a tub to bring with me so cold beans and rice it is. (Washed cutlery secreted safely in bag.)

I am surprised to find Ivan moving over to position himself beside me as the next patient enters. This is a mum with a babe in arms and a boy of about eight, though when asked mum says she doesn't know his age. I notice the baby has tiny shoes on and realise it is probably a small toddler. By contrast the boy has bare feet and is filthy. His shorts and well-worn long-sleeved sweatshirt are peppered with holes

The boy stands to one side, his arms folded defensively across his chest. His eyes are swollen and the woman explains he has a fever. She answers Hannes' questions, 'No diarrhoea, cough or throat pain.' More antihistamine and Panadol prescribed.

As I sit up from the drug box two girls wander past the door with matching blue socks and rucksacks. There must be a school nearby. A large open truck has pulled up outside with about twenty-five men onboard. The next lady is given Brufen for backache and Ivan in a tired voice explains 'one tablet at night'.

A man in long, cream, cargo-style trousers and smart short-sleeved shirt sporting a large watch (which would definitely qualify as 'bling' in my other life) takes a seat. '*Problemo?*' Hannes asks. As the man gesticulates indicating back pain and discomfort in the epigastric area I notice gold thread running through his shirt fabric; it glints as the light catches it. Hannes gasps and clutches his stomach by way of asking, 'Is it better when eating?' He is wondering if the man has a virus and is doing a great job communicating. Ivan by contrast, appears to be fading.

'Yes? OK is it a struggle to swallow? No?' The patient is indicating soreness around his middle. He says he has no rash but feels very hot. (Beside me Ivan crumples, head in hands he mumbles, 'They forgot our lunch.') Hannes presses on, 'How long has the fever lasted? Oh, four days?'

I am just thinking it is fortuitous that this patient speaks so much English when two less than pristine children slip in. They place two worn-looking but loaded plates and two cracked plastic cups inside the door. These nestle beside the oozy swabs from the blister that lie where Ivan dropped them earlier. Ivan looks up and gazes longingly at the waiting food. I silently thank God for the prompting to bring my own!

The well sounds have finally ceased and there is a stillness that comes with the midday heat. Through the window a solitary woman leans into the well to fill a cup with water and the door of our vehicle is now visible again. Only two men remain. As I look up they are both just standing staring straight at me. Hannes announces the chest sounds are clear but an x-ray would be helpful in light of the back pain, his eyes flick to the plates of food and I notice a third plate has arrived ... Help!

A mum and baby enter before anyone can move towards the food and Hannes does a toe prick. This gives a drop of blood that within fifteen minutes will let him know if the baby has malaria. He indicates mum should wait outside.

Monday evening

A man who is familiar to Hannes steps in and says he is 'better'. He is in a khaki uniform and before he wanders off Hannes warns him that the leg pain medication he takes will influence his blood pressure.

Another man rapidly takes his place (a low moan from beside me as Ivan loses heart altogether). The patient announces, 'Mycosis,' and indicates his groin and armpits. Hannes leads him into the exam room and then sends him on his way handing him the gentian violet. With his free hand he beckons the waiting mum to return and tells her the test is positive. Baby has malaria.

Hannes looks hopefully at Ivan at this point as it is clear mum is not really comprehending. Ivan is now suffering a particularly boisterous bout of hiccoughs but rallies. Hannes is giving something to mum for the baby to take twice daily for the next three days. Ever patient Hannes turns to Ivan, 'Does she understand about the treatment? She is meant to repeat back the instructions.' Big sigh from Ivan but he does turn to the lady and get her to repeat several sentences. Hannes is satisfied and declares it lunchtime before the next body can come through the doorway.

Inevitably, try as I might I cannot stay hydrated and not need the loo all day. The time had come. I'll just say that it was a huge relief to discover the appropriate space at the far side of the second half of the hut did in fact have a door! This had been wide open and folded back into the shadow. We briefly ate together before resuming clinic.

As the first afternoon patient appeared Ivan turned to Hannes and said, 'What is the current treatment for gonorrhoea?' Had I missed something? No. As it turned out the question just popped into Ivan's head.

'Problemo?' The patient indicated he was worried he had 'weak penis' (erectile dysfunction to us) and with Ivan's help Hannes explained this can sometimes be a problem with diabetes and also hypertension but if it is anything more complex he is unable to help. Ivan takes this moment to confide in me that he plans to go to university next year to be a doctor. I have no idea if this is a dream, a vague hope that I may offer to sponsor him or a journey he is genuinely on and the next patient who was a young lady, I guessed in her twenties, is already sitting down opposite Hannes.

I don't think I can tell you about all the others because I have already been writing for ages but hopefully this gives you an idea. We saw several more patients (about 28 in all, some were mums with more than one child but that counts as 'one' in the system) so you can imagine what a full day for the Doc!

Hannes diagnosed more malaria and advised mums how to treat vomiting and diarrhoea to avoid dehydration. There were more people with mycosis and a possible case of the bilharzia parasite. (You remember that thing that can be in the rivers and swims up into your bladder? We heard about it from Grandpa in Zimbabwe. And I remember as a teenager wondering if I could swim with my legs crossed!)

We got back from the clinic late afternoon and I felt a real need to do something at least vaguely familiar and preferably unchallenging. I made myself useful picking up litter for half an hour and then settled to write in bed (it's amazing having my own room as I can have the light on).

Am really ready for sleep now…hope there may be a time of staff worship to join tomorrow evening.

I feel drained just recounting it all Ma and I have no real way of

Monday evening

processing the enormity of the day. No grid that even vaguely transposes from my life at home. Thanks for praying for me as I am sure your prayers are undergirding me, especially in those moments when I feel totally out of my depth (which is most of the time).

I'm doing it, Ma; I am really here in Pemba. God said so clearly to come I know he has a purpose. I do wonder if it will be some time after leaving Mozambique before I can even discern what that is but I am happy to know I am walking in obedience. I know deep down there is something more, some treasure to be mined. I am feeling overwhelmed at times but 'mining' is by nature hard work, isn't it? I am irresistibly lured to go deeper. God spoke about 'keys' and I am longing to be plunged so completely into him that the world around me really is changed by love.

Really gotta go. I should probably get some sleep now Ma. Can't believe how much there is to tell you. Don't worry about me as I am in good hands!!

Love you so much Ma, more soon x x

P.S. I prayed again for the guard, that God would release the money he needs for hospital. I am uncomfortable, not knowing if he is really thinking I should give him money, but it will be amazing when God provides and hopefully he will be inspired to ask God for help before approaching visitors in the future. I don't know but I wonder if Iris actually assists their staff with medical things. Anyway, I want him to feel loved and valued and can do my bit to encourage. More soon x

Tuesday morning

Dear Ma,

I have prayed, 'Lord, if you wake me early I will get up and meet you in the prayer hut,' so when I woke at 4.30 I got up and dressed. Unusually there is heavy cloud about so the sunrise was quite different today. I had all sorts of random thoughts as I sat gazing out to sea.

Two gorgeous Swedish girls have arrived and intriguingly both are named Hela. Some of the young Mozambican men appear to be afflicted with a kind of dizziness and are hovering with puppy dog eyes.

Inevitably the vivid picture of the lady with Aids is on my mind; I cannot get her out of my head, that hideous tumour on her tongue. I think the tumour was a Kaposi's sarcoma, which Hannes explained is indicative of the end stage of the disease. How grim, the HIV undermines other body systems so the immune system is compromised and all these other horrid conditions then just move in on the already ill, defenceless person. Out here without early help the patient is at the mercy of the virus. I just wonder where she is now … still alive even?

Tuesday morning

By 5am there was a discordant orchestra in full swing. Birds welcoming the morning, the call to prayer tape seemed to be stuck (but I may just lack discernment), a cockerel was loudly strutting his stuff and not harmonising with a transistor on a local pop station, voices already floating over the base as villagers prepare for the new day and all undergirded by the steady pad padding of flip-flops bringing guards and *tias* to work. (*Tias* are the Mozambican women who are like house mothers and care for the children in their various living areas.) I slept really soundly after yesterday and as I think about the day ahead I thought I'd start my next missive.

I have been mulling the pictures of me in the outback, round a campfire, in a truck, camper-type vehicle. Pondering what they could mean. The Holy Spirit reminded me of a scripture that God highlighted back in 2012 during the time of 24/7 prayer we had at church. It's from Isaiah 45:2-3

> *'I will go before you and will level the mountains; I will break down gates of bronze and cut through bars of iron. I will give you the treasures of darkness, riches stored in secret places, so that you may know that I am the* LORD, *the God of Israel, who summons you by name.'*

As I was thinking about this and some other scriptures about water gushing in the desert I had a clear sense of something amazing being on the far side of barriers and challenges. A sense of purpose unfolding as I considered again Heidi's teaching about being filled with the 'knowledge of his will', so that we can live a life that is worthy and pleasing to God.

That *is* how I feel, what I want more than anything. As I poured it all out to God a solitary white feather floated down beside me, overwhelming me with a sense of awe. He is so gentle Ma, so gracious. The feathers are a constant reminder that I am 'covered by his wing', sheltered, safe. Surrounded by angels. He will never bring me to a mountain that he cannot deal with. I've stuck the feather in my journal. What a blessing.

I am already feeling queasy and ... daunted is probably the best word. This is the day the 'big prison' visiting happens. Sol and Dan head this up and having been to the jail with them last week I do feel safe. That said, I can't imagine what conditions will be like or how I can in any way bless or encourage men in such dire circumstances; but I do feel to go. More trusting.

Have been getting to know some of the other visitors. (Clara and Jojo left with the rest of their team deciding needs must: funds did not materialise in Clara's account as she had hoped.) They said they would return at a later date. I don't think from any angle, be it Mozambique law or Iris policy that a person can rock up here and just announce they are staying but there we go. I did get my watch back from Jojo and sharing days with them and Molly has only enhanced my time here.

Karlie, Nina's friend, is Jamaican born then moved to America. Working in the same office as Nina she is an eco-scientist and has considerable insight into issues surrounding western workers in developing nations. She was fascinated when we went to Kauri on Saturday as she had never seen tidal ocean and the sea literally goes out miles there, well almost a mile! She couldn't wait to walk right out to the water's edge and did so whilst I had that delicious swim.

Nina is obviously used to the MSG thing and prepares all her own food. I can't imagine the effort and planning that must take. Poor Nina had some kind of fall in the night and is resting today due to the mi-

Tuesday morning

graine the fall triggered. Thinking about it, maybe the onset of the migraine caused her to fall? I don't know but tough to be unwell here.

My initial hunch about Sophie is proving accurate and it is clear to me why her son is rather quiet. She often captures Aya and me in the kitchen area as we return with our meal. Having cleaned everything in sight she insists we sit and eat together. I had a sense ... it feels a bit like commanding an audience. Aya is no mug and her response is to chew whilst studying her plate and listening to sermons, her headset firmly in place. That leaves yours truly as captive audience.

I'm sure Sophie means well but, for example, yesterday she launched into a story of going to meet with the 'head of this region' (whoever he may be, but it couldn't just be a 'connection' or a local leader, had to be 'head') as she knew him as a child when he attended school in South Africa. She speaks of Heidi as a long-lost friend and I'm just aware of that 'name dropping' thing some people have.

Hey ho, her next question was, 'Have you met the Queen because I have?' (I wasn't far wrong then!) I got the full tale. Somehow Sophie and the Queen ended up in the same hotel in Namibia (of all places) and Sophie was fascinated as the Queen wore stockings and high-heeled shoes every day. The Queen even offered Sophie a gift. (Surely she must have asked for it? I can't imagine Her Majesty trotting around the world giving out signed photographs of herself to all and sundry; but who am I?)

Haven't had any feathers yet today. I am wondering what I can have prepared for the prison if we are asked to share as we did at the jail. I feel desperate that prisoners should know they are never alone. Sol says there are a number of Christians among the inmates. Am wondering about what to share. The picture of Jesus driving the car of our lives came to mind but then perhaps none of them have owned a vehicle? Or maybe something about walking at night and Jesus holding a torch? Maybe not. Maybe better just not to say anything. Praying is probably better use of time.

So much to think about. I'll sign off now but will let you know how it goes ...

Love you x

Tuesday evening

Hello again Ma,

Just a quick note before I get horizontal. Another big day but not as we know it! Nothing went as planned ... and then I remind myself, oh yes, I'm actually here trusting for divine plans to unfold. Feels to be a steep learning curve and rather startling how unnerving; how out of control I feel as days are allowed to, well, almost as if the day simply slips the wrapping off its contents in its own time. It is an amazing journey, learning to live with so little structure and what there is, is so unfamiliar I am playing constant catch-up!

Sol had spoken to me at church on Sunday and I understood him to say that to be involved in visiting the prison we needed to be at the prayer hut at 7.30am on Tuesday (today). I love the way the activities are bathed in prayer and it gives us a chance to connect with those sharing the experience before we launch (again in my case) into the total unknown.

A small group of us gathered. I spotted Dan on the main track. He made as if to walk on past the pathway that leads straight to the prayer hut but then hesitated diverting at the last moment. He approached us with a cheerful greeting, 'What are you all doing here?' After explaining, we asked if he was coming with us to which he replied he had to be elsewhere. He kindly used his phone, called Sol on our behalf, then left having assured us Sol would join us shortly.

Sol arrived a while later and proceeded to explain that prison visiting is on Thursdays, (today being Tuesday!) Then again, it is sometimes on Tuesday but only on weeks when there is extended bush outreach. He was sorry for the misunderstanding and encouraged us to return to meet him at 2.30 this afternoon for hospital visiting, which he affirmed would definitely be happening.

I had been psyching myself up for the prison venture and felt a bit flat. I wasn't quite sure how to spend the morning and then remembered that Nina is teaching her course each day in the vocational school.

Should (if things go according to current plan, haha) have a nice chunk of time tomorrow to scribble so will aim to fill you in on the rest then.

Weary tonight so should be a good sleep.

Love you so much Ma, night night x x x

Wednesday

Hello hello,

Woohoo!! Oh Ma ... here I am sitting on white sand under a shady canopy of the brown woven raffia that is everywhere here. It's a huge umbrella; you could probably fit six single beds side by side beneath it. What joy to be able to collect my thoughts and write in peace.

Back at the base all activities were stopped today as it is a public holiday. Nina and Karlie were game to visit a beach some way away in an area known as 'Bush Camp'. A young man Nina has known for some years offered transport and, true to form, we ended up paying a huge amount for a short journey in the vehicle of one of his cousin's friends.

I understand living is hard here but it is so uncomfortable being constantly viewed as a target and those Mozambicans working for or with Iris are well looked after. It feels bemusing when those ostensibly Christian seem to think it's perfectly OK to use people, to take advantage. Honesty and faithfulness (as in keeping your word) for example, are not simply characteristics of western culture but they are kingdom. It is easy to feel

Pemba Pennings

defensive; lots to learn and I am constantly mindful that I did, as it were, invite myself here.

I am now some way from the main road down a track so rutty that four-wheel drive is imperative. I'm told Bush Camp is well known locally (I presume mostly among expats because there is an entrance fee) as a popular place for time out. It is run (and maybe owned?) by a South African couple who welcomed us in person.

In a large clearing just back from the sand there is a central grassy area where they have built a rustic bar and basic café area and they have a few simple options on offer for lunch. They are obviously establishing a business and live on site as I had the impression that 'lunch' would be made in the kitchen of their home.

Once in the camp area there are kayaks available, sun beds and various (to my mind completely dubious) 'attractions' such as paddling with the claw crabs in a nearby stream or taking a fifteen-minute bush walk to a 'hot mud pool'. I did take the walk but the possibility of sharing what looked like a big hole in the dunes full of sticky black mud with any number of hungry one-clawed crabs held no attraction.

The camp owners enthusiastically shared how those who do get up to their necks in the mud claim their skin has never felt better. There are supposedly invigorating minerals and various elements in the mud that can also ease inflammation, such as joint pains. Hmm ... I remain unconvinced but Nina, all credit to her, decided to embrace the opportunity. 'Just because I can,' she tossed over her shoulder as she set off. The mud is very glutinous and the colour of soot.

Some while later what appeared to be a walking tree blackened by fire came swaying along the bush track requesting photographic evi-

Wednesday

dence be recorded. At this point only startled-looking white eyes peeping out defined this apparition as human. Karlie obliged with a photo shoot before Nina plunged into the sea to scrape it all off. She and Karlie also went kayaking but I just had a long, leisurely swim.

We are in a sweeping bay I think on the opposite side of the peninsula to Kauri but not sure; as you know my sense of direction can leave a bit to be desired. It is very different terrain here. Not a wide-open, firm, sandy beach but small sandy coves in the soft, deep sand with what looks similar to a kind of pampas grass growing right into the shallows. Feels a bit like the mangroves up in that area near AJ's place. The bottom is mud but not so soft you sink into it (I hate that). I am just soaking up the opportunity to think, pray and write.

Earlier on today as we sat gazing out to sea I found myself sharing with Nina what already (mysteriously) begins to feel like 'my Aboriginal story' unfolding. She was wonderfully affirming and encouraged me that it sounds just like God and she senses him moving in me in a profound way. (Help!) I have also realised how powerful telling my story can be.

As we drove to Mieze on Monday Hannes asked me all about how I come to be here in Pemba. As I recounted how God has led me and spoken to me excitement filled the atmosphere between us and he spoke of being very encouraged. I think I need to learn to be more willing to open up and trust the Holy Spirit can use my words. It was amazing to recognise a person can gain encouragement and strength for their own journey just by my being willing to open up. (Doesn't come naturally as you know but it has helped motivate me to keep trying to get this experience down on paper.) I'll try and fill you in!

Where to begin? Sigh … The last 24 hours has been amazing (just for a change!). You may want to make a brew and put your feet up Ma, because there is no short way of telling you about it all. Interestingly, there has been a noticeable shift in the general vibe on base to 'upbeat' now Heidi is home. Yesterday I woke with my day pretty well mapped out but then ... this *is* Africa.

So, as I said last night, days got a bit muddled and I unexpectedly had the morning free and remembered Nina was teaching. It had crossed my mind when reading the material that it could well be a brilliant tool down the track in remote Aboriginal schools.

Need to hop back to last week now but hold that thought ... Nina teaching a class.

Oh gosh, it feels enormous to be thinking of putting it into words. I'll have a go though because I know you are praying and I would certainly value this part of my journey being soaked in prayer for wisdom, courage ... well anything God shows you ... I can't imagine ... Right. (Having to deep breathe just sitting here, as it feels so outrageous!) I think the best place to start is here.

So, before the students left last week God spoke to me very clearly. I didn't tell you about it at the time; strangely it felt too deep ... too significant somehow to commit to paper but I'll try now.

It was lunchtime and we were all sitting around. The students got to chatting about their love of mission trips and began talking about where they were hoping to go next. Various ones spoke of unreached people groups and others elaborated on needs they plan to address in a number of developing countries.

As the conversation rolled on I felt more and more the odd one out. It became clear that they were all set on moving from one experience,

Wednesday

such as we are having here, to another and see themselves as being 'sent as missionaries' to take the good news around the globe. I, on the other hand, came here trusting that through this 'stepping out' experience God would encounter me and deposit something in me that I can carry back into my everyday life. Something that will cause the lives of those around me to be transformed by the power of heaven's love; love overflowing from my relationship with Jesus.

I am very happy where God has planted me in Australia; the last thing I want is to be 'sent out'. But then I wrestled with doubt as the discussion continued. Did this mean I was less yielded?

I felt uncomfortable with the perspective that 'mission' could be defined as what felt like a kind of 'culture hopping'. It felt is if those present were picking random Aztec tribes or little-known people groups out of the air and declaring intentions to go to them. Several shared they were already booked on their next trip or two leaving me wondering if they ever intended getting work. How is it all funded? As the group continued to enthuse I increasingly felt like a square peg in a round hole.

Then it dawned on me. In the moment, it truly seemed that the column of light from the fluorescent strip above us polarised to become a blinding spotlight shining directly at me. As yet another of the team listed the specific needs of a remote tribal people group somewhere on the far side of the world that she intended visiting, I experienced a physical jolt of realisation. The list of needs was completely familiar.

The Aboriginal people have lost their land leaving them struggling to find their identity; their traditional culture is under threat, families are fractured, fathers are absent, addiction is rife, teenagers are taking their own lives as hopelessness takes over, crippling poverty is the norm, they have no clear voice in the nation (only having been classified as 'human' by invading white man in the 1967 referendum). Education? It's unusual to find an Aboriginal student in university. Plagued by profound health issues life expectancy is less than the average white Australian. Who could need Jesus more?

I wriggled in the glare of the bright light feeling totally conspicuous. (In reality, nobody else had any inkling of the significance of the moment for me.)

A question arrived unbidden. So what might it look like to be called to a people group that you could value and serve without ever leaving the country you love? Dumbfounded I experienced a shudder of breathless anticipation as Holy Spirit wings fluttered. Maybe He is calling *me*? Could I be a 'sent out one' (such as I read about in Heidi's book) after all? Without ever needing to leave the beautiful land that is now home? What a crazy idea … Yes. It registered; SO crazy it could just be God!

Who else would come up with the wild scheme of planting me in a wonderful, prosperous, optimistic, thriving, stunningly wild land, cause me to lose my heart to its untamed allure and then bring me to Africa to highlight the gaping need right at the very core of my nation? Hideous inequality is rife but the glorious potential of loving the first people of our nation into relationship with their Heavenly Father so they can rise and take their rightful place of honour in the nation? Sounds exactly like God.

Could it even be that heaven is inhibited from fully blessing Australia until we address this issue to his satisfaction? I felt inspired, challenged, excited, daunted, elated, overwhelmed and awed all in a wave of … I don't even know what … Presence I suppose. All I do know is if I had

Wednesday

been spoken to I would have been unable to reply.

Suddenly I had to be alone. Hoping my legs would carry me under the weight of revelation I slipped away to humbly lie on my face feeling very small but inexplicably excited.

There you have it Ma. Something profound is unfolding and God is so awesome, he even gently showed me his pleasure that I already said 'yes' to leaving home and family when he asked me to emigrate. As if he were saying, 'You completely qualify as a sent out one!'

Right. Back to yesterday and the non-prison visit. I decided to act on the thought about Nina's class and sought out Karlie whom I knew had attended the previous day. We walked together down to the vocational centre, which is situated right by the road at the entrance to the base. Nina shared her excitement about a visitor called John who sounds quite high profile, to do with a scheme for improving farming in Africa. She told us he would probably speak at staff home group.

I was only half listening. With not having a specific activity to focus on, my thoughts were swirling again and this incredible sense of personal destiny unfolding has been feeling as if it is literally swelling my stomach. I've really been just 'holding it' and asking the Holy Spirit to take any opportunity to confirm what I'm sensing.

I found it difficult to concentrate on the class though I am impressed with the content of Nina's work. She told me she has been able to promote the material in a number of nations and the government of Uganda has already introduced the course in their schools. How brilliant is that?

An hour in we were breaking into small groups for a 'round table' session. As everyone was moving around I held back because they were

Pemba Pennings

all in groups from the day before. At that moment one of the full-time missionaries called Grace slipped in and we got chatting. She was genuinely interested in how I come to be here, in Pemba and whether God is speaking anything specific.

Almost without meaning to I found myself sharing about this growing sense of purpose involving Aboriginal people. As I finished speaking she reached silently for her phone and after pressing keys handed it to me smiling broadly. I know it sounds wild but I read,

> *Cheese, tomato*
> *Cheese, tomato, ham*
> *Cheese, tomato, aborigine ham*

I kid you not! The word leapt out as a stone from a slingshot. Ma, I was so stunned by this message from heaven I just gawped at Grace.

'I know' she said. 'Pretty amazing, hey? I took this photo of the pizza menu in the restaurant last night!'

It was so incredible to me that God would write that very word on a menu somewhere in Pemba (they have pizza in Pemba?) and then cause me to sit by the very person who had thought to photograph that menu.

It was not till some time later in the day that it dawned on me that it was actually a spelling mistake and should have read 'aubergine'. Yes, I know, shock horror, obvious to all. BUT not to me. I was literally awestruck by this message of confirmation straight from heaven. It was too much. I hope I was coherent; I said … something … and excused myself.

It was late morning by now and very hot as I staggered outside. Tears and perspiration mingled as trance-like I meandered up the main sandy track towards the familiar outline of the prayer hut. I was overcome,

Wednesday

disorientated, gasping and gulping for air. 'Lord,' I spluttered, 'I am only a girl, what can I do? What can you do through just me? How can we tackle such a huge issue?' Desperate for solace I was drawn to the prayer hut but as I got close I could hear voices and realised it was full of people. A staff meeting.

Unable to walk any further I crept behind the hut and sank onto the ground — dirt, rubbish, bugs an' all. My body seemed to drain out of my feet as my legs folded under me in the shade of a bush. I pulled my cotton scarf over my head as if it would make me invisible and had a fleeting thought about the prophet Elijah.

As I shifted slightly to avoid a particularly sharp stone in my left buttock a clarion call reverberated from the heavens (it was actually Heidi's voice but in my heightened state in that moment it came straight out of heaven).

'So, I feel right now God is clearly saying we are to stop saying "we're just us, we're only small" and it is time to rise up as he equips us for the task.'

I may have swooned under the weight of the Holy Spirit's presence; I may have fainted in the heat. Either way I lost time and when I came to some while later I still couldn't move.

As things gradually came back into focus I became vaguely aware of someone asking visitors to introduce themselves in the hut. I heard Sophie's confident tones as I finally managed to heave myself to my feet. It had never been suggested to me I attend the group and introduce myself and I knew I was incapable of speech at that moment. I remember strangely hoping I wouldn't be in trouble (bunking off a meeting I hadn't known about).

Pemba Pennings

As I walked very slowly away I fleetingly presumed the 'visitors' in the meeting must be linked with the farming man and wondered how Sophie was involved. I think at some level I must have looked how I felt because Gina (the young volunteer I told you about last week) greeted me ever so gently in the visitors' centre and sensitively offered me a cup of rooibos tea. Nectar.

You remember she came to serve in Village of Joy for three months and has been helping Christy with the toddlers in the playgroup whilst also providing childcare for one of the families on base. She returns to the UK in two weeks. The tea was a treat and we just chatted amiably (no idea what about or if I was coherent) for a while.

I wasn't hungry when supper time came around but was feeling more 'with it' and mindful that last Tuesday night we visitors had been included in a great time of worship and prayer in the prayer hut. This week there had been some mention of 'homegroup' so I wondered if this was a more intimate evening for staff and not appropriate for visitors. I was nervous of intruding but toyed with the idea of taking a chair into the dark nearby so I could savour the worship that would likely be part of the gathering in the prayer hut. I went to the hut to pray for a bit first.

I was still there when other visitors arrived and it was obvious they were settling in, anticipating being part of the meeting. I decided to be bold and assume I could stay. The acoustics are not special in the hut but the atmosphere is. A basic microphone and a couple of Mozambican staff with guitar and bongo-type drums began a gentle time of worship.

Children wandered in and out, half a dozen mattresses were strewn on the stone floor and people sat, walked around, knelt or lay on a mattress as worship continued. At some point Heidi must've slipped in. When

Wednesday

I opened my eyes later she was prostrate on a mattress with two children curled around her feet. I had heard there was to be a talk and rather bizarrely I thought to myself, 'If Aboriginal people are mentioned tonight I'm sure I will just fall over.'

I felt I was beginning to see things more and more clearly.

The government at home has tried everything to resolve what are perceived as 'indigenous issues'. Billions of taxpayers' dollars have been thrown at the problem but not brought resolve. Symptoms are all too obvious but healing is needed for a deep wound.

Maybe it is only the love of Jesus poured out and motivating change that can impact such desperate need. People must already be actively engaged. How am I going to connect with them? Perhaps googling when I get home? Quite random thoughts really ... except I had the verse in John's gospel this morning when Jesus says, *'My food is to do the will of him who **sent** me.'*

I found myself thinking maybe I really am a 'sent out one' after all!

John spoke a good deal about God's revelation to him about the poor and our commission to love them and meet their need. He shared how he has received a method of farming from God, in what he describes as a 'download from heaven', which he is introducing all around Africa. He has wonderful stories of the benefit this has brought to many.

He spoke for over an hour, which is much longer than the usual half-hour talk at this weeknight gathering. He appealed to Heidi to allow him to finish even though it was late. He spoke for another twenty minutes and then said to Heidi, 'I am almost done if I could take just a few moments more?' She nodded and he continued, finally concluding with dropping the bomb, 'Recently I even went to Australia and connected with people who are introducing this method of farming to Aboriginal people.'

Honestly, Ma ... would you believe it? I can hardly, well, I can't actually keep up with my own feelings inside and then lying here by the ocean today, I suddenly remembered going forward for prayer at that conference I went to in Cardiff. Randy Clarke spoke about angels commissioning certain ones there and I knew it was significant as he laid hands on me. Then God reminded me of the 'key' word (remember the blouse?). Is it possible he is really asking me to take his love and hope to Aboriginal people? Is it connected to the sense I have that I will be buying some kind of truck or off-road vehicle this year?

It's true I feel fully alive in the bush and love being under the stars, living simply. With my little house to return to I could do stints in the outback for months at a time; it sounds outrageous. Anyway, if it is God it will come to pass. Bill Johnson teaches that to come into our destiny, the reason we are created, we need to dream with God and if the dream is possible without God it is not a big enough dream. Yikes!

I'm hoping Wednesday church will be on when we get back tonight despite it being a public holiday. The girls are coming over now to eat their lunch so I will finish this later. I was reading Isaiah 58 (as well as that verse in John about doing God's will being food) and felt challenged about fasting so am just having water till tomorrow breakfast.

I am desperate to be able to hear what God is saying clearly. A jovial crowd of people on a corporate day out has arrived and the barbecue waftings are tantalising. Maybe time for a last dip before we leave. More soon ...

Back at base now Ma. On hearing what we paid for the outward

Wednesday

journey the South African couple at the camp insisted on organising a bona fide taxi and rate for our return to base at the end of the day, which was appreciated.

A young man called Ben (from Taunton of all places so just up the road from Sam in Exeter) has arrived today. He is here for a month on a medical internship. He was sharing about visiting The International House of Prayer in America and how he arrived as they were in the middle of a 40-day fast (I've got off lightly with 24hrs and am thankful).

Word is, there may not be outreach this Thursday so I will probably aim to go to the prison tomorrow and then support Sara doing Rahab on Friday. Ben asked me if I have seen any miracles here. Well, not in the blind see, deaf hear sense but I honestly feel I am living in one!

Do you think God could've brought me all the way to Africa to 'unlock' my destiny in Australia? In all the years I have lived there I have never even heard Aboriginal people mentioned in church or prayed for — not once.

I remember arriving in Canberra to my new life and fully anticipating meeting and making friends with Aboriginal folk. I was excited to think people living out there may actually introduce me to the Australian bush but ... in six years I have never encountered any of the First Peoples and I am in the capital city.

It was a mystery and a disappointment. It was confusing that the topic of indigenous issues in general was guaranteed to kill a dinner party but life got busy and I have come to understand that for most, it is a huge issue that has cost literally billions and for which they feel no resolve can be found.

There is no conviction, or even hope, of true healing from the deep wounds of a troubled history. Well, never dull with God, Ma.

Hope to be back to the page tomorrow. What a wild adventure.

Love you, and thanks because I know you will pray into this for me; I really need it. X

Thursday

Dearest Ma,

You won't believe it ... after all the 'it's on, it's off' of the last 72 hours there *is* to be outreach this week and what's more, Heidi is leading it!! I can't believe it and have agreed to go. Gremlins are rioting in my gut. I don't feel as anxious as I would've expected about bugs and things so God must be doing something.

Brace yourself ... I have learned that the laundry curfew has a deeper meaning!

One of the lovely Swedish girls (the Helas that I mentioned to you — the one who reminds me of Daryl Hannah in the old movie where she is a mermaid) has discovered a raised circular area on her wrist and it is likely it is one of the worms I have only just learned about.

Said worms burrow under the skin and grow. Typically flies lay 'eggs' in damp laundry, which hatch and the larvae burrow into the skin. We have been encouraged from the beginning to hang laundry out for only the briefest time necessary for drying but I admit to thinking this was to avoid theft.

Pemba Pennings

Not sorry I didn't have worm details earlier as having done several bits of laundry with no ill effect I will continue and trust. Poor Hela was quite distressed at first and I think the area is sore. The worms do have to be fished out so she is off to see Hannes before we go bush today; or it may be tablets to kill the worm? All will be revealed.

She seems calm now she knows what it is ... the complete opposite of how my dear sister would respond I'm sure. Can you imagine Sis finding something was living under her skin ... that she could see moving? Oh my word, the fun just keeps on coming!

Yesterday afternoon Sophie decided to empty the communal fridge and has made it clear that general standards of housekeeping are less than satisfactory. I don't use the fridge and I'm keeping my head down. This kind of living inevitably means that various things get left or forgotten and human nature doesn't lend itself to volunteering for cleaning up after others.

I nip in now and again and do some cleaning which, to be honest, I find therapeutic at one level; it is after all the only familiar ritual in this wild experience. Being frustrated is never going to achieve anything and nobody wants to be ill. (I did pluck up courage to mention my safety concern around the gas cooker and I'm glad I did because it was checked and found to be somewhat lacking in requirements, even for a missionary base in Africa! A replacement is somewhere in the system but on its way, using the term 'system' very loosely you understand!)

Church last night was better than the icing on the cake of a special day. (It was the 'Wednesday church' that I told you about that is new.) There were definitely more of us there this week and more visitors have arrived. Rolland was preaching so joy was the order of the night.

Thursday

We were strewn across the filthy raffia mats that cover the cement floor just in front of the stage; I lost my glasses somewhere in the mêlée but Zena retrieved them for me unbroken (phew). Joy just seemed to usher in rich, heavy Presence. There was laughter and hilarity in a delicious childlike loss of inhibition and many of us just lay soaking for a long time as worship washed over us. Intoxicating freedom.

I am, well, not stewing exactly, but before he left I had opportunity to talk to John yesterday evening. I asked if he could give me a connection with those he mentioned in Australia. I was dismayed Ma, when he spoke of Aboriginal people as 'a hopeless case'.

He went on to tell me of missionaries who have given them up as 'a lost cause'. I don't know how much of that is based on the fact that the First Nations people in Australia are not generally understood to have been farmers but rather nomadic hunter-gatherers. No great surprise then if his scheme has not been pounced upon as the best idea since roo burgers!

To be honest I was astounded by his confession in this context where the impossible is unfolding every day in front of our eyes. I felt deep sadness. How disappointed the people who made that statement must be. Something in me rose up but I didn't know how to express it so I accepted the contact names he offered and said goodbye.

I felt something physical when he used the words 'written off'. Shockingly countercultural in this environment. He finished our conversation by stating that Aboriginal people are the most over evangelised people group in the world. Where is the fruit then? I wonder if he is including the misguided efforts of those who were involved with the stolen generations?

Pemba Pennings

On the upside of this rather dampening exchange, the dream of seeing this people group enjoying relationship with God, restored within their own cultural context and recognised as true citizens in their own nation, just gets more and more impossible which, according to Bill Johnson's teaching, is simply an indicator of God's intent. I don't want to embark on a dream that I have the ability to fulfil in my own strength.

More and more I want to be in a place where supernatural intervention is essential. I feel a surge of excitement as I write because I've been reading in Isaiah 49, and loss of hope (desert places), huge challenge (mountains), and need (drought), all link in with God stating his intent is the release of streams of living water gushing in the dry land. I drifted off to sleep pondering ... what if he really can use me?

And then on waking this morning my thoughts were tumbling around. I wandered over to collect my bread roll for breakfast and experienced a barrage of negative thoughts, doubts. Golly, Ma, they all came rushing round the corner and stood blocking my way. Maybe it's inevitable?

As I write, we are all gathered in the hut that was being roofed on my arrival and now offers a shady area with a locked kitchen cupboard type space. This is for the primary use of visitors who are invited here to minister in some way (it may be preaching, counselling or consulting for instance) as opposed to those of us who have applied to visit Pemba as volunteers.

There are a couple of double rooms at this 'deluxe, invited guests only' end of the centre with basic 'en suite facilities' and at a glance it appears one room even sports a mini fridge. I think the Koreans had one and John the farming man too. (I think his programme is called 'Farming God's Way' but it's not easy to pin people down to detail here and so

Thursday

much is going on as visitors come through.)

Adam is a young Mozambican on staff here. He summoned us all to meet at 9am to learn about preparation for the bush outreach but I brought this to write knowing it could be quite a wait. I'm thinking I may pop to the baby house for a bit later on this morning and offer some cuddles to the little ones before taking some time to prepare my kit (and my spirit) for the excursion ahead.

It will be amazing if there is opportunity to just briefly connect with Heidi but I think it will be quite a large group of us going. All the younger women are visibly 'aflutter' with the anticipation of being around Heidi.

Hela (not mermaid one) is really distressed. She had to leave the table halfway through her porridge this morning to vomit, and is writhing on her bunk with tummy cramps. I feel so sorry for her. Her first wail when realising she is sick was, 'I came all this way! I can't miss bush outreach with Heidi!'

I think I'd love my own tent but that may be impracticable. Lucie from Dunedin arrived yesterday and it's her first time in Africa but she is jumping straight in.

That doubting moment this morning Ma, I was having all these thoughts like, 'What was I thinking? God, using me with Aboriginals? What am I gonna do? Drive into the outback in a truck and wait for people to come and strip it bare? Then once I'm stranded, what? Go low and slow until there's a thaw or miraculous connection? I must be dreaming!' Then I got to thinking. I would need a connection first. Some regions I even need a pass to enter as a 'white fella'. Maybe I should pray for a partner? I surely won't make any impact alone? Maybe a team?

Pemba Pennings

How could God possibly use me to initiate change at a people-group level?

Stories of white fellas being ill-treated when going into remote areas to 'help' are not uncommon. How would I love people where I am not wanted? I can't think what possessed me to even consider that God could be speaking to me about Aboriginal people. In reality, working to see the purpose of heaven released on a national scale; what could that possibly look like?

You get the idea. I'm pretty sure a remote nursing post isn't the answer to anything. I just can't work out my feelings — I know we don't live by them! Preparing for outreach gave me just a few things to think about which served as (I was about to write 'welcome distraction' but that creates entirely the wrong impression) well, distraction anyway!

Then I give it all back to God. I need to quietly hold it all Ma, and see what he says or does next. If he truly is speaking then he will release all I need to accomplish the task. He will certainly have a next step in mind so I will try to rest, wait and keep listening.

Adam arrived about 9.20 and breezed past us, all patiently waiting, into the office in the corner. Frustratingly I can see him from here apparently skyping a friend on the work computer. I guess the opportunities are rare. Just after 10 now. I have a disconcerting sense that somehow this excursion into the bush is going to be more than this middle-class, churchgoing white girl is bargaining for!

Oh, the lovely Lucie has just leaned over to say she would love to share her (brand new for the occasion) tent with me. I sense she may be nervous to sleep alone and it will be fun to get to know her. It may be small but I doubt there will be much time lingering in any tent.

Thursday

Every now and then I think of Pop going off to the office in his suit and bowler hat and then ponder him visiting missionaries all over the globe in his Regions Beyond and Tear Fund roles. How did he manage? His upbringing was positively Victorian, and you must remember he never came on a single one of the holidays you took us kids on. Not if they had the remotest resemblance to camping. I never even saw him wandering around in bare feet at home. I hope he would be proud of my efforts if he could see me now.

Adam emerging now, Ma, so ... fill you in when we get back. Fasten your safety belt! (Parachute may be of more use!) Me? Ejector seat has most allure!!

Love you so much x x

week three

...was I about to witness a miracle?

Late Friday night

Dearest darling Ma,

Tucked in already. So much has unfolded.

I found the bush outreach trip overwhelming, unlike any previous experience.

I feel somehow dismantled in my inner self, maybe like a stripped engine; pared back to the core. It's a struggle to find words.

Don't think I can even write tonight but letting you know I am safe and back. Well ... 'safe'? I'm thinking Narnia when Lucy asks if Aslan is safe. Mr Beaver says, 'Safe? He's not safe but he is good.'

God is still dealing with me. I will try and share my outreach experience with you but think it will have to wait till tomorrow.

Imagine God bringing me all the way to Africa to enfold me, press me right into his heart and then unlock my future. (Am sensing the whole 'unlocking/key word' is all to do with the First Peoples in Australia and my ... I was going to write 'next season' but then the word 'calling' came to mind: yikes!) This was immediately followed by, 'What about income? Funding?'

Oooh Ma. This is serious ... Real.

Nina says I am totally 'hi-jacked'. It feels wild to hear such a contemporary American expression but I do indeed feel confronted on every level spiritually, intellectually and emotionally. I can only hold still on the Master's anvil. I will just tell you something really encouraging because it's not about me.

Remember I told you poor Hela was ill and desperately disappointed? She told me it was her life's dream to go on outreach with Heidi. We all sat around after she rushed from the table that morning and I wondered aloud if we should pray. One of the others said they didn't think so 'this time'. I wasn't quite sure what that meant. I was thinking how terrible it would be to be left alone in the centre feeling ill; and then Hela's crushing disappointment would surely make it ten times worse.

I haven't seen God open blind eyes as you know but we *are* in a place where it is recognised he heals and moves in power all the time. I slipped into Hela's room and offered to pray. She gratefully accepted and I decided to step out. I could hardly bear it for her. I commanded the vomiting to stop, the cramps to relax and the sickness to leave her body. Then I prayed hope and comfort into the disappointment in Jesus' name.

When we left she was sleeping.

Well ... picture the scene four hours later when we are all setting up camp in the bush and a vehicle draws up. Heidi had arrived. But who should be sitting glowing with pleasure in the passenger seat next to her? You guessed it. Hela!

She shared that within two hours she had recovered and rushed to let a staff member know who then promptly arranged for her to travel in the only vehicle that had not yet left the base. Isn't that fabulous Ma?

Late Friday night

She was not only healed (been well and eating normally ever since) but also got to travel for a whole two hours ... actually sitting beside Heidi. I thought she was literally going to self-combust with joy. So delicious to be a part of his plan; I felt like a proper 'handmaid of the Lord' just as it were, 'delivering' healing.

Loads to fill you in on once I can process the experience (holding your breath not advised!) could be a while.

Once outreach was over we got back and I had no time to process. It wasn't that long before (Friday again) Sara appeared for Rahab orientation. Another opportunity to bless local street girls with pedicures and love. A couple of visiting missionaries had arrived in the centre and I felt a measure of reassurance about doing something that was practical and familiar. Ben and Wilf were happy to come as security, which Sara was pleased about. A good-sized group with the two new women and us and we all agreed we would be ready to go straight after supper. It being Friday, supper was a tiny one-eyed fish with a boiled potato each and rice. We all lick the bones clean knowing it's protein but also it's a great flavour!

When Sara pulled up in the Land Rover for Rahab I felt like an old hand. I confess I hopped straight in to the front seat. (Not terribly 'go low and slow' I know, but after Monday bending over the drug crate all day, the truck journeys, sitting on the ground and then leaning over to pray for countless people, my back was feeling really sore by then. It's better today after a couple of days stretching and sleeping flat on my firm bed.)

Sara explained clearly that the evening is not about getting the girls to say 'Yes' to Jesus or agreeing to attend church. Even so, there was still a bit of a tricky moment mid-evening when the two new visitors demonstrated a different perspective. It caused a bit of tension later in the night and Sara handled it really well.

Armed with the usual wet wipes, lotions and nail polish we welcomed the girls in. I noticed Karlie was moist eyed at one point; Sophie was in full swing with her ability to communicate. Having language is an amazing benefit. Sara picked up on some of the swirling after outreach not being helped by the tense spot in the evening and when we got back, kindly offered to pray and spend time with anyone who would appreciate that. She spoke to Hela who was still visibly processing.

I mentioned to her that I would love to bless one of the Iris girls in her group that I felt God highlighting to me. Sara said after church on Sunday may be an opportunity to give my gift and share the encouraging word. I really respect the way she filters and weighs things. It must be challenging. Like accepting hundreds of visitors to your home each year with many thinking they have something to offer the precious children in your 'family.' I trust her so if she is not comfortable or prefers to just leave the gift that's fine with me.

The evening was marked for me by a terrible shrieking that filled the night air. I keep thinking about the things that happen in the ceremonies around puberty.

And now to bed, struggling with mind pictures.

Sorry so short Ma, will hope to write more tomorrow.

Big hug. And thanks so much for praying as I went x x

Saturday

Good morning Ma ... Never the same!

I was really hoping my head would feel enough above water this morning to give you a good description of the last 48 hours but I find myself still in the deep fathoms of God's presence. What does that look like?

Well, conversation is an effort and tears are building behind a fragile defence as images flood my mind ... a sick child in filthy rags consumed by high fever, a tribal king wearing diamante reading glasses, an eight-year-old girl with a baby on her back and a toddler clutching her threadbare skirt, a boy of five with puss running out of his left ear, a mud church with bamboo pews, a woman afflicted by an evil spirit thrashing around, a live chicken tied by its feet and suspended above my head, Heidi, freshly made up and stunning in a cerise sarong, black short-sleeve top and flip-flops with sparkles on, pouring Starbucks coffee into plastic beakers. And children. Runny nosed, staring, everywhere.

Thankful there are no plans for today. Really in need of re-group, processing time. I'll try and start at the beginning.

It was back in another life on Wednesday evening when word suddenly went around the visitors' centre, 'Bush outreach is happening and Heidi is going.' Bearing in mind for the previous two weeks it has been happening ... then not happening right up till the last moment: I wasn't holding my breath.

Shem is a warm, smiley Mozambican man on the staff here who has chatted to me a few times. He has a more mature feeling about him than many of the younger men. I have no idea of his age but not a teenager. On Wednesday evening as I left church he asked me if I was going on outreach this week, so perhaps he knew it was planned. As we sat in the visitors' centre later that night a number of us agreed it could indeed be a dream come true if we ended up on outreach with Heidi. I had a hunch that God was setting me up, positioning me to be in the right place at the right time.

I was still feeling acutely aware that Heidi is officially not due to be home at this time of the year. We headed for bed reminding one another not to get our hopes up as all decisions here seem made to be changed. But on Thursday morning, when the message to assemble at 9am came through, a definite frisson of anticipation shot through the centre. Perhaps it really was 'game on'.

I mentioned before about wondering if I should pray for Hela and how the lack of enthusiasm from others around the breakfast table left me a bit ruffled; I felt buffeted by negativity, doubt happily wafted over me and I felt ... out of sorts. Adam (who summoned us and oversees the organising of outreaches) just nonchalantly wandering in at 9.45 and keeping us waiting still longer whilst he caught up with his social diary

Saturday

did not help this feeling.

I felt as if hurdles to test us, in terms of process, were being erected in the face of an already huge day, as he demonstrated a complete disrespect of our time. Obviously those feelings were more to do with my apprehension and still trying to adjust to the event-based rather than time-oriented culture here.

I am here as a volunteer so in a way my time is theirs to waste as they please. It's just a colossal shift, Ma, and I do want to absorb the good parts about it. Not fretting about timing and clock watching would be a good start.

Eventually Adam joined us and as he went over the list of dos and don'ts and things to bring I was able to explain a few things to Lucie, which calmed me down a bit. We agreed we could share sun block and insect repellent. Adam motioned for us all to step outside the gates of the centre where immediately on the right-hand side is the container where all the camping kit belonging to Iris is stored. I expected there to be a powerful stink when he creaked open the big doors but just the usual cloud of dust wafted over us as tents, bedrolls and other well-used camping paraphernalia met the daylight.

Most visitors leave their camping equipment here deliberately and this is a giant container stacked with resource. (Similar to the shipping containers we used but much larger.) Those who haven't brought kit are able to rummage and everyone somehow emerges with all they need for the outreach.

I was thankful for Lucie's generosity with the tent and had brought Nathan's bedroll to sleep on. Lucie and I put our bits in a pile ready to go. She went off to do something with what was left of the morning and we parted with the exhortation to 'remember to eat whatever you may be offered on outreach and always take a friend when visiting the 'bath (hole in the ground) room' ringing in our ears. I couldn't settle to anything useful.

My emotions were in turmoil (surprise surprise). Half of me dreading the inevitable challenge; the other half in awe, stunned that God had made a way and I could well be on the cusp of a life experience many Christians only dream of.

Lunchtime came and went and we had been instructed to assemble near the main gate at 2pm. The sun is high then and the assembly area is about half a kilometre or more from our rooms. This cultural adjustment thing is still in progress but I couldn't help thinking we could easily have assembled near the centre and they could simply drive the vehicle up to us; and then I checked myself. Overheating and perspiration can easily influence one's perspective.

I thanked God aloud for the joy of a spare rubbish sack and the old cushion I had gleefully stuffed into it along with my pillow. Pillows are not on the list of things to bring but I have done enough camping to know my sleep is not enhanced by the zipper on a sweatshirt nipping my ear or the corner of a bag sticking in my neck. A pillow is good and I also had a plan to help alleviate the backache I got in the old cameon previously.

I was increasingly agitated though about how to physically get to the main gate with sufficient water supplies. We had been instructed as visitors to bring a supply for Mozambican Christians who would be joining us in the form of a local pastor and assistants.

I'm no wimp but with six 1 litre water bottles, a bedroll, change of

Saturday

clothes, basic wash kit and a kaftan to sleep in all to be carried to the main gate, I was challenged. I was also taking a couple of small tubs with leftover rice and beans for the same reason I had taken them to the clinic, and a muesli bar that one of the US team had left, sunscreen and of course tissues for every eventuality. Those baby-wipe things are marvellous. I didn't think of bringing any but the American team had packets left over and I am blessed but they are quite bulky.

Keep in mind that I am also in full boy scout mode and determined to be at the ready to repel all borders at any time. I can't pretend this is a pretty sight but ... safety first. I am wearing a long skirt with long-sleeved though lightweight top. Sunhat. Some reckless individuals are embarking on this expedition in shorts and flip-flops; not so this girl! Beneath my long skirt I have been deliberate and very thankful to have borrowed a pair of trusted leggings; a pair that reach right to my ankles. These are fetchingly tucked into the top of some socks; a pair of sturdy trainers finishes off the whole effect nicely.

As I was preparing to strap various bits of gear to my anatomy and use a backpack in order not to have to repeat the steamy trudge to the far-off assembly point, Gina appeared. In that moment, as she smiled and offered me help, she sprouted wings! (You remember she is the young woman here for 3 months offering childcare to a family working for Iris?) She was on outreach last week but has some kind of training day to attend so not able to come this week. She was a bit wistful when she learned Heidi was going but so warm and positive I felt my spirits lift slightly.

We walked together down to the assembly point near the main gate. I felt ashamed as I wrestled with my feelings and struggled in another hot, sticky wait, to get my attitude right. Gina had previously shared with me that she was unable to pray aloud. (You'd relate Ma? Nudge, nudge!) But I was desperate so I appealed to her to please pray for me. Sweet victory in the midst of upheaval as she bravely stepped over the line into breakthrough to pray peace over me and I immediately felt better.

Peace came but I'm sorry to say was quickly ruffled as 2.30 then 2.45 came and went. At 2.55 a throaty, basic lorry clawed its way over the dirt towards us. Behind the enclosed cab it had a deep back with an opening on either side in the canvas tarpaulin that enclosed the metal frame. I know by now that we all pile in but I wondered if I could just get a seat on the benches that would be under the 'windows' then I could prop myself so my back would have some support and hopefully I could be as forward facing as possible to alleviate travel sickness.

All the provisions and huge cooking utensils are stored in a shed at the assembly point and the loading into two vehicles is done by the team of Mozambicans who are coming to cook, build the fire, erect the movie screen, do the sound, etc. Our boxes of water and other bulky items are packed to hold things in place on the bumpy route. It makes obvious sense to have everyone gather with all luggage at the storage point; I do see that.

I was very glad of leggings and trainers as we clambered up into the back of the truck. Shock. No benches. Even in this vehicle, often used for very long journeys, someone had decided they had a better use for the planks that had served as primitive seats last time I looked. Grateful to be by one of the windows I wedged myself in between several bedrolls and sleeping bags that were stacked up and angled myself slightly to be facing the back of the front cab whilst still able to see out. Others clam-

Saturday

bered up. Some chose to sit on the floor and didn't seem to mind which direction they faced. Then we sat and baked while various discussions were had. Several things were unloaded and then reloaded.

A cheerful young man sprung into the back of our truck and introduced himself as our leader for this outreach. I knew a wave of relief as I recognised Micah, one of the men known to Nina. This link, albeit tenuous, offered me some reassurance. A number of the Mozambican team leapt in at the last moment and piled themselves on top of the stack of equipment that had gone in first and was now piled up behind the cab.

As this groaning hotchpotch on wheels lumbered past the guard and out of the main entrance I spoke to myself firmly and took a deep breath as I prayed. 'Lord Jesus, in spite of all my struggles I truly want your agenda for this trip.' Something rolled off my shoulders and out of the flapping window space. Peace at last.

It was 3.20 as the truck gained momentum and I welcomed a fresh lightness in my spirit. It would be getting dark in a couple of hours and I was really hoping we would get to wherever we were going to erect our tents and set up camp in daylight.

We had only been underway about four minutes when the driver pulled off into an area behind the line of *barracas* where we host Rahab. It's land Iris own (I think) and there is a collection of dwellings, many appearing in need of repair, where more Iris staff live. (The main base where I am staying is known as Village of Joy, Arcos Iris.)

There stood Sophie with a number of bags. There was a spot left in the driver's cab and blithely announcing that she would be our (as in 'the volunteer visitors' context) leader she hopped into the front beside Micah without looking back. Her self-assured confidence was almost stabilising in that moment though I don't think she has ever been to Pemba before so I wondered how this would play out on outreach. I suppose living in South Africa makes a difference.

It seemed we were finally getting underway. Various roadside stalls and *barracas* were in clusters along the route. A larger area on a junction had racks of garments hanging. It is a mystery to me how the white items are so white despite the dust and dirt. My attempts at laundry still leave my clothes ingrained with a rusty hue. Every now and again I see a man in a pristine white shirt. I have no idea how the women achieve it. Fruit and various knobbly shapes (could be vegetables?) are strung from multiple makeshift rails or branches along the way.

Just as I think we are now surely heading for our destination we swerve onto the forecourt of a petrol station. There appears to be a heated debate about which pump should be used. Sophie jumps out and boldly purchases something called 'cassava'. It is passed around for tasting but I am fasting till after the mountain of the evening ahead is conquered. The cassava was brown and looked like a deformed root, not dissimilar to fresh ginger; it is a nutty-flavoured, starchy tuber, which is popular for snacking here.

And then at last we really are on the way. As we hit the open road I waved goodbye to anxiety. As the driver put his foot down I clutched my glasses in one hand and clamped my hat on my head with the other as the delicious breeze coming through the gap in the canvas gained enthusiasm, chuckling amongst the motley crew of evangelists.

I feasted on the view as the willing truck steadily ate the kilometres. We passed the airport and seemed to be heading directly south on the tarmac. Mozambique unfurled like a beautiful, rolled-up tapestry with

Saturday

a multitude of colours and textures. I gazed at the blue-grey mountains always in the distance and decided, 'This is a God adventure. All will be well.'

As we trundled on, leaning around the sack pressing against him, Carl in perfect English introduced himself as the Mozambican pastor coming with us. He explained he was leading the outreach. (Three 'leaders' now so we were well covered!)

Someone unhelpfully shared a story from a previous outreach when his tent was slashed in the night. Since punching is not really an appropriate option on a mission trip, I managed to suppress a strong urge towards inappropriate body contact (the same one I get at home when some … person, feels the need to tell shark stories as we are on our way to the beach).

I wanted to stick my fingers in my ears but instead resorted to praying in tongues under my breath whilst studiously gazing out across the landscape. Divine intervention cut the tale short abruptly as with no warning the driver swerved left and hit the brakes. We were plunged unceremoniously into a heap and kept busy recovering as yet another Mozambican man hopped in to join us, exchanging cheerful greetings with the cooks as he almost landed on one of them.

In the swerve I crunched my cheekbone on the metal frame holding up the canvas and in true pioneering spirit ignored it, deliberately choosing to focus on offering heartfelt thanks to heaven that I was not feeling sick. There was one more stop for the men to disembark and reappear with a load of firewood, which joined us in the jolly jumble. We rumbled on. At one point we came to a halt near a turn off and a number of the Mozambican regulars debated directions. The decision was made that it was not the turn we were looking for so we continued on further along the main road.

At last we slowed to a crawl and then the driver swung right, into more of a gulley than a road. Rocks and sand, which was paler than the red sand around the base, scrunched under the wheels but the truck ploughed on. I noticed plenty of trees and lush green vegetation. We rounded a bend and were suddenly engulfed in a broiling cacophony of shrieking, grinning children all madly gesticulating and jumping up and down.

As the driver stopped the truck we were instructed to remain in the vehicle whilst the pastor and Micah went to check on the plan. Little bendy arms sprouting twig fingers were thrust at us through every available crack, hands wanting to touch. It was obvious we were expected. Visible through the back opening of the vehicle was a fence in the familiar woven bamboo, forming what looked like a small compound.

A man waded through the crowd of children and arrived at the rear of the truck. He pulled himself up and stood on the back bumper. (Not to mislead you, by 'back bumper', I mean the angular piece of metal protruding from the frame that we had used as a step to hoist ourselves up and into the truck.) As he perched he welcomed us to his village with a broad smile and introduced himself as the pastor of the local church. Iris has helped local Christians establish churches in many thousands of villages. Where possible they provide a simple church building as a focal point and place for gatherings.

The pastors, often fairly new Christians themselves, visit Pemba regularly for training. Rolland and Heidi have established a Bible Training School and numbers of pastors come in from the bush, often with their

Saturday

wives, for weeks of study and tuition. This regularly runs in tandem with the Iris Harvest School of Missions Training that attracts students from all around the globe. This runs twice a year. (Golly, can you imagine living here for almost three months, Ma? You'd have to be some kind of hardcore missions person ... Brilliant way of raising funds though as I gather students pay considerable fees. I understand every school has more applications than can be accommodated.)

We clambered to ground level and the pastor ushered us proudly into what was obviously a specially prepared compound just for us. The dirt had been swept and cleared of rocks for us to be able to put tents up easily. A small child, more inquisitive than the others, crept through the opening and into the compound where he was shouted at and chased out by the pastor.

He showed us a mud house, bigger than the average hut, which was empty so felt spacious. He indicated this was for storing all the cooking stuff and water supplies. I only learned later that this was in fact his home so I don't know where all his family were. So gracious and so keen for us to be there in his village they moved the whole family out.

In a flurry of activity the cooking equipment and firewood were unpacked and the cooks set to work building a roaring fire. I was so thankful it was still light enough to see any potential creeping visitors and get the tent up and firmly zipped. I had my head torch which has been a lifesaver on this trip but it's all much easier in daylight. I like to put my bits in the tent in a specific order so I know exactly where things are. Then I can reach in for tissues or insect repellent without opening up completely thus inhibiting anything flying or crawling past from diverting into my sleeping area. (I was going to write sleeping bag then but it's so warm I only used the actual bag in the hours just before dawn. I just brought a cotton single duvet cover from home. That way I am still 'closed in'.)

The sleeping mat borrowed from Nathan is thin but it cleverly inflates itself and I found it surprisingly comfortable. You use all your weight to expel the air as you roll it up in the morning. (I confess after all that happened the action of kneeling in the bush next morning and gradually forcing the air out took on proportions akin to that of a victory roll by a Spitfire but at this stage that was many hours hence.)

There was one lovely tree with spreading branches roughly in the centre of the compound and Micah instructed us girls to put our tents in a circle with the tree in the middle, then the boys put their tents around the outside of our circle.

Not far outside the enclosure the young men in charge of showing the Jesus film began setting up a generator and unpacking cables, plugs and lights. It all came together rather fast and suddenly sound was crackling into the night air. As the sun went down people morphed out of the darkness often only visible by the whites of their eyes or in the case of children their teeth. It was rather eerie ... how did so many people know we were there and what expectation did they bring with them?

In a far corner of the compound a smaller bamboo screen was erected and behind this a hole in the ground served as bathroom facilities. I wondered again why so often the latrine is situated on a rise; the bamboo is not solid and I'm always careful where I shine the lamp in the dark. I did survive and the idea of going with a friend definitely helps as their body acts as an extra shield. This was Lucie's first encounter but she too lives to tell the tale!

Things happened pretty rapidly from there. A crowd formed and

Saturday

as we emerged from the compound I was immediately waist deep in children wanting to touch me. Brushing any part of my anatomy they could reach they squeezed or patted and then passed on to the next team member. Some lingered a bit longer to nuzzle in.

One little girl pressed into me preventing me walking on. She reached to my sides for my arms and wrapped them around her bony little body. I just held her for several moments sensing love being sucked out of me. (By the way my knee is scabbing over nicely after that fall in the showers. And don't worry about infection as I am wiping it regularly with some of the anti bacterial wipes left by the team from the US.)

There was a tangible ache in the atmosphere around the small children and I recalled Sara telling us they are breastfed till they are two, which in this culture relieves the mums of the expectation they are available for sexual relations. Then they are handed on to a sibling for care, traditionally having no further physical contact with their mother. As a mum it was gut wrenching. I was bemused. I floundered in the weirdness of being greeted in a manner more suited to the Queen or Father Christmas.

The focal point was the truck, which was parked sideways on to the people and now had a screen suspended from the roof taking up the whole side. Suddenly the 'team' were summoned over the microphone by Carl and instructed to line up facing the crowd. In the glare of the huge spotlight I felt a rush of empathy with rabbits (and in that moment filled with just about the same level of blind paralysis).

We were told to introduce ourselves and a microphone was thrust into the hands of Ben who appeared to be a step ahead of me in the rabbit-shooting scenario. He rallied and taking a deep breath introduced himself then quickly turned to hand the microphone to Hela (mermaid)

Pemba Pennings

who said a great little speech about loving being in Mozambique and something about Jesus.

I was busy running my clammy palms down the sides of my damp body and wondering if heaven would have mercy and release the rapture right then. But instead the microphone relentlessly approached and found its way into my hand. In that moment I received a sharp nudge as Lucie, who was coming after me, helped me step forward. I have no idea Ma what actually came out of my mouth. But I was rehearsing something along the lines of how blessed I am to be on my first visit to Mozambique and how honoured I felt to be invited to their village.

As the last team member stepped back and the film soundtrack burst into life I thankfully melted into the nearest patch of darkness. Light from the screen flashed over the crowd illuminating bodies all squashed in, lying, sitting, standing and squatting all over the ground.

I had the impression of men hanging back slightly. They hovered in clusters around the outer edges as scenes from the Jesus film, with commentary in a language I didn't recognise, unfolded. Having felt so conspicuous (and to be honest downright uncomfortable) I was relieved to be able to melt into the blackness and sank gratefully onto the dirt with a small child on either hip. It's humbling and rather shocking to feel that just because I am white I am perceived as having some incredible capacity to meet need.

At some point the headlamps of an approaching vehicle flashed behind the truck. Peering over I could see a shimmer of pale skin. I wondered if Heidi was now among us and as the interior light flashed on was delighted to see a beaming Hela in the passenger seat. What would happen next?

Saturday

I squeezed another bony body that had draped itself across my lap and gained a measure of comfort in offering what I hoped felt like love. I don't know for how long but as time passed I was neck deep in a jacuzzi of bodies with small people wafting, touching, squeezing.

As the film seemed to be winding down I raked the shadows looking for Heidi's blonde head and staring again in the direction I thought she could be I discerned a new, uneven, hump-like outline rising from the ground. Was someone leaning over to pray for a sick person already? I decided to investigate and began pressing through the mass of limbs and torsos.

I hesitated, apprehensive, then spoke firmly to myself. I'd come this far; it would be mad to get here and then 'be British'. Galvanised by the thought that this could be it, I might just witness Heidi praying for the sick, even see a miracle, I pushed on till the hump-shaped mound became more clearly defined to reveal a pile of young boys with a pair of white feet protruding from beneath one end.

With a jolt I realised this was a scene from Heidi's writing. She was preparing to minister.

She was on her face in the dirt and the children who had come from the base with her were praying for her. I had heard that she always brings boys with her. I became aware of Annette standing quietly to the side. (I told you that Hela had recovered and had travelled with Heidi so she was already somewhere in the crowd.) The film ended, the boys parted and Heidi glided out from under the pile to gently take centre stage.

Heidi had the microphone and immediately asked that the spotlight be dimmed. It was blinding so prevented her from being able to see the people and it was duly adjusted. Then she indicated the rope cordon that

Pemba Pennings

formed a flimsy barrier separating her from the throng of eager bodies now visible and sitting expectantly in the dirt.

One of the young men involved with showing the film leapt to dismantle the cordon but was quieted by a signal from Heidi and withdrew. She greeted and blessed the crowd, then, with the backdrop of the frozen shot from the movie of Jesus wearing a crown of thorns, there was an energetic drama depicting the story of the Good Samaritan. The beating up of the poor unsuspecting traveller was clearly a favourite part of the story with both crowd and actors.

Heidi returned to the stage (which you'll appreciate was just the piece of dirt in front of the truck) as the drama ended. Then with an interpreter (that part is now a bit of a blur) I think Heidi spoke in Portuguese and Macua — anyway, a minor detail. Heidi gave a short talk about Jesus stopping for us and then dying for us and invited anybody who wanted to know Jesus to raise their hand.

My impression was a sea of hands responded; Heidi prayed a prayer and a rumble of voices repeated it. Then seemingly in the same breath as 'Amen' she turned in the general direction she had emerged from, 'All visitors join me here please. You are going to pray for the sick.' (Think … cliff edge Ma, no parachute … only Jesus!)

At that moment, as if by magic the rope cordon was no more and as we moved to join Heidi, a seething, black ocean of limbs enveloped us. As the tide swelled, wave after wave of need was building. Any hope of 'working in pairs' or imagining 'safety in numbers' immediately dissipated as the current swept in and each team member was caught in a rip. We were quickly separated.

Think I need to take a break Ma. So sorry. You may or may not

Saturday

understand once I recount the full story but right now I can't write anymore. I am fully trusting that this experience ... this process I find myself in, is really God and part of his intention in bringing me here, but right now it is so alien, touching something so deep down in me that I can't absorb, process or begin to evaluate, only be 'in the thing'. I need to pause and rest.

Love you so much. More when I can ... x

Saturday afternoon

Back again Ma.

As I was saying …

It was noisy, dusty and very hot. Need was a seething cauldron of desperation and I couldn't speak a word of language. It was chaos as people struggled to reach one of us or pushed their sick child towards the front. The pressure of bodies caused me to begin to lose balance but I was rudely up-righted by the weight of longing as the throng leaned in.

I wondered how Lucie was doing in this massive 'stepping out'. Uncomfortable physical contact was not an option as men pressed in. It was potentially intimidating and not a bit like church. I don't know how long I stood there or what I must have looked like but a less than gentle nudge from one of the Iris team with the directive 'start praying' galvanised me into a state of suppressed panic.

ME! What could I offer? How did all these people suddenly think their needs were going to be met? I've never healed anyone. Not in the direct supernatural way that was obviously expected. A glimpse of Ben

Saturday afternoon

looking pale and moist eyed across the mass of bodies let me know I was not alone on the edge of a deep chasm of overwhelmedness! Self-talk needed. 'Deep breath, Haze. Jesus, it's all about you.'

I was immediately nose-to-nose with a teenager with one blind eye. I laid my hands on his head trusting something from heaven would flow through me into his body and prayed in tongues. I prayed in tongues as if my next breath depended on it. An older team member was suddenly beside me. He began praying as a parent pushed a small boy wearing a blue beanie into my legs and indicated he was deaf and dumb. I didn't see who prayed for him.

I suddenly felt a strong urge to be nearer to Heidi. Over my right shoulder, back towards the truck, I became aware she was with a young girl. I pushed in her direction as one of the regulars on the team grabbed the microphone to bring a word of knowledge, 'Is anyone here troubled by an evil spirit? Come forward. Jesus will heal you now.' There was a collective thrust as many people fought their way forward to respond. We had been told that the people are all familiar with the supernatural and witch doctors' curses are common.

I backed towards the truck and then could see Heidi clearly. She was sitting down now, perched on the truck step with a young girl who was wearing a pink dress in her lap. Heidi held her close and closed her eyes as she leaned over the skinny little body. I inched closer. There were only a few people in the space between us now. I held my breath and was frozen in that moment. Was I about to witness a miracle? Heidi opened her eyes and spoke to the little girl. The child appeared rather dazed and … replied!!

I stood transfixed, eyes glued to the tableau unfolding right in front of me. A man was hustled out of the throng and yes, he confirmed he was the girl's father and yes, she was totally deaf. Was she born deaf? Was it an untreated infection? Trauma? Was she dumb as well? I have no idea! The luxury of questions nowhere in sight, I just stood under the stars; awed.

I caught my breath as the healing was announced over the microphone and also the little boy in the blue beanie was now hearing and speaking. I anticipated a riot of hallelujahs and outrageous applause but the seething mass didn't even pause for breath. The clamouring for prayer just continued unabated. I whooped and threw my arms in the air. I couldn't help it! I caught Heidi's eye and mouthed 'Brilliant!' She smiled back.

No time to ponder. Urgent hands were patting my back and pulling at my clothes asking me to lay hands and pray. Quietly emboldened, Jesus is here! Another deep breath, no fear, I gently placed my hands on the nearest head, then moved to placing my hands on separate heads as even though people tended to move slightly after prayer, the number pressing forward gave no hint of diminishing. I found myself praying blessing, releasing hope and courage and resource (I didn't fully realise until later that many had just given their lives to Jesus a few minutes earlier). God's presence was tangible as I spoke healing and wholeness into people who had no other hope.

I felt about two-inches tall and time stood still. I didn't (and don't) know if there is a right or wrong way to do it. I know Jesus prayed for his Father's will to be done 'on earth as it is in heaven', where I'm certain poverty, distress and sickness are conspicuous by their absence. I have felt myself growing in boldness and authority in recent weeks as this truth takes root in my life. What was God doing? Mostly I have no idea

Saturday afternoon

BUT he was there. There was no possible chance of 'feedback' with no language and so many people. Those who received prayer were visibly at peace and looked relieved, lighter somehow after being prayed for.

Determined to reach the front, many only children themselves, pushed younger ones into me. Hoisting them up to my waist level and pointing fiercely at a swollen tummy or some other part of the child's anatomy. I felt equally desperate to comprehend but could only continue blessing and praying in tongues trusting their heavenly Father would meet them. And all the while dust hovered. We were all suspended in a pink mist.

I just have to stop for a bit Ma; tears come with the vivid memory. The well of need was bottomless and sensing God flowing through my grubby, sticky body, totally humbling whilst at the same time, as though 'commissioning' me, as a daughter of the King, to love and serve the poor on his planet ... too much.

Monday morning

Hello again Ma,

Sorry about the gap ...

Can hardly believe it, only a few days left now. I didn't write more over the weekend. Such a deep thing happened in me on the outreach I feel I am in recovery and then God has touched me again as I read and pray. And then also in church yesterday.

I really want to try and finish telling you about outreach.

As I continued laying hands on people love flowed. It was literally as if I was in a river of liquid love, it was flowing through me to meet need. I knew in that moment that God is enough. He brought me across the world and I wanted to faithfully embrace the whole encounter (never mind the entire thing feeling like a complete 'out of body experience'). I pressed on, totally in awe of being part of a scene I had read about in Heidi's books.

One of the older men in the team came beside me commenting, 'You're obviously used to this ...' (I know! Outrageous or what?) I al-

Monday morning

lowed myself a rueful chuckle, made some kind of response and pressed on. As each person received prayer they seemed to melt away and then four more pairs of pleading dark eyes moved into the space. Wave after wave after wave. Then Heidi's voice over the microphone.

One of the young boys with her, he looked about ten, had a word of knowledge, healing for stomachs. 'Team, please come with any words of knowledge.' Immediately, out of nowhere, I had thoughts about AJ. It's very hard observing changes in a brother who has a life-limiting blood disorder but probably doesn't believe God would touch his body. I remembered a particular time his cells were all out of balance and we prayed and the next blood test results were in normal range. God did it.

Crushing the immediate unbidden thought, 'I can't possibly bring a word of knowledge … ' I reached over to grab one of Heidi's assistants and shouted by his ear to be heard above the clamour of the night. The word of knowledge was given out in Portuguese. I wasn't aware of any response and could only clearly see those immediately in the glare of the trusty spotlight.

Then it struck me. If anyone did have a blood disorder how in the world could they know? They surely wouldn't have a district nurse popping round to do blood tests. No time to dwell on that. More laying on of hands as the crowd stretched back as far as ever.

After what seemed like a few more minutes, Heidi was on the mic saying we needed to stop. I had no idea of the time but clearly much longer passed than I was aware. Immediately a human cordon of local people, presumably primed, was pushing the crowd back.

We were ushered deliberately behind the truck and into a tiny hut. By torchlight we could just make out seating. Pews! They were simple bamboo fabrications and then at one end of the oblong hut a mud step formed a small platform. This must be the church then.

Indecision was in the atmosphere and I think a time of prayer and sharing testimony may have been planned but we were not alone. A lady with a tormenting spirit had responded to the word of knowledge and was causing disruption in one corner as some of the team prayed. I had a million and one questions for the 'feedback time' but Heidi immediately shepherded us back to the little compound where a large vat of spaghetti simmered over a campfire.

There was a vague smell of fish. Those returning from outreach last week chatted about quantities of oil being used. My stomach was all churn from the night's events so I was thankful to sink to the ground in the deep shadows and savour the familiarity of my cold rice and beans.

Heidi moved quietly from one to another, often hugging one of the boys who were never far from her. I suddenly remembered I had taken a number of glow-sticks as gifts and asked Heidi if I could offer them to the boys. They loved them and ran around waving them excitedly in the dark.

Around me the familiar plastic plates loaded with mounds of glistening, slippery spaghetti and tuna were hungrily being devoured. It felt utterly surreal yet somehow completely natural to be sitting in the dirt around a fire, chatting with Heidi as she asked me about challenges faced by homeless people in Exeter.

The boys capered about as the hardworking cooks began clearing up. People gradually melted away and headed for their tents. Lucie doesn't eat fish so had brought something else to snack on and having eaten we decided to hunker down ourselves. We stood on guard for each other on

Monday morning

a final toilet stop and then used those large baby wipes on our hands and feet to shift the top layer of dust at least. I had a final peak at the stars and thought with longing of the outback and the Southern Cross before firmly zipping all fastenings. Thank you Jesus. What a night.

Lucie's tent is a compact three-man so quite comfy for two with a small backpack each. As we lay down, the cooks, having cleared up, were enjoying some downtime and I drifted off to sleep to unrestrained chuckles as they teased each other.

A first for me, I slept in leggings but bravely removed socks and trainers! My kaftan was adequate cover till the early hours when I covered myself loosely with the sleeping bag. Each time I surfaced I found myself thanking Jesus and marvelling that children who were deaf yesterday could hear today. I felt I was literally glowing with praise; no words or thoughts of gratitude seemed adequate!

How can life be the same? I was physically standing there Ma, as the impossible happened. Waking at dawn I heard a cock crowing and wondered how it would feel to hear that sound for the very first time?

As we headed for bed, word had gone around that church would be held at 6am. I felt excited about what that was going to be like, especially after so many miracles.

The initial start to the new day was bathed in peace. A soft clear light stole over us as birds sang, water burbled on the fire and we pottered about greeting one another, each slipping away to find a space to clean our teeth and rinse freely into the scrub. I heard various ones congratulating each other as if they'd survived shipwreck rather than a night under canvas.

Once it was daylight I could clearly see one of the large plastic bins

Pemba Pennings

(like the ones I told you about in our showers at the visitors' centre) with plastic mug handles poking out. Beside it sat boxes of bread rolls that had come with us. Stacked in the truck I had watched flies visit them eagerly as we travelled.

I was praying earnestly about food Ma. It was a given that any food offered in the village was to be gratefully received and eaten. Refusing this honour is not an option and would be very rude. I had brought a cereal bar and was anxiously praying I would not be offered any local fare. (I know ... trusting God ... but only to a point. SO much to learn.)

Tents were rapidly dismantled and piled compactly in full view with a 'guard'. It is impossible to gauge the feelings of a person who has literally nothing viewing a whole pile of items, which could change their lives if obtained, piled up under a tree right there in their own world. Tents are valuable commodities here. Items commonly go missing on outreach.

As we cleared our camping gear the empty space was quickly filled with a large tarpaulin. It was laid out on the ground in front of the pastor's house, which had a narrow, mud sort of shelf acting as a walkway-come-veranda around part of it. As if responding to some invisible piper, dozens of children began to file in from the far corners of the village and seat themselves on the tarp. In the background I noticed the cooks were busy as piles of bread rolls were spread with red jam.

An energetic young man held the children's attention as with great enthusiasm he got going on a string of children's choruses, all with actions that felt far too strenuous for 6.40am! I was thrilled to see the blue beanie in the second row as the little boy from the previous evening did his best to join in.

I moved to the back of the rows and sat on the ground amongst the

Monday morning

older girls and women who had congregated. Many had babies with them. Siblings? Their own? Orphans? The perturbation I felt dislodged something in my core as I gazed on the ocean of unloved, hungry, hollow womanhood in front of me. Many of the older girls, hardly teenagers, had haunted, expressionless eyes.

I possibly looked just like myself but inside deep disruption quivered and a paradigm shifted. Heidi told a story based on John 15 using a tree as a visual aid. Then 'church' was over.

There was movement in front of the hut. A variety of things that could be sat on comprising of two plastic chairs, a rustic-looking bench (the word 'sturdy' not springing to mind), and a three-legged wooden stool appeared to form a rough line on the mud shelf serving as a veranda.

Heidi disappeared at this point and I wondered if she had slipped away to return to the base but was told she had gone to locate the chief in order to honour him. No more information was offered so I was left wondering what 'honouring the chief' would look like. Perhaps she had taken gifts to his hut?

There was a general milling as slabs of bread and jam were hungrily devoured. I guess the children know the routine: they attend 'church' and then they get fed. Heidi often speaks about 'fresh bread' and the children received both kinds. More adults from the village joined the gathering.

Some while later Heidi came walking into the compound from the rear corner. She was at the head of a line of people, a rather motley looking crew. All eyes were on her as she escorted an elderly but upright gentleman in full military regalia. I learned this was a general's uniform from the war — yes, that would be the one that ended in 1975! This was clearly a very important occasion for him. Just behind him were two women in bright *kapalanas* and elaborate headscarves. Then followed several men in a mixture of western and Mozambican dress.

As these dignitaries settled themselves on the various seats now facing us Heidi moved among us visitors. As we sat on the ground she bent down and explained the 'General' is the king of the village (which was spread over a considerable geographical area) and we were going to honour him. She stated that meant each of us visitors would be individually 'presented'.

The women in the entourage were his wives, one of them being his queen, and the men were local elders. I think one was also the pastor but I couldn't be certain. I find it so hard to determine individual features. I wonder if other nations find our white faces equally confusing? Heidi told us to just remember, 'go low and go slow'. 'Low,' she elaborated, meaning be careful to be lower than the king at all times, 'being sure to support your right hand with your left as this is a sign of humility.' She quickly made some motion with one arm supported at the elbow by the other.

Anticipation (or raw tension in the case of yours truly) was mounting. I could feel my upper lip growing very damp as beads of nervous perspiration formed. Right under left? Left over right? Which was it again? Was this to do with bottom wiping and eating hands? Was it a custom that carried a penalty if muddled? What if I let the team down?

I felt a knot in my stomach and my breakfast muesli bar froze in position. Ben started to show me the posture but I could see three of him. I vaguely became aware of Sophie glowing with purpose and belonging

Monday morning

as she took up position at the king's shoulder. Heidi had asked her to translate. Fluent in Portuguese, she is a very useful visitor.

My heart sank as two more men joined the greeting line causing everyone to move along as a very low daybed was added for seating. I would have to be on my stomach. How would I get along the long line on my knees without flashing a thigh albeit a legginged one? How would I know what to say? I'm bound to blow it. Heidi will be disappointed. Oh Lord, please beam me up now!

The children pressed around me wanting to hold a hand, stroke an arm. My heart ached. Runny noses and coughs at every turn. They need your love Lord. I felt an urge to rush into the little church and left the compound. I met one of Heidi's boys who I'd noticed was coughing and coughing. I stood to the side with him and offered to pray healing from the chest infection, after which he said he felt better. I left him to slip into the cool dusk inside the little church.

I perched on the end of a 'pew', emotions reeling. I noticed some old tins on the basic table that served as an altar and thought sadly, 'more litter', then seeing a few bedraggled brown stems in one realised they were being used as vases. (Imagine being so poor the only receptacle you have for flowers is an old tin you salvaged, most likely from someone else's rubbish; unthinkable.)

I lingered but no angel appeared to rescue me, make me invisible or even turn me into a lizard, which would at least have meant I could hide (eat your heart out Cinderella!). I reluctantly emerged. Right outside, Heidi was sitting in her vehicle with the door wide open. She appeared to be searching the front footwell. It seemed natural to ask if she was okay.

Pemba Pennings

Heidi shrugged and explained she had been robbed and her phone (surely a lifeline?) and an amount of money were gone. Yes, she said, the vehicle had been locked overnight and only one of her team (Mozambican) had access to the keys. I felt physically sick that someone close to her had taken advantage, but she said it happens. She locked the door and went to rejoin the gathering leaving me feeling violated by being so close to robbery.

What might it be like living on the front line yet not being able to trust those close to you? How do you absorb betrayal and skip on with your day? I noticed the little book *Jesus Calling* between the front seats in the Land Rover and thought to myself that I must give using that little book another try. I didn't click with it when I last tried to read it. Must have something if Heidi finds it a blessing. You use it too don't you Ma? It made me think of you anyway but the thought was almost a pain as I thrashed around internally longing for something to stabilise me.

I don't think I can find words to really describe what it feels like to be surrounded by people who have literally NOTHING and for some mysterious reason are happy that I am here in their village. I have no idea what appropriate emotions are but I felt stretched way beyond my capacity. The caring was a physical sensation that threatened to crush the breath out of my chest.

As I stood beside the vehicle I was adrift. I was jolted by one of the team grabbing my arm, 'Ben needs that little first aid kit you brought. There is a boy with an infected dog bite on his leg.' Wordless I followed the voice to the pile of bags and tents and retrieved the first aid kit. I handed it over, briefly wondering how Ben's medical heart was managing all this. The imprint of him, white with shock, fending off body parts as

Monday morning

he swayed waist deep in the black sea was still clear in my mind. (Think fully British, Ma!)

I joined other team members and tucked in on the edge of the seated throng. Focus was now on those seated in front of us as Heidi presented gifts and gave a little speech. The 'General' received a pair of reading glasses (the plastic ones we all buy in Walmart, Tesco and Coles). Well, maybe not exactly like we buy; the frame of this particular pair was black and white zebra stripe with diamante studs. The king was delighted and proudly put them on grinning with pleasure. I don't recall seeing him again without them.

As I desperately tried to extrapolate some vague shred of normalcy from my situation, this vision of glamorous bling atop a full military uniform, on an ecstatic Mozambican king, in the bush, did nothing to help me. Incongruity beyond my mental capacity to process.

Along the line the other important leaders accepted gifts of *kapalanas* and fruit. In return Heidi was presented with a live chicken (received with all the pleasure and appreciation of a person being gifted a ready-to-go garlic and lemon rotisserie chicken for their lunch) and some peanuts. (We're not talking Planters' roasted and salted; these were the real kind in their shells, lovingly wrapped in a bit of sacking.) How can these people offer gifts? They have nothing. I felt a catch in my throat and stood up dazed.

I missed the next bit of the proceedings as I was distracted by the appearance of our cooks entering upstage right. On an invisible cue they staggered out of the hut, and came around from behind the king to take up their position centre stage. The staggering was due to the weight of a vat of hot tea that slurped and sloshed between them. A third young man was behind them lugging the same old blue bin again full of the plastic beakers (presumably 'washed up' behind the scenes?).

But what really had my attention was a mirage involving objects that were exactly the same shape as cafetières and a number of plump packets. Coffee? My brain couldn't compute. Heidi announced that we would like to honour the king, queen and elders now by offering them a drink of tea or coffee.

It wasn't a mirage! The packets actually bore the word 'Starbucks'. Lunging towards the lifeline that was suddenly thrown I arrived beside the packets and heard myself offering to help serve the drinks. Pouring tea and coffee? Serving? What mercy! This I can most definitely manage.

Heidi smiled sweetly (could she read the panic behind my sunglasses?). She explained that she likes to honour local dignitaries, such as those in the line, and especially the visitors by serving them herself. She took a moment to say how wonderfully helpful it is for her work that people (like me) willingly come from all around the world. The local people consider it a huge indication of favour when foreigners visit their region. Fortunately she continued right on pouring, leaving no space for comment. I was speechless.

Imagine, Ma: absorbed by my preoccupation with how huge the trip felt for *me* ... I know, ' ... me, me, me' you could be forgiven for thinking. It had just never occurred to me that this could be a holy opportunity to be making a valid contribution to what God is doing. The whole western mindset of a person 'getting to go to Pemba' and the real need for me to grit my teeth, punch fear in the face and take a step of obedience, somehow muddied the opportunity for any servant-heart thinking. I sense a permanent shift unfolding in the way I think, Ma. I guess when we see fruit I will know it's Jesus.

Monday morning

I think I spluttered the word 'Starbucks?' as Heidi continued, 'It's a tradition on bush outreach that I like to bless all visitors with a cup of Starbucks coffee.' I nodded dumbly. I was at a loss as the rope of familiarity fleetingly thrown over the side was swiftly reeled in. Once again I was madly paddling to stay afloat without a whiff of a single lifeboat on the horizon.

Now my focus was on the beakers cheerily swilling around in the bin with flies and ants happily coming and going as multiple inquisitive little fingers reached in. This was the doorway to coffee but would it be safe? Too late. Heidi thrust a beaker into my hand.

I gawped as the king requested no less than eight... yes, that is 8 spoons of sugar in his tea and along the line four spoons was the minimum request. My brain wrestled in vain to find the 'Starbucks' shaped pigeonhole. It was futile. I was still trying to process the 'giving' of the chicken and nuts and asking what could possibly motivate this incredible, costly generosity?

I took the few steps back to where I had been sitting and sank to the ground to savour my coffee and try to think what on earth I was going to say when introduced. My mind was stretched blank by the overload. Sophie was in her element and doing a great job as the slow process of introductions began.

The fifth man in line wanted Lucie's telephone number. The man next to him wondered if Hela would like to be his wife. I gazed at Heidi smiling and chatting, freshly robbed by someone she loved. I gazed out over the people sitting in the dirt. Babies crying, women with faraway faces, children aching for affection, girls who should have been in school sitting with babies on their backs and a toddler in tow, childhood over. And what lay ahead? More of the same with the pressure of finding a man (several to be safe) who would share his food in exchange for her body, leaving her with more babies to rear. Where are you, Lord? How can you bear it?

Something in the core of me trembled. I was aware of a visitor on one knee at the front explaining adamantly that she did not want to part with her watch. My head was swirling. A voice beside me placed my hand on Heidi's handbag 'for safe keeping'. I clutched it trying to keep my balance even though I was sitting down.

The need in the atmosphere hurt my chest. Heidi came by and gently placing her hand on my shoulder she again said something kind and appreciative about the value of visitors coming to the bush like this, and the great help it is because it is such an honour for the villagers.

Shem was suddenly crouching down. Built like a rugby player, solid, he squatted filling my horizon. A shining smile and a gentle question,

'How do you find visiting my village?'

A strange sensation rumbled at the back of my throat. Heidi retrieved her bag and slipped away.

The padlock on the door of emotion ruptured. I don't know which happened first but tears gushed and I was aware of an eerie sound. As muscled arms reached out I realised the sound was me … wailing. I could only sob and tremble. As Shem quietly prayed in tongues I felt I was being pressed into God's chest.

I was overcome with uncontrollable, rasping pain. At one point I was aware of this sensitive stranger even wiping my wet face with his shirt. He just kept praying and holding me as if western females fall apart all over him at breakfast every day. His quiet strength held me back from a yawning chasm. Bleak, dark, endless need. So much sickness, hunger,

Monday morning

longing eyes, lonely women, children, children, children everywhere. I was choking.

I was totally overwhelmed right there in the dirt surrounded by people ... Talk about 'un-British', embarrassing, humbling (whoa Ma ... just realising as I write that those are exactly the things from Heidi's story that bothered me from that book I told you about ...) My nose was streaming, tears splashing and sobs and groans that seemed to go on for ages. As if an invisible dam had burst and I was utterly helpless. I could literally do nothing but let each wave of emotion erupt and wash out of me.

At some point Shem gently withdrew saying he was sorry but he had to leave. Eventually the eruption settled and I could get my breath. Then I sat with my head down for ages wishing the earth could swallow me. Surely everybody must be staring. I felt I had made a total exhibition of myself.

Then gradually I became aware that everyone was carrying on, introductions were well underway, people were milling around. In that moment I had a strange sensation, as if I had been in a bubble and invisible to all around. It was a deep, intensely personal experience that felt totally spiritual. I know it sounds peculiar Ma, unfamiliar in terms of 'the normal Christian life' and I haven't got it sorted in my head yet, but something profound happened in those moments and I sense it's to do with a deeper yielding.

I didn't feel as if I could stop the wave but I have been praying and asking God to take me deeper, what if this experience is part of him allowing me to feel his heart for the poor? Maybe I prayed myself into it? I've got that Aslan feeling again, you know, 'good but not safe!' It's all still raw Ma: I feel bruised but peaceful, hope-filled somehow.

I'm trusting I will understand more as the days unfold. I think God is starting to show me his wildness and it's totally alluring. It feels momentous; though much of it remains unquantifiable ... I have heard the Americans speaking about 'being wrecked'; I wonder if this is what they mean?

One of the other visitors gently leaned in to ask if I was okay. I was dazed and never felt less equipped to meet a king and queen. My turn to be presented. I have no idea Ma what I looked like or what I said. Somewhere along the line one of the men asked for my cap (I am being careful to always cover my head, as it's so easy to get heat stroke here) and I dumbly handed it over.

At the end of the line I could sense some tension; something about there not being enough gifts. A couple of men joined the line late, didn't they? I don't know the detail but I got to the end of the introductions and just hovered, still on my knees from shuffling along the line and 'going low'.

All around me jovial people were gathering. The pastor and his wife smiled and laughed with Lucie. Other happy members of their congregation chatted with team members. Just me trapped in a bubble, disorientated, unable to communicate, with no language. I loitered with no sense of direction. I felt weak-kneed and more than a little limp around the edges.

Earlier there had been talk of 'house-to-house visiting'. That surely won't be happening now? What about food and water? Half bottle of water left. I had eaten, drunk or given away the rest of my supplies.

I became aware the crowd of children had dissipated but as I looked,

Monday morning

adults approaching in ones, twos and small groups were replacing them. Some had a child in their arms. What were they doing? Nothing made sense. I was just thinking that we should soon be following Heidi back to base when Lucie slipped her arm through mine and gently said, 'Come on, let's pray. The pastor wants us to start over there.'

I meekly followed where she led, briefly thinking I must find shade as my now cap-less head was throbbing. I was definitely feeling the impact of the five calls to prayer that had pierced the tent at 4am. Does the average Muslim really get up and do the prayers each day? No time to ponder.

A man with a small child pushed his daughter abruptly into my personal space, protruding abdomen first. He indicated he would like prayer for her. All resistance had been flushed out of me as if the yielding had cleared the way for a torrent of compassion. (I can see this now Ma. In the moment I could do nothing but surf the love wave.) As people kept coming I prayed as though my life were at risk. Inviting heaven to invade body after body with healing power and love that would sustain. Yet again I ached for language, for meaningful communication.

A teenage girl came with a swollen cheek and severe toothache. It must have been a dental abscess. I will never forget the one I had when we were travelling. We were visiting Uluru, do you remember? I was watching the clock for my next painkiller dreading that the terrible pain might break through. But I did know a dentist would be at the end of the trip and I was on antibiotics. This scenario with no hope of relief? Unthinkable.

I prayed fervently in tongues and with help asked if it was any better. Her father shook his head as he shifted his weight to support the girl who was clearly unwell. I prayed for another few minutes. Any improvement? No. Another shake of the head. I went again, 'Lord, it cannot be your intention for this lovely young girl to suffer in this painful way. I command infection to leave and pain to go now in Jesus' mighty name.' I lapsed back into tongues knowing I was praying in accordance with his will. A fourth shake of the head and I grabbed Lucie. 'Please can we pray together in tongues. This girl has pain and infection in her mouth.' I don't know how many minutes passed but joy oh joy, when I looked again into the face of the young woman she smiled and indicated the pain had gone. (Interesting, hey Ma? 5 times I prayed.)

No time to gape in wonder or dance around the compound but we clapped our hands and laughed aloud as she walked calmly away beside her father. An older but not elderly lady hobbled towards us. Every step looked absolute agony. As she reached me she bent down and lifted her *kapalana* to reveal knees that resembled small melons.

I wondered if untreated arthritic knees blow up like this. They were red and inflamed looking. And so swollen. In a moment I thought of all the physical chores this lady would face in a day. Fetching and carrying water, sweeping her hut, all food preparation and cooking done at ground level, the list goes on. How in the world could she manage it all and in such obvious pain? How was she surviving?

I don't know how far she had walked but tears came as I realised this woman was placing hope in us. I knelt in the dirt and indicated I would like to lay my hands on her knees. With her permission I gently did so. Praying in tongues I let love flow. I was spent. 'Lord, I have nothing to offer this beautiful woman but she is your daughter, reaching out for help and you can make these knees well. I speak to swelling and inflammation

Monday morning

— Go.' More fervent tongues. I stopped and indicated she should move her knees, try to bend her legs.

Gingerly at first she slowly bent one knee and then the other. (Ma, it was so incredible. Heaven literally kissed earth!) Her weatherworn face crinkled up as she smiled. Light came into her eyes. She did it again but lifted them higher this time and then ... honestly Ma ... she did a little hop, skip and a jump kind of movement and simply danced away back in the direction she had come from. I know ... mind-boggling!! Wonderful. Fantastic. Amazing Jesus.

There were other people pressing in for prayer but suddenly we were herded into two groups and told to go round the village to pray for those unable to leave their huts, and not to take longer than two hours. I remember thinking, a time limit? Not very African.

This was the moment the pastor had been really moving towards and he was visibly excited. He took one group and strode off towards a cluster of huts. (Thinking about it I guess if a bunch of people, known to carry power to heal and deliver, came to our town and offered to pray for the sick we would get pretty excited. And we typically have access to doctors, healing rooms and 24-hour pharmacies in some places.)

I was in the second group with Carlos who could translate. I felt like a leaf caught in the draught as the group set off. What God had just done was so above and beyond I had no reference point. All I could do was float in the wake as the group began seeking out sick people. I clutched the few swallows of water that I had left to my chest and followed.

The group came to a halt in front of a woman who squatted in front of her hut holding a small, limp child on her lap. A couple of the team laid hands on the little one and I'm sure they prayed (I was so dazed by what had happened I felt not fully awake, with every sense heightened but somehow out of focus) and then we moved on. Carlos led us to an older Muslim man wearing a skull cap. He was in a chair by his home and looked weak. Again he was prayed for.

As I turned to keep up with the group I spotted a listless child lying outside a hut on one of the low daybeds. As I approached I could see the little boy was burning up with fever. He must have been feeling totally wretched in the searing heat. His mother hovered in the doorway of the hut as I approached. I must have indicated that I would like to pray and she nodded.

Diarrhoea and dehydration are common. I felt prompted to offer the boy some sips of my water. I felt so desperate for him to feel better I would happily have given everything I stood up in but mercifully the Holy Spirit only said 'water bottle!' I prayed in tongues and was so relieved when his body cooled under my hands. Isn't that fantastic Ma? I don't think any food was in the offing but I felt to keep moving and looking around I saw the group had moved on quite a way.

As I approached everyone had their backs to me and I could see they were clustered around a man who looked somewhere in his 30's though, as I've said, I find it so hard to guess ages. He was sitting on a baked-earth step under a flimsy porch-like construct on the side of his hut. His feet were together, his knees splayed open and his upper body hunched over.

As I walked towards the group I could see straight through a gap in the bodies clustered around him. His shoulders were heaving. He was working hard to breathe. He raised his head as I approached and staring eyes locked with mine.

Monday morning

In that moment I suddenly remembered (Holy Spirit brought to mind) reading a story in one of John Eldredge's books, about three women away together, I think on a prayer retreat. One of them out of nowhere suffered a bad asthma attack, which the others recognised as enemy activity. Still a little distance from the back of the group I stopped where I was. In a quiet yet authoritative voice I rebuked the afflicting spirit and commanded it to leave in Jesus' name. The man immediately stood up, flung his arms wide and grinning broadly demonstrated to the group that he could breathe normally. I know Ma, awesome, wonderful … off the charts.

I only fleetingly registered this miracle as my thigh was being nudged. I looked down to find a young girl beside me. She pushed a small boy into me pointing very intentionally at his head. Then I saw a rivulet of yellow pus flowing out of his left ear. Some was congealed on his little cheek and more flowed freely. (More tears as I write Ma; how much pain must he have suffered with an infection like that? No wonder so many children here suffer deafness. Living in an antibiotic-free zone … it's unimaginable.) Flies collected ecstatically in tears and gunk stuck in the corner of his eyes. I prayed, aching to swab it clean and to see the cloud of pain lift from his face. I presume the little girl was his sister. Her eyes were pleading. She wanted his suffering to end. What a weight for a small girl.

My mother's heart cracked again. And then unbidden I was caught in another wave of — I can't quantify what Ma — emotion, compassion, empathy, longing, heartbreak? Whatever God was doing, I was weeping again. I had to blindly stumble away. I ploughed through scorching soft sand in what I thought must be the vague direction of the truck.

Pemba Pennings

Head down, my red scarf around my shoulders and pulled up over my head shielding me from the sun with my long skirt flapping. I was hot and dirty. I had the peculiar sensation of being in some kind of biblical scene. Staggering blindly I had to get away. Then I was suddenly aware someone had fallen in step beside me. My head was bowed. All I saw were blue canvas sneakers as gentle hands, wordless, touched my shoulder and my elbow.

I let kindness gently guide me till I could clutch the back of the waiting truck. I clambered in and hunkered down against the piles of loaded gear. I never saw the face that went with those sneakers and have no idea who it was, where they came from or went to. What was the matter with me, I wondered? How are all the others just able to carry on? Was this what Heidi meant? Could this be the 'wrecked' they all talk about? I felt a total wreck and must definitely have looked like one. Still in process Ma, can't tell you any better than that. Perhaps time will bring enlightenment. I am wrung out, spent.

Naturally departure was protracted. There was considerable debate over where the chicken would best travel. It was understood that Heidi would bless someone with it once we got it back (as a meal I presume, as it was a cockerel). That said, it was a mystery to me why the poor thing had to suffer the whole journey either strung up with its legs tied together or being passed around as the cooks had a bit of fun.

As children flocked around we were waiting for two women who hadn't come with us but who would be riding home in the truck. At last they joined us happily sitting on the floor amidst boxes, random bags and our accumulated gear.

As we pulled away the children began running around the vehicle,

Monday morning

some attempted to hang on the back for a few moments before dropping to the ground laughing midst cheers from their friends. We kept grinding slowly towards the road and as we approached the turning, without warning, a man leapt into the back of the truck. It startled those sitting by the opening but there was a collective relaxing of shoulders as one of the women greeted him like a long-lost brother. With their delighted cackles of laughter rattling around the truck and children still scampering to wave us off we pulled onto the tarmac and began the long journey back.

You'd think that nothing more could possibly fit into one 24-hour outing, but there was more. I might get time this evening to tell you about it. I still have to catch you up on the weekend Ma. I know this is really long but it feels so important I couldn't just leave it out. I do feel I can never be the same again but it may be some while before I can begin to quantify the impact of this whole experience. Trusting my heavenly Dad. Let's face it. This entire trip was all his idea!

I love you very much x x x

Monday evening

Hello, Hello Darling Mama,

Before I get into the weekend news I will just finish off the outreach journey.

At some point the man who appeared to have hitched a ride at the last minute hopped out. (The truck did pull in and slow to a brief halt for him to get out, unlike when he joined us.) The journey is a bit of a blur for me. I was wrung out.

I was aware of chat going on around me and in one of the 'pass the chicken' games closed my eyes and hoped fervently its scaly feet were not going to get caught in my hair. (Sis would've been beside herself!) On more than one occasion in the last few weeks I have thought 'if only they could see me now ... ' but by this time my internal engine was seized. (What do they call it when a car blows up? Is it when the head gasket blows?)

Remember I told you we drove out past Mieze where I was at the clinic with Hannes? So when we got back to that same piece of road,

Monday evening

the driver just turned in and standing there in front of the clinic building was Hannes himself. He was waving his arms as we turned off the road. I think the driver was dropping something off. I thought Hannes looked anxious. I wondered what he was doing there and with no vehicle in sight. He looked into the back of the truck, saw me and beckoned me to come.

Feeling like a dead thing walking I joined him at the doorway to the clinic and he quickly explained he had a very sick child. I couldn't absorb what he said about blood test results and current observations (as in pulse, respirations, etc.) but I caught the urgency in his demeanour. My stomach cramped as he stood aside and indicated the rickety daybed. The spectre of death hovered. Ghoulish recollections hissed. No happy memories.

A distressed father knelt beside the flaccid, unresponsive body of his nine-year-old son. A woman I presumed to be his mother stood rigid and gaunt at the foot of the daybed. Grief stamped on every cell of her body. Heavy loss already engulfed her. The father was agitated and pleading for help in a mix of local language and English. Hannes explained to me, 'The boy is so ill I don't think he will live till morning without treatment but he needs to get to hospital and they have no money.'

I looked at the little body, then the parents, and my eyes diverted to the now waiting truck. The density of so much anguish packed into such a small space threatened to suffocate. Words were trapped in my throat but as I struggled to articulate, Hannes reached to hold my arm. 'Is the truck full?'

It was really but this is Africa and this was an emergency. He was clearly amazed and thrilled that we should be passing at this exact moment. The rasping sound that emerged sounded nothing like my voice, 'We could probably go past the hospital.' So before we had even drawn breath or assimilated the encounters of outreach here we were slap bang in the middle of the next crisis.

I vaguely remember protocol demanded the potential diversion and extra passengers be accepted by Carlos and Micah as leaders, and there was a wait whilst they weighed up if we should help or not.

Relieved when it was decided we could do something to help, everyone willingly shuffled around and a *kapalana* was laid in the small space made on the floor of the truck. Hannes and the father between them managed to lever the limp body into position and the father squeezed himself in beside his son. Looking around he repeated a sound several times and we took him to be saying thank you. Thank you? Your little boy is dying. Of course we want to help.

The mother was not coming. It was terrible Ma. She stood like a statue where she had seen her son lifted into the back of the truck. Hopeless desolation enveloped her. I'll never forget the picture because I could see her clearly all the way back out to the road. She stood upright, cloaked in dejected resignation. I'm convinced she was saying goodbye.

I could only think of the horror of living in circumstances that dictate a mum is deprived of being with her child at such a crucial moment and is forced to let him go to die among strangers in an alien environment. She was still there when we finally turned onto the main road and then she slipped from view. Who knows what commitments awaited her at home.

Several of the team set to praying healing for the sick boy. I prayed in tongues for several moments but couldn't stop thinking about the moth-

Monday evening

er and struggled to even look at the father. How could I begin to connect with yet more pain? I felt numb but completely raw as if all my nerve endings were exposed.

We stopped at the hospital, the patient whimpering in pain as we hit the bumps on that appalling road. When we got back to Pemba I was thankful the truck drove right up into the base and we dropped off all the borrowed kit at the container on our way into the centre. My little room felt like a palace.

A short while later, having caught our breath we congregated around the big table in the kitchen hut in the middle of the visitors' centre to attempt a debrief. Ben's conclusion was straightforward. 'Never again.' I knew he was struggling and felt for him. But he is here for three months and his medical input will be valuable on outreach so I hope he has some better experiences.

As we chatted (well; I listened — I couldn't begin to process aloud what was still unfolding on the inside) one of the Helas withdrew weeping and distressed. People tried to share a bit but we were all pretty overwhelmed.

It was agreed it was exciting to see some healings but the chaos had been a struggle for most and ministering in a context that was unrecognisable as 'church' more challenging than anyone could have anticipated. We drifted off for showers and unpacking. I had a pray with Hela and after skyping her family she felt better.

Remember how Saturday is a rest day for staff on the base and the day has a quieter rhythm? I could really have done with tackling a pile of laundry but somehow didn't manage to get to it. (As I wrote then I was in need of recovery time, and I felt thankful for the opportunity of a quiet day myself. I wrote to you in chunks.) I actually woke very early and headed for the prayer hut. I was reading again in John where Jesus speaks about reaping a harvest where others have sown and then says, 'My food is to do the will of him who sent me.' I decided to take the day to fast and pray. I sat for a while just still in his presence.

Once awake and up everyone else wandered off to the beach for a walk and swim but I lingered alone with Jesus. I journaled, trying to process and starting to anticipate church the next morning, knowing it would be my turn for the tradition of visitors receiving prayer and a gift of beads.

After a while Dan (the Australian missionary here for two years) joined me in the hut as he prepared for his weekly visit to the local mosque. We got chatting and he shared that he is passionate about Aboriginal people and has a number of friends back home who are working with indigenous folk and may be great contacts for me. (Of all people to rock up to the prayer hut Ma!)

As we chatted I felt a heavy presence over me like a peaceful mantle. Feeling rather silly I tentatively spoke about the growing impression I have that I am to get into the truck that God will provide (only seen in pictures during worship so far) and drive to a community where there are Aboriginal people living and just hang around. Anticipating caution or a reality check from a seasoned missionary, I was taken aback by his immediate response, 'It may well be God speaking that to you.'

What God is doing feels so deep I didn't want to be with people; only savour the holy sense of presence and ponder.

When the others got back to the centre they had two stories. Wonderfully Ma, someone met the boy's father (from when we dropped the sick

Monday evening

boy at the hospital after outreach) as they were walking on the beach. He said that his son received treatment and is making good progress. Isn't that just fantastic?! Great rejoicing that he is going to make it. I would love to be able to see him reunited with his mum but the nature of this kind of trip means lots of open endings. Just need to be thankful for each opportunity to love, serve and bless. We could easily never have known that we got him there in time. How kind of God to cause that chance meeting on the beach!

The second tale involved a man approaching the group as they sat in a café. He was offering to buy one of the girls! There was talk of a time of worship together which I felt I was aching for but in the end they all went out to celebrate a birthday. I sat a while then simply went to bed and had a deep sleep.

Early on Sunday morning I read some great scriptures in the Old Testament during time in the prayer hut and felt a weight on them as if God were speaking into my future. 2 Chronicles chapters 14 and 15 are about God moving on behalf of an obedient king with the verse, 'But as for you, be strong and do not give up, for your work will be rewarded' feeling like a personal promise when I am tempted to feel completely daunted. (I'm going to encourage Dan with it too.)

What I am sensing unfolding can only be hard work, Ma. Then the first part of Psalm 41 with promises of protection and health if I care for the weak and finally Isaiah 58 particularly verses 6-9 and then the amazing promises of verses 11 and 12. The references to feeding the hungry, releasing captives, providing for the poor, seeing the yoke of oppression broken, all feel very pertinent. And the promise of constant refreshing with life and hope to give away, fabulous in the context of so many Aboriginal people living in desert places — some quite literally — but as a people group, hope of meaningful change has seemed completely remote.

As I sat journaling and praying I suddenly became aware of a number of busy ants where I was sitting. I got up to move a few feet along the cement bench and as I turned there was a feather, just one solitary feather right there on the seat where I had been sitting. I've kept it to stick in my journal and no ... not another feather in sight!

Mulling the scriptures and in awe about the feather I wandered back to the visitors' centre for breakfast. I could feel a weight of Presence and was trying to just absorb the sense of being called up into something way beyond my natural ability to fulfil. But also entranced by God, the Almighty Creator, painstakingly reaching into my prayer time to reassure and confirm what I think he is speaking. This is turning out to be a completely extraordinary trip Ma.

I returned to the kitchen area and was sitting quietly but Nina accosted me and waved her Kindle in my face. Positively fizzing with anticipation she asked if I was familiar with a new version of the Bible called *Mirror Bible*. She thrust the Kindle into my hand declaring I must read the page immediately. It was marked as Colossians 1, which I realised straight away was the passage Heidi preached from last Sunday. She was focusing on verses 9 and 10 about 'knowing the will of God' which now, after a few short days, feels as significant as the difference between life and death. Nina was bouncing up and down as she pointed to the passage in Colossians. 'Read that,' with a jab of a finger, 'you are totally hi-jacked!'

I sat down to read. In this version it is translated, *'Go on a walkabout tour*

Monday evening

to explore the extent of the land that is yours under his lordship' finishing with, *'You are empowered in the dynamic of God's strength; his mind is made up about you! He enables you to be strong in endurance and steadfastness with joy.'*

You can imagine, 'walkabout tour'?! I was as dumbstruck as if an angel had just sat down beside me. Whoever heard of 'walkabout' being in the Bible? Nina was beside herself with glee having sensed my need for reassurance as I'd recounted the story so far that day by the beach.

But Ma ... 'walkabout' is so totally indigenous in context. I still can't get my head around it; not sure I ever will. Couldn't have imagined it, dreamed it up or actually believed it if I hadn't got it in print in my hand. Coming on the back of the scriptures I was digesting and the deep sense of being drawn up into something way, way beyond any current experience or understanding, I could only hand the Kindle back without a word.

I had to get alone. Be by myself. Be still. And quiet. I sat behind one of the buildings for some time struggling (and failing dismally) to manage feelings of profound conviction colliding with stunned disbelief that a supernatural power was targeting my future. It's not processable, is it Ma? Whatever is going to unfold? I don't think I can afford to even try to think or guess.

I don't know how much later it was when I felt recovered enough to make my way to church. It felt completely delicious to feel 'at home' walking in, familiarity offered welcome comfort. I moved to be among the hungry women already prostrate on the altar.

As worship began I greeted a young Mozambican mum. She lingered, holding my hand. Suddenly Holy Spirit Presence enveloped us both and I began trembling uncontrollably. I sensed she was praying for me and felt totally privileged as God touched me deeply. Tears came, and then deep sobs. I suddenly saw myself in the outback and then Jesus with an arm around Sam and Nathan's shoulders. These are now recurring pictures.

As the song 'Come Away' began I heard myself cry out, 'Yes Lord. Show me what is next.' This is a song I have learned here and the words are Jesus speaking to us saying things like 'it's never too late, come away with me, it's gonna be wild and I have a plan for you'. All of which feel very significant.

At 55 I feel my brain is literally boggled by the revelation that God has a whole new chapter. Nina approached me weeping and repeating, 'it's never too late'. I was aware of someone leading prayer for Dan who had fallen ill overnight, and then I opened my eyes and saw that at some point Heidi and Rolland had slipped in.

I was surprised as knowing Heidi was due to speak in Westminster, London the following evening I presumed she would have left, but I guess the time difference is minimal. I think there is a daily flight out of Jo'burg mid-afternoon so she is probably flying overnight. Someone said that after the UK she is going on to Singapore and then to speak at the Shine Conference in Perth. (That's the one near where cousin Julia lives that I have booked to be at.)

Another song, the offering and then it was time. Visitors to the front. Gina came to pray for me, which was lovely. She shared a picture God had showed her of a stream in a desert and then she said, 'The thing is, in this picture God is saying you are the stream bringing life to dry places.' I was so encouraged as this linked directly with the verses that had felt important only a few hours earlier likening my life to a 'well-watered garden' and 'a spring whose waters never run dry'.

Monday evening

There was a time of exuberant dancing led by the young men and boys in the church and then Heidi spoke from Acts about when the Holy Spirit fell on the disciples and they received their heavenly languages. She spoke about the power and boldness they received. This week she was wearing a simple black tunic dress with leggings and a wide headband. As she concluded her talk she said God had shown her the Holy Spirit was coming to visit us in power and she asked Rolland to join her on the platform.

Then there was a baby dedication (you never know what is coming next!) and the baby was passed around midst lots of that amazing sound people born here make with their tongues. After another worship song Rolland had the microphone and asked, 'Who wants more Holy Spirit? Come forward.' There was a general surge towards the front and people also went onto the platform where a whole bunch of them immediately fell to the ground chortling.

I went right around to the back of the stage and lay on the ground on my stomach with my arms stretched out wanting as much of God as he could pour in. I was aware at some point of Heidi kneeling beside me with her hands on my back. She prayed, 'Take her deeper God, deeper than she has ever been. Right here as she lies in the dirt, overwhelm her.'

I lay very still for a very long time and then came to with the disconcerting thought that I was lying alone in church. Had everyone else gone? Were the musicians just playing and waiting for me? How awkward. Obviously those thoughts came all in a rush in the moment. I forced myself to come into the present, like surfacing after an afternoon nap that became a deep sleep, and managed to push myself up on my elbow.

I clambered in a rather ungainly fashion to my feet and realised there were dozens of people in similar state. Heidi was saying, 'Take the hand of someone near you and begin to prophesy.' I was blearily aware of a young boy beside me looking vaguely uncomfortable. As I reached to put my hand gently on his shoulder someone approached me from behind and simply blew on the back of my neck.

Just like the tower of Babel, and with no hint of my ladylike heritage, I collapsed back all over Rolland and spent another period of time overwhelmed by God's presence. I did at one point pray for my own eardrum as I had somehow managed to fall pinned against the drum kit which subsequently burst into life. Nobody could accuse Africans of a lack of enthusiasm in worship!

Once the hubbub had died down people in various stages of Holy Spirit inebriation could be seen staggering towards the dining hut for lunch. I stopped on the way back into the centre to pray for the guard's hernia again and then sank gratefully onto the bench beside Nina who was showing her teaching material to another visitor.

The conversation ended and Nina turned to me to tell me more about the *Mirror Bible* translation. (I think it may be New Testament or sections thereof, I'm not sure.) I took the afternoon just quietly again. The Bible seems to have come alive with verses about the weak, the poor and deserts. Funny that …

So now it's early Monday evening and I finally got my laundry done this morning. It was quite therapeutic actually thrashing various unsuspecting garments on the stone slab. I got straight into it after writing in the hut first thing. Sophie left today. Mo has been around sorting a few things like light bulbs and the notice board.

I am meeting Sara and the young girl I told you about later on. I feel

Monday evening

a bit nervous as I never really know with the teenage girls what they are thinking much less saying, I have tried to reach out a few times but then even English girls of 14,15,16 can be unfathomable! I hope she will be blessed.

I have a slight sore throat and my left ear is aching so I have prayed healing and am just taking this time out to write. (Knee completely healed up though, thanks for prayer.) I want to feel on form tomorrow as I'm hoping to go to the big prison with Sol (and Dan if he is better) and if I'm brave enough I may do hospital visiting in the afternoon. I think Ben must've gone to Mieze today with Hannes and I keep wondering how he is doing. No doubt we'll hear tonight. I still can't believe he is from Taunton when I am just down the road in Exeter so regularly.

I am so excited and it's amazing that God has spoken to me about 'land'. I feel he will highlight an area. Once he gives me a region or particular people group I will have a framework to pray into. So much deep pain for our Aboriginal people is directly related to their loss of land. Land is quite literally where they gain their identity, which explains why so many people simply don't know who they are or where they fit in; impossible for us to understand that kind of connection with land really, isn't it?

I feel complete and yet on the brink of something so incredible equipping myself is beyond me. (Meets Bill Johnson's criteria nicely then, as he teaches that if our dream is possible without God it is too small.) I did remember yesterday that six months ago I received a word about the 'suddenly surprises of God'. I think arriving in Pemba only six weeks after the seed thought was sown and finding God commissioning me as a 'sent out one' in my own country of Australia MUST qualify? (Gosh,

I wonder if he plans to connect me with an Aboriginal person or people at the conference in Perth?)

Whew! Rather a lot to digest.

I'm really looking forward to meeting you and Sis in Sydney. There will be a huge amount to catch up on. I hope you have a great meeting with your friends on the Operation Mobilisation ship. Is it the *Logos* or *Dulos*? Sorry, you probably told me before I left.

I thought of Sis again at one o'clock this morning as I made my way to the loo. Never alone here ... there was a large green cricket-like thing right on the toilet seat. (What does a praying mantis look like exactly?) This afternoon I tried to get a close-up snap of one of the blue-tailed lizards. They are electric blue and incredibly quick and it darted into the undergrowth. Next time. They're quite impressive with their yellow and black body. Just her type of pet! To be fair I nearly trod on it so moving at speed was a good plan for survival.

OK. More soon then. Big hug Ma, not sure how this final week is going to pan out.

I guess autumn is in the air down there in Auckland? I know you love that time of year. Enjoy. Bit less humid here, which is appreciated!

I love you x x

Tuesday afternoon

Hello again Ma,

Well, Tuesday afternoon here around 3pm so I am sitting on the concrete veranda outside my room in a patch of shade. A gentle breeze often comes through about this time. I love it. In the last week the temperature has definitely dropped a bit and with less humidity it can be almost comfortable.

In the prayer hut at 5am today I was actually chilly. One of the Helas was there and had caught a great shot of the sunrise. She asked me if I would pray for her. I was suddenly aware that God is teaching me more and more about the simplicity of praying constantly.

Also I am more conscious of the mystery of how he can be working such a deep thing in me, whilst those around me are unaware, still the fruit of what he is doing can bless their lives as it overflows. What a delicious way to start the day. I deliberately had a time of praise and thanksgiving pushing back this throat thing that lurks.

By the time we returned to the others Wilf (who has come out of his shell now he is here alone) had collected bread rolls and we tucked in to what has become our usual breakfast. All the American visitors brought peanut butter with them so we are now relishing their leftovers. I was also given sunflower seeds that were surplus to requirements. Stirred in with the peanut butter and a hint of Bovril that was also unwanted, it's a feast. I could manage on a dry bread roll but nobody else is and I don't feel the Holy Spirit saying 'no' so it's all joy! Gina even has marmalade. I try not to think about Starbucks in the bush but wow ... it was a great cup of coffee.

I have been careful about using sunscreen especially with taking the antimalarial tablets. I'm often wearing long, cool sleeves but I'm still rather surprised by the pale complexion that gazes back at me in the mirror. I look like a month of night duty!

It's much quieter this week on the guest front but a young Mozambican (in his late twenties I should think) who has been in America for a while has returned and is staying in the centre for a while. He grew up here in Mozambique but I think he has been worship leading at a school in the States. A number of those who have led worship at the staff home group nights and at church are now hanging around a good deal. The presence of three beautiful blondes (as in Helas and Lucie) is no deterrent.

Yesterday evening one of the young men began asking 'innocent' questions about who among the girls enjoyed cooking. Somehow the conversation swung round, from all of us being invited to watch him cook and serve a Mozambican meal, to the girls agreeing to make a tasty meal with the chicken his mate went off to collect. I couldn't help thinking this was a practised skill.

Tuesday afternoon

I was bracing myself for a killing and plucking session and wondered how the girls would fare but when it arrived the chicken was frozen. (I thought he said he had brought it back from America but I could have got that wrong.) The result was a convivial supper together. Someone fetched rice from the usual place and Gina, who has finished her work now and leaves in a couple of days, rustled up a yummy side dish with lentils. My old room being vacant now Aya has left, I had agreed to shut the cats in overnight in hopes they would catch or at least permanently deter the rat (maybe don't read this bit out to Sis as she may have bad dreams).

It was difficult to tune out stories of rats eating their way into suitcases through aluminium foil (intended as a deterrent) and the poor missionary who ended up duck-taping herself into her room, only to discover the desperate rat just chewed its way back in. It was thought the rodent must have been motivated by the desire to nest in that space. (How sweet. The unsuspecting missionary could then have shared her humble abode with a thriving rat family!)

There are many courageous single girls amongst the full-timers. I would be tempted to comment that the alpha of the species (as in single variety) is conspicuous by his absence but that's not terribly spiritual is it? The aforementioned Mozambican males melted into the night at the merest hint of washing up but we'd all enjoyed time together so much nobody minded. Those of us who hadn't cooked just did it. I feel so blessed to be included in these random fun times and keep forgetting most of them could be my children!

The Helas, Gina, Ben and Lucie, Nina and Karlie were all doing their own thing this morning. Except for Ben they all leave tomorrow.

Pemba Pennings

He is finding the medical setup much more basic and frustrating than he had anticipated. I got up again in the night but with replacement bulbs having been found, two outside lights were working so it was much easier to navigate my way to the bathrooms. I noticed we had a new younger guard and the gates were left wide open so not blocked shut by the big rocks that the other guard always placed there.

As I mentioned before, this morning was due to be prison ministry. Dan was ill so Sol came alone to the prayer hut. We were all there prompt at 7.30am. We prayed together and Sol went through the usual routine. Again explaining we girls are required to wear *kapalanas* or long skirts and tops that cover our shoulders.

We are not meant to leave the base at any time without our ID, which is the stamped copy of our passports that we paid to have verified by officials on arriving. We knew we would be required to present these and entry to the prison was not permitted without them. Any contact with the authorities here requires ID to be shown and obviously it is proof we are legally allowed to be in the country as it demonstrates our visa status is current.

Nothing may be taken into the prison so there is no point taking phones etc. (I suppose there is the risk some keen visitor may think of attempting to get photos of men in prison?) Water bottles only may be left on the bus as the driver will park and wait for us outside the gates. At 8am we duly assembled at the maintenance area where all the vehicles are stored overnight. Amazingly at 8.05 our driver drove into the yard on his motorbike and entered the office hut.

Perhaps less cause for wonder when by 8.30 there was no sign of him and I was thanking God for my red scarf as I once again wore it draped

Tuesday afternoon

over my head and shoulders to give me protection from the sun. At 8.40 a group of men, none of them our man, ambled from the hut each with Coke bottle in hand. Sol decided to venture in to find our driver and was offered a Coke at the door before disappearing. Maybe this is akin to the first coffee of the day.

Bottle tops are just flicked into the air to land randomly around the yard. I pondered again how in this culture there appears to be no appreciation of a person's time being of value. And also no understanding of the window of time Sol is allotted for the prison visit even though this happens every week. I still don't know if drivers are local men glad of employment or if they're all Christians and connected with Iris. I think it is the former.

More valuable time was lost when we were shown the 'bus'— it being an 'open to the elements' flatbed truck, without even the canvas covering of the outreach vehicle, people needed to return to the centre to find hats and sunscreen. I was relieved to find the cab had three seats. Sol offered the spare one to the group and when nobody responded I joined him in the cab.

We left the base turning left but within a few moments swung left again onto a sandy track that was in the big village surrounding the base. So we were on the left-hand end of the open horseshoe shape I described to you. It was a narrow track and the truck only just fitted between the familiar bamboo woven fences that create boundaries for each family plot. We swung around a right-hand bend narrowly missing a small boy who was minding his own business engrossed in a game with an old bicycle tyre, and came to a halt in a dead end. The driver clambered down from his cab and disappeared into the nearest little compound.

Pemba Pennings

Sol explained that this was the home of the transport manager who had the authority to issue a docket for fuel and was inside. Only, of course, he wasn't. The driver emerged chatting nonchalantly on his phone with no hint of agitation. As if he had all the time in the world he got back into the driving seat and turned the key. Sol did not speak. It was rather quiet in the cab as we began the long reverse back to the bend where the main track had gone straight on up into the village.

We arrived at the (almost) junction and the laborious process of a three-point turn, in reverse, commenced. I gazed at a stump of protruding metal to my right where a large wing mirror obviously once resided and knew a frisson of anxiety for the little boy I had seen playing. But the driver was clearly experienced and it wasn't long before we once again hit the main road. A few more moments and we swung off the road again, this time onto the forecourt of a petrol station. We were definitely doing this the African way.

The driver seemed uncertain of something at this point and was peering at the pumps as if one would be flashing to indicate the appropriate fuel. No help was forthcoming so we did a lap of honour and then pulled into a parking space at the side. Sol explained that the boss had said he would meet us here but you guessed it, no boss! More waiting and then 'boss' did indeed arrive with the necessary docket and, fuel delivered and paid for, we were finally underway.

Sol asked if I would like to hear his story and I was delighted to listen. He told me he used to be in the military. There was some kind of riot and I think I understood that he stepped out of line in terms of army protocol and the government decided that nobody was above the law so he was prosecuted and charged. When he was serving his sentence in

Tuesday afternoon

the prison (I noticed he spoke of 'prison' i.e. where we were going, not the jail for more minor misdemeanours) a group from Iris came to visit in exactly the way we were about to. He said that at that time he was a practising Muslim but never felt anyone was there when he prayed. He gave his life to Jesus, received the gift of a Bible and his life changed.

When he was released Iris offered him work on the base and a place in the Bible school. He accepted and earned his keep and a low wage sweeping the church and tackling various menial tasks around the base. He told me he began praying earnestly for a helper in his life: a wife.

He explained with enthusiasm that he prayed often about the matter. At this stage of the story something about the colour pink and a shirt featured but I couldn't fully follow the thread. It feels rude to ask a person to repeat things more than twice so I settled for nodding sagely with an encouraging smile. The third woman he considered (who either wore pink or liked pink) commented on his shirt 'looks great on you' and this was his sign. He explained that she had no mother or father and lived with her sister and her sister's children.

Sol began to go home with her over the next few weeks. He learned that the family had had Catholic influence in the past but she had become a Christian. In a few months' time he brought her onto the base to live with him. He explained, 'to share my life and support me'.

He went on to tell me how one day the missionaries inquired if they were married to which he responded, 'We have no means of getting married, no money.' He said how completely blessed they both were when the missionaries asked them to make a list of what they needed in order to be married and together made it possible.

I knew the prison to be some way out of town whereas the jail was just at the end of a residential street in town, attached to that little office that felt like a rural police station — well kind of! We passed the usual roadside stalls selling basics with piles of fresh fruit in front, and then the now familiar shoe shop (we always seem to pass this particular corner whenever I leave the base) where one of each pair of shoes for sale is suspended on a piece of string attached to a wire strung between two poles. Strung at a height they appear like a rather weird effigy dancing in the wind.

Moving past the edges of town the bush rolls away on either side of the truck. I could see the ocean on both sides of the strip of land we were driving on so I don't think I had been that way before but of course on outreach I could only see out of the small opening in the canvas over the back of the other truck so ... who knows? Every now and again two or three women appear together. They each have more wood stacked on their heads than you would see piled in the average log basket on a UK hearth.

Here and there are clusters of basic shelters just a little back from the road. Stones of various sizes are piled up and in each shelter a young man patiently breaks larger rocks into smaller stones by smashing them with one heavy rock. The shingle this creates is a crucial building material here. A double framework of bamboo is erected and then the shingle is poured between the two and secured in place by thick mud (not sure if anything is added to give the mud longevity) to make the hut walls. Flooding is a huge issue when the rains come and you can see how easily the mud walls succumb. Perfect for keeping cool in the heat though.

We swung around a bend and another village unfolded. Huts spreading as far as I could see. Then we passed a sign for Bush Camp before

Tuesday afternoon

I recognised Mieze up ahead so I must have been that way before and just viewing the journey from a different perspective (and hardly seeing at all on that Mieze clinic day). I enjoyed being higher up in the cab and having a view over the small trees and shrubs into the village. From street level it was completely hidden.

As we passed Mieze village it was conspicuous as Iris with the play park showing off swings and a slide for the children. The clinic hut sat deserted and squat. Eyes and mouth firmly shut it had the appearance of a sleeping cartoon character, slumbering but ready to pop open like animated eyes on Monday morning.

After a while we took a turn left on a wide sandy track that brought us quickly into another sprawling village. Sol pointed to a hill indicating the long, low, white building in the distance was the prison.

As we journeyed on women chatted, children played, countryside unfolded and over it all the brooding prison. I wondered how it would feel if a member of the family was in prison for a number of years and all the time you could see where they were incarcerated. I wonder if prisoners are allowed visitors? It would be a huge walk in the heat and within six or seven minutes of leaving the tarmac the terrain was more suited to a 4x4.

The simple dwellings dwindled until all we could see was dirt and scrubby bushes. I felt for the others in the back as the truck heaved and lunged, navigating both deep ruts and sudden rocks. Eventually the truck gasped its way up onto a slight plateau at the far end of which a solid wall with large entrance gates rose up out of the dirt.

The driver pulled up some distance away from the wall as if he was reluctant to be caught in the ominous aura exuded by the weighty barrier. We handed our IDs to Sol and subdued by the barren landscape, we quietly stepped away from the vehicle. I was relieved to hear an exchange between the driver and Sol that gave me hope that, unlike the jail truck driver, this time the vehicle would remain ready and waiting to scoop us up when we emerged. Intimidation lurked in the atmosphere.

We moved as one into the 'no go zone' and I had the impression of being on a movie set. I glanced over my shoulder at the wide-open bush behind. It sprawled forever to merge with the horizon. I thought of Alcatraz. My goodness, if anybody managed to escape from here they would be exposed for miles with no cover between the gates and the village. An easy target. I shivered, blinking away the mental image of rabbits scattering under fire and turned back to the group.

I wondered if we were being watched as Sol led us right up to one of the massive blue gates. As we got there an invisible hand slid one huge gate. On grinding rails it opened enough to allow us to pass through. Sol and the guard, who only became visible once we were fully through, exchanged a greeting. I avoided eye contact and didn't dare stare but I was aware it took the man his whole body weight to get the solid gate to clank shut behind us.

The surreal sense of a movie unfolding was sharply heightened as the weighty sound of the gate bolt settling ricocheted around us, echoing finality. No going back. But the surprise was that this side of the gates looked much like the outside. We huddled in the shadow of the wall taking in the scene. Stretching out for some distance was more dirt. Further away towards the centre of what appeared to be a massive enclosed area, low scorched-looking bushes with scanty foliage rose up dotting the terrain.

Tuesday afternoon

The wall just went on … Swiftly taking in the new vista I saw some way over to the right the actors in this scene. They were just visible as they bent over bushes flinging wet garments out to dry. Must be laundry day. Further away there were shadows that could be huts. Then some way behind those in the far right-hand corner of this massive enclosure a stark oblong building rose up. I had the impression of solid, windowless walls. A brooding womb of suffering.

Squashing an unhelpful and graphic report from a team member last week of 'suffocating heat and claustrophobia' I recalibrated myself to the present. Still immediately inside the gates, on the left stood a small hut, a booth really, not much larger than a tollbooth on the motorway. One low step up and through the open door a man in uniform stood behind a basic desk. Reaching out an open hand he accepted the pile of ID documents Sol handed over. Several other men lingered in the small space but none of them wore uniform. Their silent staring only added to our unease.

I didn't feel anxious in the way I did in the jail but apprehension clung to us as we waited. I don't know what happens if ID is not accepted. It's obviously a great help that Sol comes regularly and some of the men had greeted him cheerily which I found reassuring. The guard indicated he would keep our documents; there wasn't time to claim victory over the fleeting anxiety that turned my tummy at that point: we were moving.

Oh my word, Ma. It was very hot, very dry and how conspicuous were we as we began the long walk across the expanse of bare earth between us and the building? (Strains from *The Good, the Bad and the Ugly* as who knows how many pairs of eyes monitored our progress.) There was plenty of time to take in some detail. One of the men doing his laundry stuck out because he appeared to be wearing a surgical mask. Hayfever? Allergy to laundry? Or was he carrying some contagion that required a barrier between him and his fellow inmates?

The darker shadows took on form and became visible as simple shelters. Too far away to see clearly they appeared to be basic workshops and several men in each looked as if they were doing something fairly simple with tools; perhaps it was carpentry but they were too far away for me to see. We trudged on towards the building ahead.

A breeze wafted over us and I was mystified as it carried with it what sounded just like worship. We reached the building and stepped gratefully into the shade afforded us by the rudimentary covered veranda at the entrance. A solitary figure sat at a table. Open in front of him lay a hefty, ledger-style book. A large bunch of keys like a prop in a Dickens' drama rested on a big metal hoop beside him.

He greeted Sol warmly (Sol later told me that this man was a guard when he was an inmate and they have been on good terms ever since) and Sol explained quickly to us that between 8 and 11am each Tuesday the men are permitted 'Religious Activities'. We learned the men had been worshipping since before we had left the base, as this is the only time they are allowed to sing corporately.

I think Sol signed in the ledger but my attention was by this time focused on the narrow gateway that clearly led into the building. It was made of iron bars, the entrance to an enormous cage. Men were pressing up against it. A mound of squished limbs and distorted faces full of haunted eyes. The scent of desperate need mingled with body odour. Smells my nose struggled and failed to recognise were thick in the air. Fear prickled the back of my neck. Help me Lord!

Tuesday afternoon

I glued my eyes to Sol as we waited for the guard to fumble with the lock. At the same time he was roughly ordering the men to get back, to quiet down and clear the way. It seemed ages but as soon as the gate swung open Sol stepped in.

I felt a bit protective of the younger girls but only Lucie was near me so I tucked her in behind Sol and then followed them in. Obviously this is all completely familiar for Sol but even if he had tried I don't think there is anything he could have said that would have prepared me.

As the crowd of men moved back from the entrance and my eyes adjusted to the gloom we were just on the narrow end of the huge rectangle-shaped building. It was long and split down the middle by the narrow corridor we now stood in. Either side of us were solid, bare cement walls that went up very high, and then above the corridor all the way through the building was a raised narrow strip of roof with small panes of glass running down each side that let in the only light. (Actually what I saw was probably just daylight posing as panes of glass.) It could have been 40-feet high so the light was a long way from us. I'm not brilliant at measurements but if two people sat on the floor hugging their knees on either side of the narrow passage we stood in, a person could just step through the gap.

Trying not to gasp out loud I swallowed my breath as immediately on our left I noticed a space in the wall about seven-feet high and six-feet wide with bars. An actual cell, like in a Wild West movie! Staring, my eyes picked out the shape of a body.

The man was lying on his back on the filthy cement, limbs akimbo, wearing only some kind of loin cloth. (I guess it could once have been a pair of shorts.) His face was frozen and his eyes completely unseeing.

Words flashed through my head as I struggled not to visualise beatings, demons, rape and viciousness. How long had he been catatonic? Is medical help available? Do the guards do this to prisoners? Jesus, where are you? This was all in a flash.

Two prisoners stood idly beside the bars, leaning against the wall and leering in our direction. Sol pressed forward telling us to stay close and follow him. Almost immediately there was an open doorway off to the right and a glimpse of rough blankets. A fleeting image of men in various postures of despondency and boredom on rows of basic bunk beds suggested that this was a gigantic dormitory.

I kept my head down and we had to press against the wall on the left to allow prisoners moving in the opposite direction to pass. The men stared unabashed at the girls as we walked by. (I willed the attractive, gregarious brunette in particular, who is less than sensitive at times, not to attempt to connect.) The men streamed by in the opposite direction, often making incomprehensible comments the tone of which strongly implied something less than holy purity.

Suddenly we had to step around a body in a ragged shirt and stained shorts. The man lay wedged against the right-hand wall of the narrow passage. He was almost in the foetal position so men going the other way literally had to step over him causing single-lane traffic at this point. I stared down as we waited for men coming towards us to pass.

Only eyes moved as we continued past this shell of a man, pools of liquid despair. (I'm still processing from outreach Ma, but something about yielding in a deeper place and compassion are linked to create profound change because, filthy and out of it as he was, all I wanted was to sit beside him and hold him ... not exactly the me most people have come to know and love ... go figure! ... and when you do, let me in

Tuesday afternoon

on the revelation because I am so deep into this thing, this journey, this process, can't even think what to call it, I hardly know which way is up anymore. I think this deep experience is somehow key in terms of motivation for wanting to see Jesus do miracles and a daily life that enables consistent release of his power, who he really is.)

I was still churning over whether the man in the cell behind us was being given food and water. I wondered how long he had been there. (The memory is making me cry Ma, such utter helplessness, how could you not lose the will to live in such conditions?) It was overwhelming and many of the men looked young. Phrases from the story of the Good Samaritan flashed through my head.

The singing grew louder and the acoustics were impressive as some of the men harmonised. As we moved deeper into the building we suddenly could see that the corridor was in fact split-level.

About half-way down, four quite deep steps were carved into the cement floor meaning the remainder of the building was set a few feet lower. At the foot of these stairs the men who were singing sat on the ground, either side of the corridor, with about twenty men in each line. We could see the passageway extending some way beyond and men from that direction then trickled constantly up the steps between us, many carrying what looked suspiciously like makeshift urinals. Thankfully nobody tripped over so my suspicions remain unconfirmed.

The men who were worshipping cheered a welcome and I felt two-inches tall again in the face of such blatant joy in suffering. They were clearly delighted to see Sol. He told us to stand still and we gathered at the top of the steps as he went down to greet a man at the front of the line.

At this point I noticed the walls were in fact a dirty white and some way above us there were some slit windows, air holes really cut into the wall. It wasn't too hot but I could appreciate the potential for the visitor who had spoken of heat and claustrophobia. A bird was flying around above us but nobody took any notice.

Sol indicated he would stand on the bottom step and we were to arrange ourselves behind him. Gratefully we sunk to nearer the men's level. Two of the girls were on the left and then three of us on the right. I was thankful Wilf was acting as rear guard on the top step. Sol said a few words of greeting and then it was straight into rousing worship.

The men all stood up and there was enthusiastic clapping and swaying such as the limited space allowed. One man took the lead and strangely he was wearing a blue Billabong t-shirt (traditionally Australian ... pang!).

Just like at the jail and on outreach we all had to introduce ourselves and then Gina gave a brave testimony about a time when she recognised she had a 'huge hole' in her life and how Jesus filled it. Sol translated and the men listened attentively. All the while random prisoners wove their way between us as they moved from one end of the building to the other. A few lingered at the top of the steps; some wore the skullcap worn by Muslims. As Gina finished her testimony Sol prayed and then he invited those who would like prayer to raise a hand. As one they raised their hands and surged to the foot of the steps.

I can't really describe how it felt, Ma, to stand gazing out at a sea of worship and praise; such joy and none of these men would be going home any time soon. Their faith is their lifeline. In the face of gruelling hardship they wanted to praise ... and they had been going since long before we arrived not wanting to forfeit a moment of their 'legal' wor-

Tuesday afternoon

ship time. I struggle to process such courage. I was aching, longing that the Lord would cause me to be a blessing.

Towards the end of Gina speaking I began to feel the feeling I get in my stomach when the Holy Spirit asks me to step out. It's a churning kind of sensation that is only ever alleviated by me obediently doing the thing. I had the thought that I should sing over the men and the song 'Holy Spirit You Are Welcome Here' was in my head. Sol beckoned us all to step down and move among the men to pray and bless.

I knew it was then or never so took a deep breath and asked him if I could sing over the men as the others prayed. He nodded and I still don't know if he was disappointed, blessed, surprised or pleased that I stepped out. I do know it's not about positive feedback and I have an audience of One. Just tell that to my legs, which by this time were feeling suspiciously as if bearing the weight of the rest of my body was a demand they could no longer meet.

I leaned against the wall for support and dragging my reluctant legs with me I sort of slithered backwards up two steps to create space for the others to come and pray. The feeling in the pit of my stomach intensified. I looked at all the eager faces hungry for prayer then closed my eyes, took a deep breath and launched into song.

There was a steady burble of prayer and conversation but I could hear my voice resonating in the corridor and focused on worshipping and welcoming the Holy Spirit. It didn't matter I needed the wall to keep me upright. There was a delicious sense of Presence and courage slipped her arm around my shoulders enabling me to sing the chorus twice through.

And then it was time up. Sol raised a hand in blessing. He thanked the men for hosting us and indicated we should leave directly the way we came. Foreboding hovered as the bars of *that* cell approached. I couldn't march past without looking; it would feel like contributing to the humiliation. The body had not moved.

The guard was hovering (it must have been 11am already) and unlocked the gate to let us out. The lock must have been sticking because the sound of keys rattling followed us for several minutes as in a collective daze we made our way in silence back across the scorched earth. A short pause for Sol to collect our documents from the little hut, the man on the gate slid it open just sufficient for us to pass through, and we were back in the truck.

The journey back and the afternoon are a bit of a blur Ma, as I attempted to process … and failed miserably.

Going to have a rest before staff night this evening.

Love you x

Tuesday bedtime

Tucked in but just before I settle.

Sharing in staff night this evening was a gentle relief (more tomorrow).

Another huge day Ma, and the accumulative outcome of these weeks can only be profound change. This visit to Pemba is indisputably the most challenging God adventure of my life so far. Something permanent, something profoundly good is happening deep in the fabric of who I am.

But don't ask me what it is or to quantify the process because it's beyond my comprehension. I just know something at the source of who I am has shifted and it will be seen to influence every area of my life. Oh my goodness … I still can't quite work out how from attending a conference in Wales I have landed myself in literally 'darkest Africa!'

Still, the good news is … I don't have to!

And now for a night of well earned slumber.

More childlikeness, Ma! Keep it simple — that's the answer.

More tomorrow. Love you x x

Wednesday early morning

Morning Ma,

So Karlie and Nina left early. I really appreciated time with them. They offered to pray for me before they left, praying that my writing will be a blessing to many. We say Amen to that! Sounds like a pipe dream but then I remind myself that if someone had already written this I would have devoured it before visiting Pemba, so ... who knows?

Early on yesterday evening we had a sweet time of worship in the prayer hut as it was the staff gathering night again. The new headmaster of the school here on the base, for hundreds of children from all around the area, spoke to us from the story of the man at the pool of Bethesda. He challenged us to be deliberate about pursuing things in our own lives that need healing and not sit back like the man in the story, basically taking the attitude, 'God knows where I am; if he wants to interact with me or heal me, I am open.'

The mattresses were strewn with worshippers and the sound system was struggling as usual but God was there and that makes everything

Wednesday early morning

totally worth it. I was completely surprised, honoured and nervous when Sara, who was leading, asked me to come to the front and close in prayer.

I stood still, silent, holding the microphone. It was a profound and humble moment, as I recognised I was standing in the very spot Heidi had stood that day she encouraged the team as I sat out of sight under the bush. My legs were jelly again but I prayed from a full heart and wandered back to my room.

Only a couple of days now till I leave but today is looking like another adventure in its own right as Tina has invited me to accompany her to visit a village that is part of the Iris sponsorship programme. There are multiple facets to the way Iris is loving and serving Mozambique. I am not sure what the programme is exactly, but we are going to a village that is some distance away to deliver things. This isn't part of the normal visitor programme and to be invited feels a privilege. I am hoping to encourage Tina and get to know her a bit better.

Will let you know how we go. Should be back in time to write this evening.

Big hug x x x

Wednesday evening

Hello dearest Ma,

Well, I was right to anticipate a special day with Tina!

Not long after enjoying my breakfast roll I made my way down to the transport area where we had arranged to meet. Frenzied activity (for this part of the world) was already underway with four young boys busy loading a large truck. Trudging to and fro two boys moved sacks, dumping them heavily on the tailgate where the other two dragged and pushed the goods. They were piled well back under the high canopy that enclosed the back of the vehicle. I don't know the exact weight of those being loaded but it's not uncommon here to see women carrying sacks of rice or beans weighing 50kgs on their heads.

The boys worked steadily stacking and wedging to fit a surprising volume of goods on the back of the truck. It was a large metal flatbed-style tray behind a triple-seater cab. A Mozambican lady was giving them instruction whilst Tina, who appeared to be looking for something as she paced around the vehicle, was overseeing the movement of bulging bags and the large sealed sacks.

Wednesday evening

As the last bags were loaded Gina joined the group and, smiling broadly, declared she was free to come with us. I felt pleased for her Ma. She has obviously been faithfully serving the family with young children but had been out with Tina on a previous occasion and told me how much she had enjoyed it. With only a short time left here she had confided in me that she was really hoping to be able to come for the day.

In a puzzled tone that creaked with controlled patience, Tina inquired of one of the workers as to the whereabouts of the driver. 'He's gone home' was not the response she was hoping for and the accompanying shrug did nothing to sooth the threat of frustration. (Another busy morning in Pemba, I quietly thought to myself. But exercising discernment I decided against any attempts at humour.)

The other boy loading chimed in with a comment about the driver retrieving a key. Tina turned and explained to me that as a policy there are no spare keys available. The particular driver of a vehicle is held accountable if anything untoward occurs so more than one key could make him vulnerable.

Gina encouraged me to return and leave my camera in the visitors' centre for safe keeping whilst collecting extra water supplies for the day. Realising there was to be a short (or possibly not so short) pause in the proceedings whilst we awaited the driver's return, I took the opportunity to do what she suggested.

As I walked back to the truck one of the *tias* working in the baby house emerged with a large basket of laundry perched on her head. She moved slowly across the track some way ahead of me. What caught my attention was not that she was carrying this huge load on her head with apparent ease but that the basket was snuggled into a nest of fluorescent curls. Her hair was literally every colour you see in those garish sets of pens for children including the blinding, glow-in-the-dark lime green, which the sun's rays seemed to hit and then explode out of. The vibrant play of colour and light rendered a successful impression of a giant, walking firework making me glad of my sunglasses. I have no idea how she achieved this extraordinary hairdo and caught myself chuckling.

Whilst we waited in the shade of the huge baobab tree that conveniently grows just outside the transport enclosure, I chatted with Tina. She is in a time of change as God spoke to her through the man who told us all about the new method of farming suited to Africa that is producing great crop yields. Tina told me she plans to embrace a role introducing this method in the wider region; staff are already praying for a suitable replacement for her here.

The driver joined us as the boys finished loading some gifts for the particular children on the sponsorship programme, but relief was short lived as he quickly became engaged in a heated exchange with the driver of a passing vehicle and promptly strode over to make his point.

I couldn't understand what was said but gesticulations and body language made it pretty clear; the other driver was asking why the large left-sided wing mirror on our truck appeared to have returned from a wild night out. The metal stem was completely kinked and the mirror protruded at a skewed angle. I noticed the right-sided wing mirror sported a splintered glass mosaic. A man rode past on a motorbike wearing just a cap. Then I recognised the cap as belonging to Wilf, Sophie's son. The back tyre was bulging ominously.

Finally our driver seemed to get over his offence and returned ready to set off. Gina, the boys and two Mozambican ladies who materialised at

Wednesday evening

the last moment, all travelled happily together in the back. I was thankful to be in the cab with Tina and relished a happy sense of anticipation as we pulled out of the main gates.

We could see a dozen or so people on the beach hauling in one of the huge fishing nets they use here. The ocean sparkled tantalisingly as we passed the usual stalls selling bananas and fish on the roadside and made our way slowly along the coast. We pulled into a rough layby before leaving the built-up area, and sacks of salt were loaded before we finally got underway. I think it was over an hour later (could have been more or less, I lost track of time altogether) that we turned off the road onto an area of sandy scrub on the edge of a village.

As we travelled I asked Tina about the sponsorship programme that was being talked about. I felt excited as I began to understand that I was living in the end stage of a journey I had witnessed beginning many times. In meetings around the world people are exhorted to commit to giving regularly, to 'adopting' a child in Africa. Many friends have endearing photos of small African people stuck on their fridge. Most sponsors never have opportunity to physically connect with the children they bless. But here I was about to meet a whole host of families receiving tangible evidence of the love and support of God's family. The generosity and long-term commitment of Christians around the globe is releasing hope and life in this corner of Africa. What a privilege Ma!

Tina explained that all children 'adopted' are listed and through the sponsorship programme their families receive regular supplies. Yesterday this consisted of bags of rice, beans, corn, sugar and salt. Each family also received a can of oil for cooking and some laundry soap.

Then for the children themselves we had a new backpack for school,

Pemba Pennings

a toothbrush and tube of toothpaste, a warm blanket and then, as a treat, a small fizzy drink and a packet of cookies. Having been on bush outreach and seen how most people live I could understand the level of excitement as we arrived.

Although I have been here a while now and know to 'expect the unexpected' I couldn't stop the butterflies. So very many with so little. How does suffering wear such broad smiles? I was unprepared for the number of children and it felt thoroughly incongruous they were dressed in full school uniform. It was blue and grey and, clearly feeling very smart, the children wore it with pride.

Looking beyond the bouncing heads that thronged the vehicle I could see we had pulled up not far from a small church building, which sported the usual mud walls and a shiny corrugated iron roof. There were more children clustered inside and I caught a glimpse of bright *kapalanas* where the women were already seated on the floor. Tina gave instructions to the boys about the unloading and guarding of the precious cargo and then Gina joined us as we entered the little building through the door that faced the road.

It was clear we were going in at the back since in front of another open doorway at the far end of the building and to the right-hand side, uniforms hovered in lines as more children on the programme formed a choir. Older women were clustered immediately inside the church door sitting on the dirt floor. They were mainly to the left of a makeshift aisle space that snaked its way through the bodies to the feet of the choir. It was hard to see in the murky light. Flies were making themselves busy in the shady building as the thick cloud of accumulated hot body odour assailed our senses. Hot, sticky, dusty, crowded, noisy, cheerful. Africa.

Wednesday evening

Following Tina's example Gina and I sunk to our knees to honour and greet the older women. My pulse was racing. I'm so out of my depth in these situations; still trying not to show any reaction to the obvious poverty and shocking lack that are the norm for multitudes here. We shuffled awkwardly along the lines of wrinkles and colour, sensing the warmth of welcome though only Tina could communicate. The Mamas all smiled.

My eyes slowly adapted to the dusk. It was very dusty and sticky heat made salt trickle into my eyes but who knows how long those assembled had been sitting waiting. Probably they hadn't eaten and yet no resentment in the atmosphere. It's so humbling Ma, to be welcomed so warmly by those for whom survival is a challenge every day. My face ached from smiling and nodding. I was willing myself not to unwittingly cause offence.

The non-choir children were in a large group in front of the women. I wriggled my way to the side wall in the thick of the group and limp with relief, sank amongst the children. Relief was short lived as Tina approached from her spot across the church and leaning into my right ear explained she would indicate when it was time but in this context the talk would only need to be short ... about seven minutes. As you can imagine, clammy panic took hold. Oh my goodness; in at the deep end once again!

The pastor arrived. He entered and stood by the choir. Exuding cheerfulness he wore a bright red-checked working shirt. Clearly a few sizes too large and reaching to just above his knees he had attempted to take up some of the surplus by wearing a second shirt beneath. The luminous green collar of a polo shirt was clearly visible and, although totally incongruous, the red and green combination prompted memories. Christmas crossed my mind. He welcomed us and the children sang, though I found it hard to be in the moment and enjoy it all with 'the talk' hanging over me.

Then Tina gave me the sign. I stepped over various bodies and made my way to the front where enthusiastic applause triggered a stampede of Imposter Syndrome thoughts. I had been praying enthusiastically in tongues since Tina's whispering and suddenly knew what I was going to share.

Totally out of my depth I have always had great admiration for those who appear fully at ease in front of a crowd but it probably is good for me to be cornered in this way. (I've forgiven Tina.) I can't actually remember what I shared, I think mainly due to what happened soon after, but I know I spoke in English and then Tina translated into Portuguese and then the pastor followed with Macua.

I recall being thankful again for the pauses in which to arrange the next thought. More applause as I sank back among the children and then Tina and the pastor organised the distribution of what we had brought to the sponsored families.

Each family processed in a very un-African fashion to receive their share, a bit like a prize giving but it was woven in to form part of the service and as I sat observing the ceremony a small boy crawled into my lap, curled up and went to sleep. His tummy was bloated. My heart ached. A second toddler squeezed himself in against me and just lay still gazing up at me with deep dark eyes: far too deep for one so young.

Tina sat on a bench on the opposite side of the church from where I was leaning against the wall. By this time I am doing better about

Wednesday evening

spiders, scorpions and the like, Ma. Three weeks of being up close with those who have no or very few choices is really changing my perspectives. Checking for things that may bite or crawl inside my clothing almost looks on a par with 'white woman whingeing' in the face of the brave hearts all around me. I went clammy all over again as Tina indicated we were to move.

Gina was about five little people away from me and we both cradled even smaller coarse haired bodies submerged in sticky sleep. Gently rolling our slumbering charges onto the dirt floor we scrambled to get to our feet. Leggings saved the day yet again (not sure if I told you Molly kindly left me a pair) since the poor unsuspecting pastor was directly opposite us.

Now I think of it, men were rather scarce during the whole visit; maybe collecting of supplies is viewed as women's work? (Certainly they appear to do all the heavy work in general.) Insistent hand-and-eye signals from Tina spurred us to take up an obedient but reluctant posture on an empty mat. I hadn't noticed it on the ground up to this point but we were bang 'centre stage' in our new position, which was at the front but across from the choir. The pastor beckoned us forward and reluctantly we took our places facing the people.

I was mortified as a small human cluster approached from the back door of the church and coming right up to us children presented us with two simple baskets. Each was roughly made of some plant matter (it had the appearance of what we call raffia) woven together to form a wide shallow basket, which they carried on their outstretched forearms. Little fingers curled around the outer edge hooking the precious cargo against bony ribs. The baskets were bending with the weight of the offering. (Ma

Pemba Pennings

... think gold, frankincense and myrrh because these people are outrageous in their generosity. They absolutely cannot afford anything at all and yet here they were bringing *us* gifts.) I fixed my stare on the baskets, knowing eye contact would press the waterfall button.

First a mound of raw peanuts came into view (I did *not* want to cry). Still in their wavy, husky outer cases the edible hillock wobbled slightly as the basket was laid to rest just in front of our mat. The second basket sported plump bananas nuzzling up to a pile of sugar cane that being sweetness itself is very popular here. I was drenched with nervous perspiration.

Heidi had shown us on outreach that in order not to cause offence it is crucial to accept anything that may be offered but every cell of me was desperate to just feed the hunger that crouched behind each smile. I can't imagine how it felt to the children to be told to present us with treats they may not have eaten in ... who knows how long? I don't know, so hard to process. Tears welled. The mat prickled through my skirt, my back was screaming, the dust in my hair was itching but I hardly noticed as I struggled to stay in control. And then a mega need to pull myself together as the pastor indicated they would like *me* to bless the offering. I know! Where was Tina??

My eyes found the mocking empty space where she had been seconds before. I frantically combed the crowd hoping she would step in but no sign. No choice Ma. Talk about arrow prayers! 'Help me Jesus' was all I had time for and I wasn't at all sure I could actually get any more than a groaning sound past my vocal cords. My voice was lumpy and wet but I stumbled through some kind of prayer and somehow arrived at 'Amen'.

Everyone clapped and the small church reverberated with exuberant

Wednesday evening

ululating (didn't know the word before but Tina explained it's the celebratory sound they do with their tongues here) then I exhaled. I had been holding my breath since 'Amen'. The pastor addressed us and there was a crescendo of movement and conversation indicating the ceremony was over.

I checked with Gina and we rose thankfully to our by now filthy feet. As Tina reappeared at the side door I felt myself literally shrink. I was tight with tension and rushing relief deflated every muscle. She was clutching her phone. She wriggled along the wall back to the bench where she had been seated. I made my way through the bodies now all on the move to perch next to her.

As a gaunt young woman approached her Tina stood. Feeling uncertain and awkward I did the same. The young woman was taller than Tina, about my height, with sunken cheeks and lean blotchy limbs. She had a very small baby that looked more like a newborn puppy that was not going to survive than a child. All the limbs were flaccid and the piercing siren of a tiny sunken fontanelle shrieked to all that this child was dangerously dehydrated.

I couldn't understand what the young woman was saying but her tone suggested she was making a request. Her voice was thin and devoid of energy. She was draped in a worn out piece of fabric, leached of all colour. A second piece of tired, grubby material strapped the baby to her chest. It wasn't till I took a step sideways to steady myself I saw the second baby strapped to her back. Presuming them to be her much younger siblings I fleetingly wondered how any mother could give birth to a daughter and then encumber her in this way.

I know it is the custom for young people to care for siblings from an early age but I can't get my head around it. No childhood and certainly no concerned parenting to offer the focused attention, so widely acknowledged as essential for healthy development in the west. This poor young woman was exhaustion personified right in front of us.

Even so, I was appalled when I began to understand that she was trying to *give* her babies to Tina. (Too hasty to make judgment as ever.) The baby in front looked so ill Ma, as if it had been unable to absorb any nutrients since its recent birth. It was shocking to learn that this had not been only a few days but some weeks previously. They were so tiny. Twins. The baby on her back had more flesh, could hold its head up and its eyes could follow movement but it was clearly far from healthy. I leaned a little closer to see the baby on her back and realised with a shock this woman was not a teenager. Was she the mother then?

I felt a corkscrew plunge into my gut and turn slowly round, ripping, piercing. Surely she wasn't so desperate she was trying to give away her own babies? I tried to keep my face from showing any of what I felt but when Tina turned to explain I had to turn away to hide the shock and grief I felt in the face of this poor woman's agony. Tina brought painful understanding.

She told us that this young woman had several children of her own. Her older sister had given birth to the twins and then died. Now she was totally downcast, overwhelmed and unable to cope. Her own six-year-old was in the corner obviously ill (probably with malaria). Having heard of the baby house in Pemba this desperate woman had travelled some distance in hope of someone from Iris attending the ceremony who might relieve her of her terrible burden.

Tina was obviously concerned and spoke about the regular milk clin-

Wednesday evening

ic at Mieze. Telling me she was trying to get through to the base, to ask about space in the baby house, she stood on the bench and held her phone aloft struggling to find a signal. No joy. She headed outside.

Gina had slipped out earlier to play with children who were all milling about eager to release pent-up energy. I felt once removed as laughter and noise filtering in from the play formed a backdrop to a pitiful mewling sound as the tiny parcel of skin and bones on the woman's back began to whimper. I don't recall a sound more heart rending ... I stood peering over the edge of a deep, deep well of frantic need. Yet again confronted by unthinkable suffering with no means of offering relief.

Refusing to contemplate the inevitable outcome for these little ones if Iris could not step in I willed Tina to return with good news. In one swift moment as she reappeared, disappointment swallowed hope, gulping it down whole. Eyes down, Tina approached us. She then explained to the young woman that the baby house is full at present but that all her details were now with Iris so they would get word to her as soon as a place became available.

Tina gently gave directions to the milk clinic where the next morning powdered milk and support would be available as a first step. I couldn't tell how much was being taken in through the suffocating shroud of despondency that had settled on the three utterly pathetic human beings that hovered in front of us. Physical touch, so often misrepresented, and the injustice in the atmosphere inhibited any hug of comfort or reassuring embrace. The two babies made it physically tricky but even a sideways hug would have been confronting and intrusive as the woman's desolate disappointment froze us out.

All we had to offer was what we had just received and Tina duly gifted her a portion of the offering. Someone produced a piece of material and the produce was wrapped in it then handed to the young woman who had walked some way in dusty heat longing for so much more. I felt so sad Ma. Collecting her unwell daughter from where she sat near the door the little group shuffled out into the harsh afternoon sunlight. The ball and chain of hopeless despair weighted every step.

Tina and I just stood and watched them slowly go out of sight. I was reeling with emotion. We know God is love. He is comfort. He is a perfect Father. One of his daughters, made in his image, was carrying a load way beyond her ability to manage and we, part of the same family of humanity, were powerless to bring relief or meaningful change. How does God manage this level of heartache? And the longing? We know he wants good things like peace, food and shelter for all made in his image … so? These thoughts were wrestling in my head, an incoherent jumble of feelings.

How does Tina cope? I do understand nobody can be helped if helpers are overwhelmed by emotion. I know focusing on the lack is futile but clinging to truth, and releasing hope in the face of suffering that threatens to crush, introduces a whole new dimension to a life following Jesus. 'Bearing the burden of another' and 'sharing suffering' are familiar phrases that just become unquantifiable in this context.

In silence we turned to leave the church by the side door and I followed Tina as she headed for where we had left the truck. It was there but the driver was not. I leaned against the back of the vehicle facing the church. I struggled to corral straining thoughts; sensations and questions were wildly running amok throughout my being. Think … trying to tuck a giant octopus having a seizure into a small pouch. Hopeless!

Wednesday evening

The children romping around without an apparent care in the world jarred with my turmoil but the sight of Gina sitting in the shade, cradling a slumbering body was briefly soothing. I tried to absorb some of the peace that the cameo offered. Tina's telephone voice interjected, 'Well *where* are you?' A lengthy pause whilst presumably the driver explained his whereabouts. 'How long will you be? We are ready to go so please come soon.'

Pocketing her phone as she rejoined me, Tina explained that the driver had told her he was sewing up the sacks. If this was intended to enlighten me it failed miserably but as she swiftly moved on to suggest a 'bathroom break' I let it go recognising all would probably be revealed, sooner or later. It was a number of hours since we had left the base and with the bumpy ride back to Pemba ahead a toilet stop was not unappealing. (I am quietly amused that the Americans continue to refer to a 'bathroom break' or a 'visit to the rest room' when needing the toilet even though, in my experience, the ablution facilities here in no way resemble anything even vaguely akin to a bathroom.)

Pondering 'sewing' and 'sacks' and coming to no meaningful conclusion I dutifully followed Tina as she headed for a mound of bald earth. A small hummock I suppose you would call it with intermittent patches of prickly brown scrubby growth. After a few minutes we passed a dwelling and turning right I could see about sixty metres ahead, poised on the skyline, a skimpy bamboo screen. As we got nearer it was evident the spaces in the flimsy bamboo were more frequent than the bamboo itself. All was not lost for this modest Brit as upon closer inspection a couple of pieces of rough sacking were attached in the vague vicinity of the holes. This would probably have worked well if it hadn't been for a stiff breeze that swept up the side of the hill and whistled through the tiny shelter.

We stepped carefully over a mother hen and narrowly missed tripping over the cluster of small dusky chicks that scuttled out of the scrub as we approached. With a show of generosity (which was an attempt at disguising my apprehension) I encouraged Tina to go first and turned my back as she entered the latrine.

I presume the position of this particular hole in the dirt was designed so the breeze would transport any unwanted odours. Due to the aim of some being less accurate than others, it is thoroughly desirable that all garments maintain a safe distance from the ground.

Even three weeks in, for a girl like me still unaccustomed to managing long skirts and leggings, which seem annoyingly to drape and flop without warning, this is a particular challenge. When paired with the need for healthy muscle control in the squat position combined with flapping lack of privacy on a hillside ... I'll spare you the gory details Ma but let's just say I have had more relaxing experiences and the need to exercise a degree of mental discipline (pushing back anxiety about the risk of the sun glancing off a particularly white part of my anatomy and signalling my position to locals for miles around) well, you get the idea. (I think Sis would give up drinking water in the day if she ventured out here.)

As you can imagine all this takes considerably longer than a 'nip to the ladies room' and in my case is thoroughly conducive to perspiration. We headed straight back to the truck and I was focused on getting to my antibacterial wipes. Offering one to Tina she suggested we climb up into the cab and wait for the driver. By now it was well past lunchtime. She had some biscuits and I had some cold rice in a tub. There were children playing, groups of ladies sitting together quietly chatting and various

Wednesday evening

villagers moving through the space around the church.

We sat quietly munching and I wondered if I could find a way to put my feelings into words in order to process the situation with the twins, but I felt tongue-tied. This level of despair and need would not be new to her and I desperately didn't want to come over as … Oh, I don't even know what really, Ma. Tina probably didn't have answers but I suppose I wondered what coping mechanism she has developed. There must be a way of engaging with the Holy Spirit to keep your heart soft in the face of so much hardship.

Before I could find a way of voicing the inner churnings an elderly lady approached the window and Tina wound it right down in order to hear what she was saying. A scrunched black face looked up from a startlingly bright orange *kapulana* and the old lady asked Tina for money. Tina, direct as ever leaned out of her window to look the old woman in the eye, 'Do you know Jesus?' Without losing eye contact Tina opened her door and stepped down onto the dirt. Gently taking the old lady by the hand she led her over to a group of three ladies who had come out of the church.

A group of boys had been happily messing about with an old tyre, a steel wheel trim and a broken piece of an old Frisbee. They stopped playing and wandered over to stand staring at Tina and her new friend as the women exchanged greetings. The ladies from church sat happily together in the shade of a small tree and every now and then one would call across to a passing villager. The boys appeared to be listening and fascinated as joining the group Tina squatted down and introduced the older lady. After a brief exchange I could see they were praying for her.

Climbing back up beside me Tina explained the old lady needed

Pemba Pennings

healing and the women from church would then lead her to Jesus. (I know, just like that!) We lapsed back into silent eating. The sun continued to beat down out of a steely sky and it was warm in the cab but the humidity began to lift a few days ago and I for one am very grateful.

Tina seemed a bit tense. The driver was clearly much later than she had planned and she began explaining to me about the charcoal. Charcoal is used for cooking and out in these more rural areas it is quite a bit cheaper than in Pemba. The two ladies who had come with us work in the kitchen in Pemba and when they come to help Tina on this trip their reward is a sack of charcoal each, which they then divide up and resell to make a small profit in Pemba.

There are strict criteria for the number of sacks it is legal to move over the border and when you travel between geographical regions you are subject to possible police checks. Tina had already noted that there were a number of sacks piled up in the back of the truck and she explained that the plan had been for the women to return with the usual three sacks.

The chance to resell the charcoal is in the context of a blessing, specifically for the women, for working on the sponsorship programme all day. It is not intended to create small business opportunities. For example if it created 'smuggling' channels between the areas that would hardly enhance the reputation of Iris. Five is the maximum allowance and Tina had counted nine sacks on board (hence the slight tension I had noticed in the air). Like so many other times Ma, no time to process the plight of the twins or ask about the lady in orange as we were immediately tumbling into a whole other scenario.

As we finished our respective snacks the two ladies who had travelled

Wednesday evening

with us (having been visiting with friends in the village) clambered into the back of the truck to await departure. Gina was now engulfed in a small, curious crowd of children but we knew where she was. As I saw our driver appear from the direction of the road Tina opened her door and hopped down onto the ground allowing me to get out. She asked me to go and get Gina, saying we were running late and needed to leave straight away.

She had spotted our driver (who had collected 'a helper' whilst he had been away) appearing from the direction of the road. He walked slowly towards us and I was aware of him ambling over to the truck as I crossed the strip of bald earth to retrieve Gina. She again had her arms full of sleeping child and sat in the shady spot against the church wall. I relayed the message and she stroked the cheek of the reluctant toddler till he woke and rolled off her lap.

The children laughed and protested as, jumping and skipping, they came to the truck with us. Gina quite happily clambered in the back to join the women and I rejoined Tina in the cab. The atmosphere emanating from the driver's seat was such that I was thankful Tina was now in the middle.

Chilly looks shot across the cab and then Tina spoke to the driver's chiselled profile. He stared fixedly ahead and showed no inclination to drive. 'Why have you got so much charcoal? You know three sacks for the women is the normal for this trip. The maximum allowance is only five in any case.'

As Tina waited for his reply a Muslim family passed in front of the vehicle making their heat-hazed way along the side of the road. We were parked about ten metres back but I could see immediately that they were dressed quite differently from the villagers. The man at the front wore traditional headgear (the bright white and red material wound around his head with tails over the shoulder; it's the only time I have seen it here and he must have been roasting). He walked in a way that communicated his importance to all and wore a long white robe with golden embroidery around the neck, sleeves and in the front. The fabric appeared quite heavy and had a good quality swing as he stepped out.

Three women followed. Presumably wives in order of favour and importance, they were walking in line a respectable distance behind him, each sporting amazing bright headgear and various loud dangly hoop earrings with necklaces that glittered in the sun. I caught myself just staring. It was so incongruous to see obvious wealth walking by in the dirt. Nobody greeted or acknowledged this little group and they walked across the road opening in front of us from right to left with no distraction or interaction as if they were playing a role on stage.

I was jolted back into the present by the driver gruffly demanding lunch for himself and his helper (I presume his accomplice and partner in crime!). He had remained silent as Tina expressed disappointment in his greed. She pointed out that he is employed by Iris and paid sufficient to support his family but paid work for women is much less common and he knows the charcoal is intended as a perk for them.

I was amazed he just appeared to ignore Tina. I held my breath during a short, very pregnant silence. I for one would not want to cross Tina. His belligerent tone suggested he had no such hesitation as he merely repeated the request for lunch. Tina remained calm and in control, 'We are late. We need to get back. Please drive. There isn't time for lunch.'

Wednesday evening

The 'helper' had joined the women and Gina in the back and I thought better than to comment to Tina as the driver complied and we began chugging forward then, turning left and crunching into third gear, we headed back towards Pemba. Tina was disappointed and cross.

After about ten minutes she spoke explaining to me that if we were stopped and searched there would be a heavy fine. I felt for her because I could see that she was powerless. Removing the huge sacks was not a real option. We needed the driver ... to drive. She had no way of ensuring the women got their quota and no influence at all over what happened to the booty once we got back to the base.

The selfish greed and the domination of men over the women are obviously areas where many long to see change. I don't think those employed in the Iris transport department are necessarily Christian as Iris are committed to creating work opportunities for local people and that does not depend on their faith. Also, various stories about spare tyres and other random pieces of equipment 'disappearing' plus the whole issue with the keys all suggest honesty cannot be assumed. Tina announced she was not buying lunch and (I think by way of explanation) that she was unhappy about the number of charcoal sacks on board.

We rode along, each with our own thoughts, for about ten minutes then Tina spoke to me, 'Let's pray in tongues for a while and also for the sick woman.' (I still had no idea what was wrong with the lady in the orange *kapulana* but that's part of the joy of tongues, isn't it? So freeing to know that the Holy Spirit can pray what's needed through us!) We prayed aloud at the same time in our heavenly languages and after a little while the atmosphere in the cab shifted.

At one point the driver slowed and pulled right into the side of the road. I caught sight of the helper jumping out of the back in the wonky wing mirror beside me. Nothing was said. I found this habit of 'open travel' with random people jumping on and off at will very unnerving initially (as in the jail visit!) but I have got used to locals getting on and off transport whenever we go anywhere.

I guess any opportunity to avoid long hot walks is enthusiastically embraced. It generally unfolds that someone in the vehicle (as when we went on bush outreach) is the nephew of the mother's uncle's brother or some other relative who is in some way connected with the reason for the journey being undertaken. Imagine if each time you pulled into a motorway services at home random strangers just hopped in to join you for the next leg of your journey ... all so different here.

As the miles passed I followed Tina's lead and continued praying aloud. We prayed in English for the sick lady then lapsed again into quiet. I wondered about the upcoming police check-point. There had been a number of armed policemen either side of the road in the morning, waving various vehicles aside to be searched.

I hoped we would not be stopped though part of me felt the driver should be called to account. I think a long delay, explanations and the inevitable suggestion of bribe would all have fallen on Tina and presumably reflect on Iris ultimately as they own the vehicle, so relief washed over us as the police check came and went with no signal for us to pull over. The driver who had not spoken, was suddenly animated, 'It is the favour of God!' He smiled broadly. Tina's voice had softened but she was firm, 'I don't think so, not if it's sin.'

As we reached the outskirts of Pemba, Tina turned to me, 'I'll buy everyone chicken for lunch.' I must have looked as nonplussed as I felt

Wednesday evening

at this apparent change of heart because in response to my unspoken question she shrugged her shoulders, smiled and then as if by way of explanation she said, 'Extravagant love changes things.' She spoke to the driver about stopping to buy lunch at the takeaway chicken shop.

I had the distinct impression he had just been waiting, knowing all along she would come round to this decision. We parked on the side of the road back on the street with the *barracas*, near the roundabout in Pemba. Tina called to those in the back that she was getting chicken and then disappeared into a long, low, shack-style building which was open to the road but too dark inside for me to see.

It was clear it wasn't a KFC. (My last day Ma, and with the long journey back to Australia looming, the last risk I wanted to take was one of a tummy upset so I declined the offer.) I sat waiting beside the driver as he munched a bag of peanuts produced from under his seat. He had to crack each out of its shell with his teeth, fish the peanut out and then was happily chucking each empty husk out of his window.

As we watched the traffic a car with a spare wheel on a bracket on the rear door swerved in front of us, closely followed by another vehicle that narrowly missed swiping the spare wheel off the back of the first car. I heard myself gasp as a pedestrian almost got caught on the rear bumper of the second vehicle right under our noses but our driver didn't miss a beat as the next husk hit the road.

Golly it was hot, Ma, mid-afternoon by this time and Tina was gone almost an hour, by which time the driver beside me had moved to swilling out his mouth with water and spitting bits of half-chewed nut out of his window to join the husks on the road. A passing motorcyclist slowing in the traffic was unimpressed as a random peanut shell found its way down his shirt. I have yet to meet anyone who actually keeps their own rubbish. It's just not on the radar at all even though health and hygiene are obvious issues. Tina did eventually emerge with pieces of chicken wrapped in paper. Everyone was delighted with hot food and the smell was very enticing.

We arrived back at the base weary but feeling it had been a good day. I enjoyed being with Tina and am thankful for the opportunity to experience tongues being a powerful weapon in spiritual warfare. I do wonder about the 'extravagant love changing things' philosophy. I mean, what in this context did she mean … I doubt that relenting and buying him chicken would influence the driver's time-keeping skills or his greed for money in the context of the charcoal. His heart? How would relenting and there being no consequence for his 'sin' help him to think of the women and their needs in the future?

But then is that what the whole set-up here is committed to? This extravagant, unconditional love that does seem to have a power all its own? Stories of Heidi adopting children into the family, them straying into their old ways, often robbing her and then later being welcomed back into the family again, are numerous.

Is our western concept of people needing to 'pay for their sin' more or less like God, I wonder? Have I unwittingly engaged with some kind of religious judgmental spirit that isn't God at all? The fruit here would appear to be a nation influenced by God's love and thousands of lives blessed.

Oh my word Ma … I have so many more questions than answers. It has been another enormous day so need to end for now.

It was great to spend time with Tina. I kept finding myself thinking

Wednesday evening

about what it might be like travelling out to remote Aboriginal communities. Tina is strong and focused. She will begin her new work with the farming project towards the middle of the year. She makes no apology for being a woman alone and neither will I as God anoints me for the task ahead. Last day tomorrow, can hardly believe it. We have Wednesday church tonight so am going to have a short rest before that. Phew! A full day.

Will aim to get up early to pray in the morning and will hope to get a slot to write. What a wild adventure Ma, and I'm recognising that writing as I go has been a really good thing because how could I have ever remembered all that is unfolding?

I'm so thankful for the prompting. It will be amazing to have time together next month though, to share the experience in detail. Thanks again for all your love and prayers. Last sleep in Pemba. I feel so blessed to have had this opportunity!

Big hug x x

Thursday

Dear Ma,

Here I am again, early morning and in the prayer hut.

Today is my last full day in Pemba. I can't imagine ever returning.

I haven't mentioned the horses much but they continue to rove freely around the base. I struggled at first: you know how much I love horses and the thought of them not being cared for properly, and kids messing about with them as if they were toys, was painful. That might sound mad to many with malnourished children on every corner ... Guess you have to be a horse lover to relate!

Anyway I think I jumped to a wrong conclusion (increasingly aware of this shortcoming, echoes of AJ's warning) and although obviously animal welfare here looks very different to at home, the horses seem contented and as healthy as I think could be expected in this environment. On several evenings I have seen them being ridden bareback by some of the lads growing up here. (A far cry from your lessons in the indoor arena with Brenda, Ma.) They just canter at full speed straight up the main

Thursday

track through the base. Tack cleaning and schooling are hardly going to be on the agenda here are they?

The last two mornings as I have crept out of the visitors' centre to come to the prayer hut they have been grazing (at least, rummaging in the scrub I can't say there is green pasture readily available and to me they look thin …) right in front of me. As the sun rose this morning they chose to move downhill of me; both had a leisurely roll in an area of slightly softer, though no less red, earth. Still after all these years, there is little to match the pleasure of watching a happy horse having a carefree roll. Beautiful. With God giving me such joy in horses I wonder how he will weave them into my life in the next season. I have been aching to ride again. I don't somehow think that going 'walkabout' on horseback is what he intends; although wouldn't that be a dream? I get shivers down my spine just thinking about it.

Zena and Lucie are in the little prayer house behind me. They kindly invited me to join them but I just love this cool time of the morning out in the open air. Interestingly, since the temperature has dropped there is usually a ribbon of cloud on the skyline so not a red sunrise. The light is still beautiful at dawn. I love to watch as skeletal silhouettes of the huge baobab trees take form and grow leafy flesh.

My last day then. It has been a very long three weeks but at the same time, it has flashed by! I have managed to write you most days so I am praying I've captured what God intended and that you feel you have tasted the Pemba experience. At Wednesday church last night Andoni the school headmaster was speaking again. He spoke about Jesus telling Peter to cast the fishing nets over the opposite side of his boat. Peter was doing what he had always done but in a different way; the Jesus way.

Pemba Pennings

Andoni posed the question, 'What will you do now? What will you do that you have always done but needs to be done the Jesus way?' That is the million-dollar question, isn't it? One I can't answer from here.

I'm not sure how to spend the day. I have dressings and some surplus paracetamol and ointments to donate at the clinic and will say my goodbyes. I need to return a couple of books I borrowed. Neither one has even been opened in light of so much happening, both in activity and processing. The other visitors are all going off to outreach later today.

Ben was adamant he is simply going to focus on his medical contribution now, stating he has seen miracles and has no desire to repeat the chaos and touching of last week. He disappeared and spent time in his room. When he re-emerged he spoke in a quiet voice; as nonchalantly as he could manage he announced he thought he would go after all. This week it is more than four hours' drive and the outreach is over two nights. I don't know if Ben knows that yet. He's lovely Ma. He's twenty-two, not animated but sincere. I think he will be blessed out of his boots.

I'm praying the Holy Spirit will nudge me if there is anyone I can help today. I need to pack and get myself organised. I'm so glad I planned this next visit home to Australia via Perth. The conference is a couple of days after I arrive so I'll see cousin Julia then head to a hotel near to the venue so I can walk to the conference.

It's amazing that I booked it presuming I wouldn't see Heidi at all in Pemba. It feels really special to finish this incredible time with her actually in Australia after so much confirmation that is where I am to remain. I sense God will cement what he has been doing and saying in me here, through her teaching at the conference. *And* we will be right in the culture he has sent me to.

Thursday

No more feathers to report. Wow, God has done so much. I am going to worship for a while now and then the gong will go for bread. Whoa, just realised, I never even heard the call to prayer today. Will do some packing and then finish this later. Love you x

4pm

Hello again Ma,

This will be my last note from Pemba. Store up all your questions for Sydney. (Maybe you should bring the large teapot in your luggage since I foresee many happy hours of chat and a teabag in those hotel cups is never quite the same!)

Wilf had kindly got the bread when I got back this morning. I had a wry smile when one of the others commented on his t-shirt and he shared it had been given to him by the Pope, in person (naturally!), at some event or other. He appears to be coming into his own and is considering being here for some time. I thought maybe Sophie was pushing him but he seems quite happy to be staying on without her. They've all left now for outreach and it feels very quiet.

Something really great happened before they departed. I went to visit Gina in her little room in the centre. As a staff member her room also has a little kitchenette with table and chairs and a shower cubicle. It's a few doors along on the same side of the centre as my room.

4pm

We got chatting and she shared she had never prayed in tongues. I explained how easy it is to receive the gift and prayed for her, encouraging her to start; she was delighted to get her heavenly language. God is so good. I went down to the gate to see them all off in the trucks and on the way the guard at the gate of the visitors' centre told me it's *'bon hopital'* meaning it's all on for him to go to hospital; he has a date for his hernia surgery and the funds came in. That's great, isn't it?

It's got humid again today and I had a short rest on my bed. As I was praying I had a strange thought, 'I don't think this is a full stop.' I have no idea what that could mean but if it's God it will come clear. He surely can't be thinking of bringing me back?

Sara came to the centre and I was glad to hand over all spare wipes, nail polish remover and some trinkets I brought with me that she can use as gifts. We had a great chat and prayed together. She asked me what I felt about being here and if God had done anything specific.

I chatted a bit with her about my challenge to understand situations where there appears to be a conflict between culture and kingdom. Meaning those attributes such as honesty, faithfulness, and respect for one another and for possessions. Things that appear to be perceived as 'western ideas' but we see as part of attaining to live like Jesus. I shared the sadness I feel about so often sensing even those who have grown up here in Iris perceive me as a soft touch for money.

She spoke about some of her language learning and told me of a story she found in a textbook used by all the children in school. It's a story about a tortoise and an elephant having a race. Basically the tortoise gets hold of a laxative and hides it in something he then offers the elephant to eat. The elephant ends up in dire straits and is unable to finish the

Pemba Pennings

race thus enabling the tortoise to win. BUT in the book it is the tortoise that is hailed as wise and clever because he outwitted his opponent to win the race.

I think my chin literally hit the ground as she explained. She related to my response but pointed out that if that is the attitude you are raised with, making the change to 'prefer one another' is a profound challenge. I could see that of course. The new headmaster is the one who spoke about Peter on Wednesday. He has been living out of Mozambique for some years so I wonder if there will be changes.

Sara was very encouraging when I shared some of what I sense God speaking in regard to our First Nations people and asked how it feels in the context of being in Pemba. I admitted sensing that God had brought me here for a significant purpose.

She shared a picture likening me to a bright red flower that was blooming on the shrub beside where we sat and spoke about boldness, sticking out from the crowd and a few other things that could destine a person for a fair amount of discomfort. But the flower was beautiful and had a fragrance so there was an upside to what she shared. She also mentioned something about a role of 'ambassador', which is very interesting as this has been a theme as people have prayed for me in recent years.

Trying to 'just fit in' no longer an option then, if I am truly abandoned to what Jesus asks.

Anyway Ma, I may get the chance to write a final note on the plane and get it straight in the mail as I land. I love you so much. I know you probably feel you would never come to a place like this but I am thankful you and Pop raised me always encouraging me to pursue God. Without that I would never be here, so in that way I feel you are both very much

4pm

with me and have had a massive contribution.

As Sara and I chatted I remembered again Tom Jones (one of the speakers at the conference in Cardiff which, by the way, feels as if it happened in a previous life!) and the prophetic word he brought one morning, which resonated with me at the time. I wrote it out in my journal. He said, 'A new chapter is about to begin. It is a bold and very long chapter.' I have a feeling this has little to do with any actual book although I will have to write as I go … Listen to me! In my heart and spirit I am already 'sent'. How has God done that Ma?

Aged 55 and a whole new chapter beginning! Talk about 'more than you can ask or imagine'. Yes. Imagine … me 'called'?! I can write it but can't actually say it out loud yet. I don't know how, who with or when, but I am certain the place is Australia.

I will pray much, trust this season of being UK based is coming to a close and keep moving towards being home to settle later this year. Can only wait and see what God unfolds. I feel he will soon show me the next step and make a way for real connection with our beautiful indigenous Australians. Only he can bring about the fulfilment of the dreams and longings he is birthing.

Watch this space …

So glad you are feeling better, love to the others and travel safe. I feel I want to say I hope you still recognise me such are the changes unfolding.

Love you so much Ma, ever thankful for your prayers and loving support during this adventure.

Time here is ending but I also feel on the brink of a mysterious beginning, summoned by a, 'Come away with me' whisper. Exciting!

See you very soon x x

Author's Note

Dear Reader

You could perhaps be forgiven for thinking that within six months I would be 'out there', stuck in and making great headway in the ocean of my destiny.

Instead, I navigated an endless stream of right turns, left forks and even what looked and felt like full-on U turns.

Back home I struggled to find the God of miracles and wonder at work in the everyday of my white middleclass environment. Hunger for him alone was hard to find, demonstrative passion unwelcome, unfettered abandon seen as embarrassing, healing rarely expected and power painfully conspicuous, by its absence.

I felt less and less at home, often experiencing a sense of dislocation in church as relentless love prepared, transformed and equipped me; in spite of myself. Surely, he must be revealing himself, his supernatural hand, somewhere other than Africa?

And then, he instructed me to visit a city in California I had vaguely

Author's Note

heard of, in a nation with which I had no connection. To me it was a mystery. Thousands of miles in the opposite direction to the people I wanted to connect with; the people I thought *he* wanted me to connect with.

But God!

The next chapter in H A's story is coming soon. You can connect with her via hapennings1@gmail.com

www.ingramcontent.com/pod-product-compliance
Lightning Source LLC
Chambersburg PA
CBHW070605170426
43200CB00012B/2590